Feminist perspectives in criminology

Open University Press
New Directions in Criminology series

Series Editor: Colin Sumner, Lecturer in Sociology,
Institute of Criminology, and Fellow of
Wolfson College, University of Cambridge

Current and forthcoming titles include:

Imperial Policing
Philip Ahire

Lawyers' Work
Maureen Cain and Christine Harrington

Feminist Perspectives in Criminology
Loraine Gelsthorpe and Allison Morris (eds)

The Enemy Without: Policing and Class Consciousness in the Miners' Strike
Penny Green

Regulating Women in Wartime
Ruth Jamieson

Black Women and Crime
Marcia Rice

Criminal Justice and Underdevelopment in Tanzania
Leonard Shaidi

Censure, Politics and Criminal Justice
Colin Sumner (ed.)

Reading the Riot Act
Richard Vogler

Feminist perspectives in criminology

EDITED BY
Loraine Gelsthorpe and
Allison Morris

Open University Press
Milton Keynes • Philadelphia

Open University Press
Celtic Court
22 Ballmoor
Buckingham MK18 1XW

and
1900 Frost Road, Suite 101
Bristol, PA 19007, USA

First Published 1990

British Library Cataloguing in Publication Data

Feminist perspectives in criminology. – (New directions in
    criminology).
    1. Criminology
    I. Gelsthorpe, Loraine   II. Morris, Allison   III. Series 364

    ISBN 0–335–09933–5
    ISBN 0–335–09932–7 (pbk)

Library of Congress Cataloging-in-Publication Data

Feminist perspectives in criminology / edited by Loraine Gelsthorpe
    and Allison Morris.
        p. cm. — (New directions in criminology series)
    ISBN 0–335–09933–5   ISBN 0–335–09932–7 (pbk.)
    1. Criminology.   2. Feminism.   3. Women – Crimes against.
    I. Gelsthorpe, Loraine.   II. Morris, Allison.   III. Series.
    HV6030.F4 1990   364–dc20
                                                    90–32286 CIP

Typeset by Inforum Typesetting, Portsmouth
Printed in Great Britain by Biddles Limited,
Guildford and Kings Lynn

Contents

List of contributors

Beverley Brown is a lecturer in the Centre for Criminology and the Social and Philosophical Study of Law, University of Edinburgh. She is currently completing a book analysing the feminist critique of criminology and is also researching the use of sexual-history evidence in the Scottish courts. Her recent publications include 'Women and crime: the dark figures of criminology', *Economy and Society* (1986) and 'Debating pornography: the symbolic dimensions', *Law and Critique* (forthcoming).

Maureen Cain is Professor of Sociology at the University of the West Indies, St Augustine, Trinidad. Her most recent book is *Growing Up Good: Policing the Behaviour of Girls in Europe* (Sage 1989). She was for a long time editor and is now consultant editor of *The International Journal of the Sociology of Law*.

Susan Edwards teaches in the School of Law at the University of Buckingham and is author of *Female Sexuality and the Law: A Study of Constructs of Female Sexuality as they Inform Statute and Legal Procedure* (Martin Robertson 1981), *Women on Trial* (Manchester University Press 1984) and *Policing 'Domestic' Violence: Women, the Law and the State* (Sage 1989). She is currently evaluating police cautioning of men involved in wife abuse.

Loraine Gelsthorpe is a research fellow in the Department of Social Science and Administration at the London School of Economics. Her books include *Women and Crime* (Institute of Criminology 1981, co-edited with A. Morris), *Gender Issues in Juvenile Justice* (Lancaster Information Systems 1985) and *Sexism and the Female Offender* (Gower 1989). Her current research is on race and gender considerations in social inquiry reports. She also teaches criminology and works with a range of national voluntary organizations on juvenile justice issues.

Annie Hudson is a social work team manager working in central Bristol. From 1982–9 she was a lecturer in social work at the University of Manchester. She has carried out research on feminism and social work, young women in trouble and child sexual abuse. Recent publications include ' "Troublesome girls": towards alternative strategies and policies' in M. Cain (ed.) *Growing Up Good: the Policing of Girls in Europe* (Sage 1989).

Liz Kelly is a research fellow at the Child Abuse Studies Unit, Polytechnic of North London. She was a founder member of her local refuge and rape crisis group and is currently a member of the Trouble and Strife Collective, Feminist Coalition Against Child Sexual Assault and Women Against Sex Trafficking. She has written extensively on violence against women including *Surviving Sexual Violence* (Polity 1988).

Maria Los is Professor of Criminology at the University of Ottawa. She has an extensive publication record in the sociology of law. Her recent publications include *The Second Economy in Marxist States* (Macmillan 1989) (edited) and *Communist Ideology, Law and Crime: A Comparative View of the USSR and Poland* (Macmillan 1988). Her current interests are in feminism and law.

Allison Morris is a lecturer in criminology at the Institute of Criminology, Cambridge. She is co-editor of *Women and Crime* (Institute of Criminology 1981) and of *Women and the Penal System* (Institute of Criminology 1988) and author of *Women, Crime and Criminal Justice* (Basil Blackwell 1987). Her current research interests are female prison officers' experiences of working in men's prisons and the needs of female prisoners.

Marcia Rice is a recent graduate in criminology from both the Universities of Edinburgh and Cambridge. She is currently employed by the Afro-Caribbean Mental Health Association and is writing a book for the Open University Press on black women and crime.

Phil Scraton is Head of the Centre for Studies in Crime and Social Justice at Edge Hill College of Higher Education. His recent publications include *The State of the Police* (Pluto 1985) and *In the Arms of the Law* (with Kathryn Chadwick, Pluto 1987). He is currently working on masculinity and men's collective violence and is involved in a project on the aftermath of the Hillsborough disaster.

Carol Smart has been writing in the field of women and law/criminology for over ten years and her publications include *Women, Crime and Criminology: A Feminist Critique* (Routledge 1976), *The Ties That Bind: Law, Marriage and the Reproduction of Patriarchal Relations* (Routledge 1984) and *Feminism and the Power of Law* (Routledge 1989). She is editor of *The International Journal of the Sociology of Law* and lecturer in sociology at the University of Warwick.

Elizabeth Stanko is a senior lecturer at Brunel University. Her recent publications are *Danger Signs* (Pandora 1990) and *Intimate Intrusions* (Unwin Hyman 1985). Her research interests include prosecutorial decision-making, police discretion, violence against women and the fear of crime.

Colin Sumner is a lecturer in sociology at the Institute of Criminology, Cambridge. He is author of *Reading Ideologies: An Investigation into the Marxist Theory of Ideology and Law* (Academic Press 1979), editor of *Crime, Justice and Underdevelopment* (Heinemann 1982), and editor of *Censure, Politics and Criminal Justice* (Open University Press 1990).

Preface and acknowledgements

It is New Year's Day, 1990, a fitting time to reflect on past achievements and to make future resolutions. In many ways this is what this book sets out to do. It expresses the increasing interest of feminists in the broad sphere of what can be called criminology by critically assessing what has been accomplished and what is still to be done. A central goal is to make explicit connections between theory, research and action.

We would like to thank the contributors for taking on the task asked of them. We would also like to thank Pam Paige, Thelma Norman and Maureen Brown for their patience in typing the essays in their various drafts and Jean Kenworthy for dealing with our panics regarding the fax machine and for her general help. Our thanks also to Peggy, John, Gus, Dotty, Lucy and Amy for putting up with us during the final stages of editing this book.

Series editor's introduction

This series is founded upon the socialist and feminist research carried out in the Institute of Criminology over the last decade. It is, however, concerned more broadly to publish any work which renews theoretical development or opens up new and important areas in criminology. Particular attention will be paid to the politics and ideology of criminal justice, gender and crime, crimes of state officials, crime and justice in underdeveloped societies, European criminal justice, environmental crime, and the general sociology of censure and regulation. The series will centre upon substantial empirical research informed by contemporary social theory, and will be unusually international in character.

Behind the series is a belief that criminology cannot be limited to policy-oriented studies and must retain its integrity as an area of independent, critical enquiry of interest to scholars from a variety of disciplinary backgrounds. A criminology that wants to remain dynamic and worthy of its complex subject matter must therefore constantly renew theoretical debate, explore current issues, and develop new methods of research. To allow itself to be limited by the often narrowly political interests of government departments or the funding agencies' need for a parochial 'relevance', especially in an age when 'realism' is so often defined by short-run philosophies, is to promote its own destruction as an intellectual enterprise. A criminology which is not intellectually alive is useless to everybody. We live in increasingly international societies which, more than ever, require a broad, non-parochial vision to ensure their viability and health. The various kinds of administrative criminology may be necessary for wise government, but they can only be of general value if they remain closely connected to an independent, intellectually rigorous criminology, which, even now, actually provides them with ideas, topicality, drive, depth and legitimacy. The latter, equally, must retain a close connection with political reality if it is to achieve real insight and sharpness. Both, we believe, must be committed to a general drive towards increased democratization and justice, and the indivisibility of freedom, truth and justice, if they want to avoid a drift into the twin cul-de-sacs of 'police science' and political propaganda.

Some might argue that criminology is an outdated term in that very few people believe any more that a positive science of crime and criminal justice administration is possible. Indeed, some of the studies in this series will look more like studies in the sociology of law, or in political sociology, and their view of science is never positivistic. We have decided to retain the term criminology, however, because we intend this series to contribute to redefining its meaning, so that it clearly includes sociology of law, political sociology, social history, political economy, discourse analysis, and so on. Criminology merely refers to any kind of study concerned with crime and criminal justice. It is an umbrella term covering a multitude of topics and approaches. The task for all of us is to give it a meaningful substance to meet the emerging and exciting challenges of the 1990s. The Cold War is almost over; now, we enter a phase which will demand a new clarity on fundamental social values, and a stronger vision of the substance and form of social censure and regulation necessary to promote peace, health, growth, equity and co-operation on an international scale.

The present volume by Loraine Gelsthorpe and Allison Morris is a major contribution to the project of a progressive reconstruction of criminology in the 1990s; a project which cannot even begin, in my opinion, without a recognition of the full implications of feminist work, and without the full participation of feminists. Feminist perspectives, over the past twenty years, have not only put some new topics under the criminological umbrella, they have challenged the theories, concepts, methods and assumptions of most of the people already under that umbrella. Sometimes, perhaps, they have merely broadened the scope of exciting enquiries and suggested a reordering of priorities, but increasingly they have questioned the character and colour of the umbrella itself, the sexism and masculinity of the people holding it up, and the purpose of the whole exercise. Feminist perspectives have thus registered, once again, the fact that criminology must recognize its roots in political ideology. More importantly, however, they have begun to demonstate the sexism and hegemonic masculinity of most criminological work. Insofar as they have achieved these effects, they have played a vital part in deconstructing both the traditional criminologies and the orthodox Marxist criminologies.

The essays in this book do illustrate the challenge of feminism, but they also go further to debate the issues that it raises and the implications of its interventions. They attempt not only to reinforce the fact that the conventional definition of criminology's boundaries has been shot to pieces once-and-for-all, but also to clarify the foundations for future criminological work which will be both aware of the subordination of women and gender-conscious. In this sense, the book is very much part of a reconstructive moment in the history of criminology.

Reflections of this kind are all too necessary in a period of political thought and intellectual history when very little can be legitimately taken for granted. Foundational philosophies of various kinds are in crisis and no one can be certain of what will emerge in their place. But it seems all too easy to despair of mainstream criminology and to leave it to the administrators. Analysis of crime and criminal justice will continue; therefore it is important to sustain a culture of critical debate about the kinds of theories, concepts, assumptions, methods and purposes which inform that analysis. As long as that criminological analysis remains ignorant of and fundamentally resistant to feminism and to the critique of hegemonic masculinity, and as long as feminism remains a vibrant arena of debate containing a variety of perspectives, books of this kind will be of value in combating the complacency of orthodoxy.

Colin Sumner

1 Introduction: Transforming and transgressing[1] criminology

Loraine Gelsthorpe and Allison Morris

But y'know what feminists are like. If something's impossible, that's the perfect reason for doin' it.

(Willy Russell 1988, Act 1, Scene 1.)

The idea for this book grew out of a paper we wrote for a special issue of the *British Journal of Criminology* focusing on 'the past and present condition' of British criminology (Rock, 1988). In that paper we reviewed the impact which feminism had had on mainstream debates in criminology and concluded that although most criminologists now acknowledge the existence of a feminist critique, their writings characteristically continue to refer to it only tangentially; see also Heidensohn's review (1987). We also referred in that paper to the potential which feminism has to offer criminology. In this book we seek to explore this further. Part 1 focuses on theory, Part 2 on methods and approaches and Part 3 on action. But first we have to address some definitional issues.

To say that you are a feminist usually evokes preconceived notions of identity, role or behaviour. These notions are often negative rather than positive, and you are popularly assumed to be an aggressive, self-seeking, banner-waving woman who prefers work to family life and who, if a mother, abandons her children to a hen-pecked partner or, worse still, to the state. To say that you are adopting a feminist perspective in an academic discipline or a feminist methodology in research usually leads to puzzlement, claims that there is no such thing, or accusations of bias. There is now, however, a wealth of feminist research and theory. Leaving criminology aside for the moment and simply glancing at our own bookshelves, we can refer to recent publications in the natural sciences by Evelyn Fox Keller (1982) and Ruth Bleier (1988), in the area of epistemology, metaphysics, methodology and the philosophy of science by Sandra Harding and Merrill Hintikka (1983), in the literary world – with the development of a specifically 'feminist literary criticism' – by Toril Moi (1985) and Mary Eagleton (1986), in psychology by Beverly Walker (1981) and Carol Gilligan (1982), in political theory by Nannerl Keohane, Michelle Rosaldo and Barbara Gelpi (1982), in sociology by Dorothy Smith (1988) and in law by Carol Smart (1989). A visit to a decent bookshop, of course, would reveal much more.

Criminology, like feminism, encompasses disparate and sometimes conflicting perspectives. The history of criminology well reflects these (Rock, 1988). In contrast, the tensions and conflicts within feminism are seen as indicative of an inchoate, unrigorous and 'indisciplined' discipline. There is no one specific feminism just as there is no one specific criminology. True, some positions and perspectives will be seen as more 'right on' than others but essentially feminism, because of its acceptance of the importance of the personal, promotes tolerance of these different perspectives in its simple recognition of them (Mitchell and Oakley, 1986).

Criminology has for many feminist writers and researchers been a constraining rather than a constructive and creative influence. Indeed, in a sense our task in this book is to fracture its boundaries. We have found criminology to be impoverished and have looked elsewhere – to where feminists are working rather than criminologists – for help in understanding and making sense of our work. For this reason not all the contributors of this book would conventionally be described or describe themselves as criminologists and their essays reflect this in their use of ideas and material which lie beyond the narrow confines of the criminological enterprise.

We are wary of pursuing definitional clarification further since this seems to us to be a diversion – leading to 'false trails', endless disputes about whether or not particular writers or ideas have made positive contributions and hence, inevitably, to dead ends. We have chosen the title of this book – *Feminist Perspectives in Criminology* – with care, being anxious to avoid the difficulties of previous debates about whether or not there was or could be a 'feminist criminology' or 'feminist criminologies' and who 'belongs'. The issue is not of importance. All that it is necessary to say here, and what unites the contributors to this book, is that holding a feminist perspective means accepting the view that women experience subordination on the basis of their sex and working towards the elimination of that subordination.

Feminist (and non-feminist in recent years) writers alike have achieved a great deal. They have exposed criminology as the criminology of men. Theories of criminality have been developed from male subjects and validated on male subjects. Thus they are man-made. Whilst there is nothing intrinsically wrong with this, the problem is that these theories have been extended generally to include all criminals, defendants and prisoners. It was assumed that the theories would apply to women; most do not (Smart, 1976; Leonard, 1982; Heidensohn, 1985).

Feminist researchers have also made female offenders (Adler, 1975; Simon, 1975) and victims (Bowker, 1978; Pizzey, 1974) visible. They not only developed a critique of 'accumulated wisdom' about female offenders and victims, but illuminated institutionalized sexism within criminological theory, policy and practice. For example, they identified the way in which traditional gender-role expectations influenced the treatment of both female defendants and female victims (and hence indirectly of women generally). Thus, they showed that girls were penalized for behaviour which was condoned, if not encouraged, for boys (Chesney-Lind, 1973; 1977; 1988; Gelsthorpe, 1985a, 1989); that being a good wife or mother governed courtroom decision-making (Carlen, 1983; Eaton, 1986; Daly, 1989a) and that women who alleged abuse found themselves suspect (Dobash and Dobash, 1979; Walker, 1979; Stanko, 1985).

The importance of alternative modes of social control and their interconnections with criminal justice system controls has also been explored by feminist writers. They have made apparent the correspondences between the policing of everyday life and policing through more formal mechanisms (Smart and Smart, 1978; Hutter and Williams, 1981; Klein and Kress, 1976; Allen, 1987). Significantly, many of these writings have both informed and been informed by practice and practitioners – especially in relation to the work of rape crisis centres and refuges for battered women (Hanmer and Saunders, 1984).

Some feminist writers have gone beyond the stage of critique to unravel the confusion between feminist, women's and gender issues. Feminism does not mean an exclusive focus on women although it is often taken to mean that. Gender is both critical and central to the concerns of criminology. For example, if women do not commit as much crime as men – what Kathleen Daly and Meda Chesney-Lind (1988) call the 'gender ratio problem' – then this has profound significance for theory construction – what Daly and Chesney-Lind call the 'generalisability problem'. Theories of crime must be able to take account of both men's and women's (criminal) behaviour. They must also be able to highlight factors which operate differently on men and women. The fact that most theories do not do this (Leonard, 1982) is now widely accepted. What is not yet widely realized is that criminology, despite the fact that its primary subject matter is male offenders, focuses hardly at all on *men* and *masculinity*. It deals with men without acknowledging this and hence creates theories about criminals without a conceptualization of gender. For feminists this is a key construct.

Feminists have made other contributions too. In the USA, for example, Daly and Chesney-Lind (1988) have written about 'building theories of gender and crime', 'controlling men's violence towards women' and 'gender equality in the criminal justice system'. In our own work we have looked positively, and critically, at the shift from 'offenders' to the relationship between those who do and do not break the law, issues of social control and the use of micro- and macro-sociologies to increase our understanding of how knowledge is sustained and mediated and how structural constraints affect our everyday lives (Gelsthorpe and Morris, 1988).

Developing feminist perspectives in criminology is *a project under construction*; we would not pretend otherwise. After all, criminology has pursued many false trails and blind alleys. The task is one of re-vision – of taking into account women's and men's experiences, transforming existing knowledge foundations, transgressing traditional knowledge formations, taking tentative steps towards theory-building and creating new methodologies. This is much more than the 'revitalising' of existing perspectives of which David Downes and Paul Rock (1988) write. Feminist challenges to the criminological enterprise rank alongside the radical approaches of the 1960s and 1970s (ethnomethodology, symbolic interactionism, labelling theory, critical criminology and so on). We would argue that feminist perspectives do 'engender' both new and existing paradigms (cf Downes and Rock, 1988: 292).

In his paper on 'the present state of criminology in Britain', Rock writes that

> British criminologists know one another . . . educate one another . . . sometimes marry one another [*sic*] . . . read each other's works . . . gossip about each other . . . meet repeatedly in conferences . . . committees . . . form a social world.
>
> (1988: 67)

Rather than entering this closed world, the feminist enterprise seeks to fracture it. We agree with Daly and Chesney-Lind that 'the time has come for criminologists to step into the world of feminist thought, and for feminist scholars to step more boldly into all quarters of criminology' (1988: 498). This must be a journey of exploration for both men (and hence for men working in the criminological sphere) and women. We must not assume that women have a monopoly of understanding feminist perspectives. Women should surely be given the time and space to develop feminist perspectives in their own way, using their own language and not the categories and concepts provided for them by men in traditional methodologies; but there is a strong argument for encouraging men to consider and make use of feminist perspectives, even if they cannot completely share the emotional and political commitment which feminism entails. To promote separatism would be self-defeating in this context because it would mean the perpetuation of conventional knowledge boundaries. Our inclusion of contributions from male as well as female colleagues in this volume signifies this belief.

This book thus represents some tentative steps in this journey of exploration. The contributors between them add to the critique of criminology, review early feminist critiques, reflect on research approaches and methods, conceptualize new feminist standpoints and reveal the potential of feminism to transform and transgress both theory and the politics of research and practice.

Notes

1 We were introduced to this term by Maureen Cain.

PART 1

Rethinking criminology and the feminist critique

Criminology in all its guises has ignored women to a large extent. The construction, production and dissemination of knowledge has been dominated by men and men's discourse. Though Downes and Rock (1988) are right when they stress that women are not the only group who have been ignored, this is hardly an adequate response. The exclusion of women and others (for example, white-collar criminals) poses fundamental questions about the adequacy of the analyses.

Gender considerations have also, to a large extent, been ignored. Indeed, Downes and Rock (1988) remain unconvinced of their significance. They argue this because they believe that criminological theory has been 'crime-led' and that the subjects of this theorizing have been predominantly male adolescents. What they fail to realize is that the concept of gender includes *men* not just women.

This neglect of gender is well demonstrated in *A History of British Criminology* (Rock, 1989) which describes the development of criminology from 1870 to the present. The book presents a history of the major influences – sociology, psychology and law – which have determined the shape of the discipline; it also traces shifts in ideas from positivism through to the sociology of deviance, radical criminology and realism. But the majority of the contributors failed to address considerations of gender in any way that led them to rethink either their mode or unit of analysis. As we argued in our own contribution to that volume, references to gender have been characterized by marginalization (Walker, 1987; Bottomley and Pease, 1986), incorporation (Box, 1981; Downes and

Rock, 1988) and tokenism (Matthews and Young, 1986; Jones *et al.*, 1986).

There are now at least some signs of change and for this reason we deliberately invited two men to write about the way in which considerations of gender made them rethink their work, the writings of others and the construction of criminological knowledge itself. Thus the first two chapters are by men who have become aware, through feminism, of the inadequacies of criminological theory generally and of certain theories in particular.

Phil Scraton builds on the earlier work of *inter alia* Carol Smart (1976), Anne Campbell (1981), Frances Heidensohn (1985) and Allison Morris (1987) and presents a damning indictment of 'malestream' criminology. He documents the processes by which women have been generally excluded as both producers and subjects of criminological 'knowledge' and the processes by which women, when remembered, are presented in stereotypical terms. Remedying this, however, is not simply a matter of adding on women to the analyses since the basic framework of criminology with all its inadequacies would thereby remain solidly in place. Scraton argues instead that what is required of 'malestream' criminology is both a deconstruction and reconstruction of their frames of reference. Feminist insights aid this process by challenging the generation and distribution of knowledge and men's intellectual hegemony.

Some writers have pointed to the existence of sexism with respect to women in the criminal justice system (Smith, 1988). Colin Sumner believes that we need to augment this conception with recognition that there is also a particular notion of 'masculinity' within that system and that gender ideologies and gender-biased practices run deeper than mere sexism. Rather the criminal justice system is gender-oppressive. It is precisely these concerns which lead Sumner to develop a trenchant critique of the writings of Michel Foucault. While recognising Foucault's profound impact on criminological theorizing, Sumner argues that Foucault's work reflects a profoundly masculine perspective. Most notably, he demonstrates that it systematically ignored the gendered character of disciplinary power and the gendered character of censures of femininity and masculinity. At a more general level Sumner concludes that the task of reconstructing criminological theory is hindered by the unreconstructed gender character of its orthodoxy and that developments in men's studies and socialist–feminist analysis can help dissolve these theoretical blockages.

We have already pointed to the importance of early feminist work; see also Daly and Chesney-Lind, 1988; Simpson, 1989; Cain, 1990. This is not to say that it is without criticism. For example, early theoretical writings concentrated on inserting women into 'malestream' theories yet, at the same time, black and ethnic minority women were missing from the analyses. There was also both too much and to little emphasis on sexism.

Allegations of sexism were made without attempting to understand it in any organizational context and the possibility that men could be dealt with in a sexist way was ignored. The equality/inequality debate also took men as its norm and hence men remained the standard against which the treatment of women was judged. Furthermore whereas the stereotyping of women in the criminal justice system was attacked, the stereotyping of men in early feminist discussions of violence against women was accepted. The next two contributors provide a more detailed critique of early feminist work. We include these because the process of criticism is itself creative.

In her incisive and closely argued chapter Beverley Brown exposes the mistargeting inherent in some early feminist critiques of criminological theory because of their focus on biological determinism and their unquestioning acceptance of pre-existing critiques. She acknowledges, however, that feminists have learned from this and have begun the process of self-criticism. Marcia Rice castigates feminist research and writings for their attempts to 'insert women' into criminological concerns and questions without fully acknowledging that women have to be seen in relation to ethnicity (and class too). She shows that these writings have focused too much on the sexism of criminology and have ignored the extent to which sexist and racist ideologies interact. She also points to the ethnocentrism of criminology and feminists' failure to correct it. Her radical and important solution is to provide guidelines for the development of a black feminist perspective.

The final contribution to this part questions why feminists would want to work in criminology. Carol Smart's provocative chapter challenges the very nature of the criminological enterprise and underlines its intellectual poverty. She effectively draws attention to the wide and rich variety of feminist scholarship and contrasts it with the limited horizons of criminology. In focusing on the continuing 'marriage' of criminology to (unacknowledged) positivist paradigms she highlights criminology's isolation from some of the major theoretical and political questions which are engaging feminist scholarship elsewhere. This, she argues, is to criminology's loss and eventual diminishment.

2 Scientific knowledge or masculine discourses? Challenging patriarchy in criminology

Phil Scraton

Knowledge, academic discourse and patriarchy

> The sociologist is not what he eats; but . . . what he sees, does, and wants every day, in all his activities . . . whether as a sociologist or not . . . some sociologists I know are gentlemen–farmers or gentlemen–ranchers. . . Like other men, sociologists also have sex lives and 'even this' may be intellectually consequential. In loyalty tinged with bitterness, most stick it out to the end with wives who saw them through graduate school, while others practise serial polygamy . . . it is my strong but undocumented impression that when some sociologists change their work interests, problems, or styles, they also change mistresses or wives.
>
> (1970: 56–7)

Alvin Gouldner wrote this in his influential and widely acclaimed text on Western sociology's impending crisis. He identified and traced the direct relationship between academic sociology, the industrial–military complex and state funding, the conservatism which lay at the heart of the dominant academic paradigm of structural functionalism and the social reductionism implicit in the work of contemporary interactionist approaches of ethnomethodology and phenomenology. Gouldner's project was to establish reflexivity as a priority and so he argued for the significance of personal experiences and the knowledge brought to bear by the sociologist as interpreter of events. However, his radical route ostensibly bypassed the dominance of patriarchal assumptions within the process of interpretation. Sociologists were 'men at work' and, apparently, at play; women were related to the sociological profession as 'mistresses' or 'wives'. Radical contemporaries of Gouldner (Becker and Horowitz, 1972; Blackburn, 1969; and Shaw, 1972) shared his concern over the relationship of academia to the powerful but their analysis also did not extend to the material, social and personal subordination of women to men.

At around the same time Dorothy Smith wrote several articles concerning the systematic and institutionalized exclusion of women from academic discourses. Her initial work, introducing women's perspective as a radical critique of sociology (1973), proposed that academic discourse not only neglected women's experiences as priorities for analysis but also denied women – as inquirers – participation in the process of determining priorities. She wrote, 'women appear in a sociology [read criminology] predicated on the universe occupied by men' (1973: 7) and continued:

> How sociology is thought – its methods, conceptual schemes and theories – has been based on and built up within, the male social universe . . . the two worlds (that of women's and men's contrasting experiences) and the two bases of knowledge and experience don't stand in equal equation. The world as it is constituted by men stands in authority over that of women.
>
> (1973: 7)

Smith's position was that since women's contribution to the making of society was as significant as that of men, their exclusion was more than a reflection of a hierarchy of domination based on the ascribed importance of their relative contributions. It was also an exclusion from the construction of knowledge. Her critique was not very dissimilar to Gouldner's characterization of 'dominant assumptions'; it was just that Gouldner did not recognize the domain central to Smith's analysis. Women had experienced a systematic exclusion from full access and participation in academic work as men consolidated their circles formed around shared and taken for granted 'themes, assumptions, metaphors and images' (1975: 354). Whenever women did achieve access they remained on special licence, individuals entering the fringes of the circle on 'the terms and relevances of a discourse among men'. The exclusion of women operated on two levels: the common rooms of academia and the corridors of professional practice. This is well illustrated by Carol Smart's (1984) research into the legal profession and the administration of the law in Sheffield. She describes the experience of presenting herself to lawyers in a style and clothing which would ascribe to her the status necessary to carry out the project. It can be assumed that this episode represented, albeit in an exaggerated form, the problems encountered daily back in the academic institution.

Dorothy Smith's contribution, therefore, was to raise the importance of the assumed and ascribed *collective* authority of male academics. She questioned their authority to define, prioritize and reproduce the intellectual enterprise through the administration and maintenance of power within the profession or circle. But she went beyond the argument that women experience exclusion in terms of physical presence – as women – to suggest that women were also excluded in terms of the institutionalized denial of women's perspectives. Her position had much in common with Simone de Beauvoir's thesis in *The Second Sex* (1972), in which she presented the subject–object relationship as being the basis of women's experience of 'otherness': 'She (woman) is defined and differentiated with reference to man, not he with reference to her. . . He is the Subject, He is the Absolute . . . She is the Other' (1972: 16). For de Beauvoir this relationship of subjugation was accepted and internalized by women through the systematic employment of biological determinism. Otherness was self-evident, factual and embodied in nature rendering gender relations as universal and unchanging. She challenged the 'fixed and inevitable destiny' bestowed on women primarily through the 'scientific' claims of medicine and the social sciences. It was this proposition which was central to Smith's critique of academic discourse and women's access to academia.

As this volume demonstrates, a considerable amount of feminist work has followed the critical tradition set out by de Beauvoir and Smith. Academic fraternities have not only failed to understand these critiques but have also sought to represent them as a militant tendency from within a caricatured and monolithic women's movement. Yet the critiques, with their diverse complexity of political/theoretical analysis, refuse to be so misrepresented and their significance is that they strike at the heart of theory and method. The key question raised has been to ask how and why academic knowledge has taken shape, albeit with different emphases and priorities, in a consistently patriarchal form.

Theorizing, as with living, is a process which embodies struggles around continuity and change, which threatens established orders not only in wider politics but also in academic professions. Consequently the derivation of a theoretical framework has its roots in those theoretical traditions which it challenges. Its analysis, its discourse and its language are contextualized in the theoretical debates with – and rejection of – established theories and their methods. This is clearly evident from any historical examination of the pre-eminent traditions in criminology and their domain assumptions. Entire texts, like that of Gouldner, have been constructed to encapsulate these dialectics and analytical ground is possessed and defended by diversifying, refining and adjusting the mechanics of frameworks under scrutiny and challenge.

Foucault (1977) demonstrates clearly that discourses which engage with existing theoretical frameworks perversely reinforce their object of criticism because they recognize, and even reproduce, the prevailing distinctions. They become arguments about content rather than form, about text and sub-text rather than premise and context. While it is a dubious proposition to argue that deconstruction and reconstruction can be anything more than processes which embody criticism of, or opposition to, content (that is what is 'known'), the significant point here is the questioning of assumptions concerning the contexts in which knowledge is derived and consolidated. As with other influential post-war feminist critiques, the work of Simone de Beauvoir and Dorothy Smith has demonstrated that while theoretical debates have raged over the content and application of theory, they have neglected to consider the patriarchal essence – and substance – of the debates, their focus and their discursive priorities.

This leads to a further proposition central to Foucault's work, that of the relations between power and knowledge:

> We should admit rather that power produces knowledge (and not *simply* by encouraging it because it serves power or applying it because it is useful); that power and knowledge *directly* imply one another; that there is no power relation without the correlative constitution of a field of knowledge, or any knowledge that does not presuppose and constitute at the same time power relations.
>
> (1977: 27–8, emphasis added)

Foucault concludes that it is 'power–knowledge, the processes and struggles that traverse it and of which it is made up, that determines the forms and possible domains of knowledge', and it is this which requires analysis. While accepting that power produces knowledge not 'simply' in a determinate form which confines knowledge to the reproduction of dominant relations and also that power and knowledge are related 'directly', the significance of knowledges of resistance must not be understated. Foucault traces the extension of the technology of discipline throughout societal processes and Stanley Cohen takes this line further in his exploration of 'control talk', 'the logic and language of control' and professionalism's 'power to classify' (1985: 196). The reproduction of knowledge, which includes its language, its logic, its forms of classification, its instruments of measurement and its claims to scientific validity, is an essential part of the creative project of power. It should come as no surprise, then, to find academic professionalism, with its own reproductive capacity, directly implicated in the maintenance of power.

This does not imply a simplistic reductionism, for clearly there exists a long tradition of opposition from within academic disciplines. What it does suggest, however, is that if the liberating potential of critical analysis is to be realized it needs to be understood in terms of context within the domain assumptions of dominant structural relations and social arrangements. While state officials possess and use professional discretion in the administration of their duties, they remain constrained by their training, their role and their institutional parameters. As part of the interactive processes which comprise agency, they draw their legitimacy, status and *raison d'être* from the social structure and its attendant institutions of social control and political management (Giddens, 1979; 1984).

What is important here is to identify the determining contexts within which power knowledge relations and their consequent discourses take shape and become dominant, for structural relations cannot be confined simply to the arena of state institutional practices of political management. It is clear that identities and reputations, at the level of agency, are defined, identified, managed and policed; but these processes operate neither in a vacuum nor in a world of their own making or choosing. The work of Judith Walkowitz (1980) and Frank Mort (1987), on nineteenth-century medico–moral–legal discourses and their construction of policy interventions connected with sexuality, demonstrates clearly that the social relations of production and reproduction were primary determining contexts in the development of these discourses. Elaine Showalter's work (1987) on the history of the incarceration of women in mental institutions and the professional ideology and procedures which defined women's behaviour as mad or threatening is a further example of the need to contextualize the emergent state, its institutions, its professions and, therefore, its power–knowledge discourses, within the framework of social relations derived in the politics of reproduction under patriarchy.

What this proposition demands, therefore, is an explanation of the 'material base' and 'historical context' of patriarchy (O'Brien, 1981: 81) and its determining qualities in the creation of genderized social relations (Coole, 1988). Patriarchal relations have developed and maintained a complex universalism through the process of paternity, the means by which men appropriate children over and above women's relationship derived in childbirth. The socio–legal–political potency of patriarchy is the extension of this process into state, religious and cultural institutions (Millett, 1970; Rich, 1977). It combines the use of force and violence against women with the language, ritual, convention and legal discourses of subordination. While patriarchies differ and are complex (Segal, 1987), women's subjugation to men is a universal, structural reality (Morgan, 1986). Within patriarchy men dominate women through the threat and reality of physical violence (Kelly, 1988), through the unwaged and subordinated domestic mode of production (Delphy, 1984) and through 'control over women's labour power' (Hartmann, 1979: 14); the political economy of advanced capitalism is essentially patriarchal. While, as Hester Eisenstein has argued, it is important to 'retreat from false universalism' and to develop 'a sensitivity to the diversity of women's experiences and needs' (1984: 141), the advance of feminist critiques of patriarchy, with all their diversities and complexities, has been effectively to deconstruct the power–knowledge axis inherent in advanced capitalist societies.

These critiques have challenged the assumptions which historically have normalized and subordinated political relations based on perceived natural constructs of gender and sexuality. These assumptions are not the preserve of the everyday world of common sense; they are etched deep in the institutional fabric of the political economy, form part of the national consciousness and become central to the professionalism of knowledge. They are not confined to the arena of labour power and its utilization, nor to the administration of justice, health care, schooling, housing and welfare through the state, but they dictate the minutiae of interpersonal relations, restrict access to a whole range of social activities and place unwritten curfews on many women and some men. Most significant to the broader discussion here, however, is the permeation of such assumptions into academic discourse, their limitations on understanding and explanation and their shackling of priorities for developing critical analysis to the legacy of a genderized, masculinist and homophobic past.

If academic discourse and its patriarchal context is to be challenged it needs to be considered within a broader framework of how ideas gain currency, become transmitted and eventually become institutionalized or consolidated as knowledge. While this is apparent in Foucault's connection of knowledge to power and, in terms of patriarchy, the power that men institutionally, personally and physically exert over women, the further significant dimension is the process by which women's subordination is internalized and reproduced despite continuing grassroots resistance. Gramsci's (1972) concept of hegemony offers this dimension to the analysis since it demonstrates how dominance can be achieved and maintained without the use of direct coercion. By social arrangements, forms of political management and cultural tradition, which are the daily bread of what Wright (1978) refers to as the world at the level of appearances and which contextualize personal relations, hegemony is established. The potency of hegemony is that it is consensual and not coercive, that it reflects the reason and fairness of competing interests: it is a product of democratic pluralism.

With the relations of domination expressed through the material and physical power ascribed to men and supported by a 'hegemonic form of masculinity in the society as a whole' resides the compliant subordination of women, 'oriented to accommodating the interests and desires of men' (Connell, 1987: 183). Bob Connell terms this 'emphasised femininity' to stress that it does not preclude strategies of non-compliance by women. Also significant, however, are 'subordinated masculinities'. Examples here are the subordination of younger men to their seniors or the subordination of homosexuality to explicitly heterosexual hegemonic masculinity. Connell demonstrates that hegemonic masculinity, emphasized femininity and subordinated masculinities become the stock in trade of cultural processes, the media and policy orientations of formal politics. Further, they become the basic currency of entry into the world of work, leisure and social commentary, deeply ingrained in the initiation of induction procedures of political and economic institutions, social clubs and gatherings, and forming the basis of laws, conventions and practices.

It was with these issues in mind that Dorothy Smith expressed her concern over academic work, its structural opportunities and its priorities for research and teaching. It is within this interpretation of hegemony that de Beauvoir's man as subject, woman as object is to be found. Emphasized femininity is an expression, even a celebration, of otherness. Taken together with the power–knowledge relationship established as central within patriarchal relations, hegemonic masculinity adds the important dimension of cultural transmission and internalization of patriarchal values. While these values contrast in time, place, cultural manifestation, race and class, they embody the physical and personal subjugation of women to men, the material domination of men over women which includes essentially the domestic sphere and ways of seeing, thinking and responding which are portrayed as expressions of a natural order. The development of criminology, and the radicalization of its project, has not been free from these imperatives.

Views from the 'boys': some reflections on the criminological tradition

Criminology and the sociology of deviance must become more than the study of men and crime if it is to play any significant part in the development of our understanding of crime, law and the criminal process and play any role in the transformation of existing social practices.

(Smart, 1976: 185)

With these words Carol Smart concluded her feminist critique of criminology and the sociology of deviance. In the introduction to this pioneering text she wondered if all that it would lead to would be a token lecture on criminology courses while their main content would 'remain undisturbed, continuing to be concerned with the "real" or "important" issues, namely explaining male criminality and delinquency' (Smart, 1976: xiv). Her concern was that criminology, even in its more radical form, would be 'unmoved' by feminist critiques. Over a decade later it is clear that on many courses her fears have been realized despite the fact that a strong feminist literature concerned with analysing the history and development of criminology and its patriarchal roots has emerged. Following on from the work of Dorie Klein, Freda Adler and Rita Simon (see Adler and Simon, 1979), Eileen Leonard (1982) filled the substantial gap left by contemporary radical texts such as Taylor, Walton and Young (1973, 1975), in providing a review of five of the main criminological theories from a feminist perspective. In her conclusion she proposed a structural analysis which would provide a framework for understanding 'the connections between women and their patterns of crime'; 'the process by which a person becomes a criminal'; 'a grasp of law making and the application of law'; and 'how sex, race and class interact to produce criminal patterns' (1982: 191).

More recently texts by Frances Heidensohn (1985), Allison Morris (1987) and Pat Carlen and Anne Worrall (1987), among others, have extended the project of feminist analysis beyond women's criminality to deal with the processes which underpin it and which operate within the criminal justice system. Furthermore, women have written about women's experiences in a wide range of areas: prisons, policing, welfare, Nothern Ireland, race, public order, pornography, violence against women and mental health. Dorothy Smith's objective would appear to have been realized. Whether this breakthrough has been replicated in mainstream criminology, however, is doubtful.

Examples of the neglect of feminist analysis in contemporary writings are not difficult to find. Contributions to an Open University reader (Fitzgerald *et al.*, 1981), the first overviewing critical developments in criminology in the 1960s and 1970s (Cohen, 1981) and the second exploring six major paradigms within criminological theory (Young, 1981), and influential mid-1980s' texts (Downes and Rock, 1982; Cohen, 1985) discussed criminological theory, its traditions and the processes of social control, without so much as a tokenistic nod in the direction of feminist analysis. The much publicized *British Journal of Criminology*'s edited special issue, *A History of British Criminology*, is a pertinent example of the problem (Rock, 1988). Of the fourteen contributors all but two are men – the two women contributed a paper on feminism and criminology (Gelsthorpe and Morris, 1988). Their paper provides a useful overview of the impact of feminist work on criminology, deviancy theory and the criminal justice process. Yet it is some measure of the *lack* of impact that the other papers in the collection remain free of any references to feminist analyses and their critiques of the history of British criminology.

An excursion through the twentieth-century's developments in criminology is a journey through communities inhabited only by men, passing street corners and seafronts occupied exclusively by male youth and into soccer stadia, youth clubs and rock venues where women and their experiences fail to register even a passing comment from the researchers. When women are noted they are viewed through the eyes, comments and reflections of men or male youth. They are possessed, rejected, tolerated and defined by the experiences and judgements of 'hegemonic masculinity' and it is their ascribed sexuality which is central to such judgements (Scraton, 1987a; 1987b).

Post-war developments in British criminology heavily profiled the 'delinquent' behaviour of young men and the construction of 'criminal areas'. These developments were rooted in several decades of American work, particularly the Chicago School (Mays, 1954; 1967). While it was recognized that American theories could not be simply transposed on to British society (Downes, 1966), the emphasis remained the same: 'sub-cultures', 'delinquency' and 'gangs' were the sole province of men. The lives of young women did not feature.

As the structural functional perspective was challenged and gave way in some respects to new deviancy theory, the theoretical emphasis shifted, but assumptions about gender and sexuality remained taken for granted. In the 1970s a range of studies provided 'views from below' as crime and deviancy theorists plotted a more radical course through the streets and alleys of inner-city areas. The search was for 'social context', to define 'delinquent action' from within the communities in which it occurred and to propose that apparently mindless behaviour could form part of the politics of 'doing nothing' (Cohen, 1972; Patrick, 1973; Parker, 1974; Gill, 1977; Corrigan, 1979). There is no doubting the signifi-cance of the contribution of this work both in challenging the analytical shortcomings of established theory and practice and in giving a legit-imacy, a meaning, to the daily experiences of young men. Phil Cohen's essay (1972), for example, became a classic account of working-class youth subcultures in London's East End in which he contextualized their rebelliousness, visible in style and identity, as an expression of the economic, social and cultural changes facing traditional working-class life. Cohen's work was well received precisely because it 'took into account the full interplay of ideological, economic and cultural factors which bear upon subculture' (Hebdige, 1979: 78).

This range of critical work on youth, subcultural form, style, symbol and collective identity and action, however, fell short of a 'full interplay' of factors. While the significant contributions of Paul Willis (1977) and the various contributors to Hall and Jefferson (1976) recognized the importance of gender and sexuality in their analysis, they were not central to it. Willis did raise the issue of sexuality and the complexity of meaning ascribed to contrasting expressions of sexuality between young men and women. The research, however, was filtered through masculine assumptions; see also Robins and Cohen, 1979; Lea and Young, 1982; Williams and Dunning, 1984; Dunning *et al.*, 1988. It was as if some recognition of feminist work was necessary but that the potential of that work was neither understood nor appreciated. The occasional walk on parts of young women in these studies were matched by the occasional walk on parts of feminist work in the analysis. When it did appear, like the visibility of young women in the research, its interpretation was simply confined to the traditional role of women and women's sexuality.

Throughout the 1970s and 1980s, however, reassurances were voiced from within the academic profession: studies of young women's lives had been contracted and so soon they would 'catch up the men' – a century of imbalance would be redressed. While excellent studies have emerged (Griffin, 1985; Lees, 1986) naive constructs of equality miss the point. The body of knowledge was already in place, against which women's accounts and women's experiences were commissioned, published and assessed. The patriarchal discourse, as discussed in the first section, was established as subject – the feminist response was object. The status of 'other' was ascribed in the construction of ideas and the formulation of knowledge.

It is not sufficient simply to argue that women's accounts, experiences and researches have been absent from the overall project and that, therefore, all that is needed is something which can be added on to that which is 'known'. As Sydie (1987) and Harding (1986) have so clearly demonstrated, if the premises of the analysis are flawed, then it follows that understanding derived from the research also is flawed. As the previous section concluded, the significance of the challenge to academic discourses which are in essence patriarchal is not to rewrite the projects or reinterpret their findings; it is rather to *deconstruct* their frames of reference and to *reconstruct* a critical analysis which has at its base a grasp of the primary determining contexts which together structure and shape economic, political, social and cultural experiences of everyday life.

Resisting the 'malestream': the challenge for critical criminology

What has been created is an image of the critical debates in criminology and deviancy theory as being high-jacked by ultra-leftists whose crude reductionism and determinism removed the possibility or perceived need to engage in responsible, constructive or interventionist dialogue around crime and policing.

(Sim *et al.*, 1987: 41)

This comment forms part of a substantive critique of the work in the 1980s in British criminology of the self-styled 'new realists'. Beginning with a series of articles (Young, 1979; Kinsey and Young, 1982) and developing their work in texts (Lea and Young, 1984; Matthews and Young, 1986; Kinsey *et al.*, 1986), 'new' or 'left' realists set out to discredit the work of critical criminologists to whom they ascribed the generic label 'left idealists'. The main theme running through the new writings was that 'left idealists' were crude reductionists and economic determinists uninterested in state reform or political negotiation. They were caricatured as the polar opposite of establishment or conservative criminologists and viewed as rejecting analysis for rhetoric and espousing revolution rather than reform. In contrast, the new realists saw themselves as occupying the middle ground, committed to pragmatism and winnable political objectives. It was never clear exactly who or what constituted left idealism yet the label had a currency, particularly with mainstream Labour politics in the mid-1980s and it became a prophecy self-fulfilled. While left idealists were nowhere to be found, it was safely assumed that, Yeti-like, they existed.

The impact of this perspective on critical criminology has been profound. While the new realists chose *their* identity, they ascribed left idealisms, as a caricature, to others in the radical debate. There were no clear theoretical indicators of what constituted the full-blown sin of left idealism but, in their commentaries, the new realists selected a few paragraphs here, a few there, to point the accusatory finger. Left idealism, it would seem, was action so labelled! As with criminal or deviant reputations, however, the label soon became institutionalized. Criminology courses examined students on the new realism/left idealism 'debate' as if the latter existed and embraced their ascribed status. This was confirmed by reference to the 'debate' in a new sociology reader (Abercrombie *et al.*, 1988; see also Edwards's (1989d) text on violence against women).

In terms of advancing the project of critical analysis, the construction of the realism/idealism debate has been diversionary, regressive and purposefully misrepresentative of the advances within critical criminology since the mid-1970s. The development and consolidation of that work encompasses a full range of issues: policing, prisons, Northern Ireland, race, gender, and the challenge of alternative accounts to official discourse. Sim *et al.* (1987) correct the direction of new realism and its associated politics and present a theoretical framework directly representative of the primary determining contexts and structural relations of contemporary Western societies.

One of the main criticisms of the radical shift in criminology was that it remained gender-blind. This point has been reiterated by Susan Edwards in her commentary on left realism (1989d) and, from a different perspective within feminism, by Liz Kelly and Jill Radford (1987). It is their contention that the underlying problem is that criminology, be it traditional, critical, Marxist, or realist, remains malestream and, consequently, has difficulty in dealing with 'activism, theorizing and research' based on women's 'individual and shared experiences' (1987: 237). This construction has drawn useful criticism from sociologists concerned about its possible reductionism. In such language, argues Connell, 'a social fact or process is coupled with, and implicitly attributed to, a biological fact' and consequently produces a 'naturalisation of social processes, without question the commonest mechanism of sexual ideologies' (1985: 266). Hester Eisenstein makes a similar point in her critique of the concept of 'all women' as false universalism (1985: 134).

Connell's concern, like Eisenstein's, is that the ascription of malestream denotes an equally false universalism based solely on biology. It would be a legitimate concern if the construction was established as a category applicable to all analysis by men regardless of their theoretical position. Kelly and Radford's work, however, deals with the authoritative universalism of academic knowledge which, as demonstrated earlier, is essentially patriarchal. Their analysis is concerned with structural relations and this in no way predetermines the capacity of individuals to think or theorize individually. What their work suggests is the implication of mainstream academic discourses in the political processes of 'ideology and coercion'. As Catherine MacKinnon states:

The state is male in a feminist sense. . . The liberal state coercively and authoritatively constitutes the social order in the interest of men as a gender, through its legitimising norms, relation to society, and substantive policies.

(1983: 644)

Thus power is institutionalized in a masculine, indeed masculinist, form. Returning to Foucault, the power–knowledge relation normalizes patriarchy and its academic expression and professional structures reflect, reinforce and reproduce patriarchal relations. All men benefit from this process of normalization regardless of their intent or purpose, for patriarchies institutionalize social relationships which provide men with power (economic, political and cultural) over women and enable them to appropriate children. Further, Kelly and Radford state, 'patriarchal societies may also include hierarchies constructed on the basis of class, race and sexuality which divide men and women', but patriarchal oppression, 'like all forms of imperialism/oppression/exploitation is ultimately based on violence' (1987: 238–9).

The foregrounding of patriarchy in this way reveals a tendency to subordinate other forms of oppression to those of sexism and heterosexism. It is a tendency which has produced considerable confused and confusing debate over hierarchies of oppression and often futile discussion about the relative statuses of women and men who experience discrimination and oppression through non-comparative differences in race, class, physical and mental capability. At the centre of critical analysis, however, should not be a notional league table of differential oppression but a theoretical framework which provides an understanding of the primary determining contexts derived in the dominant structural relations of a society's history, economy, politics and cultural forms. If the experiential, daily world of social interaction and institutional reaction (that is, agency) is to be interpreted in context then it needs to be located within the dominant structural forces. These forces are·derived from a society's economy (that is, the relationship between national industry and multinational corporations), its politics (the nation-state and its international alliances) and its primary ideologies (that is, the relationship between populism, official discourses and institutionalized processes). How these forces have structurally embodied oppressive and exploitative social relations should be the fundamental concern of critical analysis.

Whatever the short-term objectives of 'realism', and its apparent faith in the British tradition of social democracy, its neglect of these structural forces and the primary determining contexts of production, reproduction and neo-colonialism suggests a tacit acceptance of a pluralist interpretation of contemporary conflict. The social relations of production derived in advanced capitalism, however, represent a more complex development of the class relations of early capitalism (see, for example, Braverman, 1974; Wright, 1978). The development and consolidation of advanced capitalism in Britain could not have been achieved without the unique contribution of the economics of slavery, colonization and imperialism (Sivanandan, 1982). The imperialist legacy remains central, economically, politically and ideologically, to the institutionalization of racism directed towards black people, others of 'colour' (Gilroy, 1987) and Irish communities in Britain (Curtis, 1984). This has given rise to a now taken for granted legal framework of differential policing and regulation (Hillyard, 1987). Beyond this there exists a mass of contemporary evidence which shows the extent to which the law, at all levels, discriminates against identifiable groups on the grounds of race (see Marcia Rice in this volume). In considering the main contexts which determine social relations in Britain, neocolonialism historically and contemporaneously is central.

The main concern of this chapter, however, has been to expose the flawed base of established academic discourses given their assumptions concerning the naturalness of gender divisions and heterosexuality. The social relations of reproduction, so much the essence of the political–economic formation of patriarchy, are irretrievably connected to the structural forces of advanced capitalism and neocolonialism and their social relations. Marginalization is not a political-economic process restricted to comparative minorities such as the poor, black or Irish people. While women collectively experience the process of marginalization, their experiences are mediated by other structural factors such as race, class, sexuality and disability.

Critical criminology, then, is a progression from unidimensional discourse and analysis. Its main theoretical construction is the synthesis and application of a framework sensitive to the interconnections between social relations of production, reproduction and neocolonialism. Within this framework there is no hierarchy of oppressions and no clearly defined boundaries to the analysis of institutional process or social interaction. To consider contemporary British society, its institutions, its social arrangements or its social

movements without prioritizing the centrality of each of these primary determining contexts is to flaw the analysis from the outset.

As Gramsci argued, the rule of law is central to the shaping of society.
The state and its institutions, including the formalization of knowledge,
are sites of struggles around class, race, gender and sexuality. Not only do
they attempt to resolve such struggles in conditions favourable to an
established order but also they seek to anticipate and prevent the mobilization of oppositional forces. Thus the state represents a series of relations
which are complex and often contradictory. While oppositional voices are
permitted a voice, established positions are defended on the basis of
alliances which cut across the state's institutional forms (the government,
civil service, education, judiciary and so on). The containment and management of political struggle is a developing process informed by class,
race and gender alliances forged in the training, selection and professional ideologies common to all state agencies. There are coincidences of
interest; there is a common or shared ideology and the hegemonic conditions which dominate contemporary British society are manifested in the
policies, priorities and practices of state intervention. Institutions, be they
legal, administrative or academic, tutor, guide and educate the broad
membership of society. They are not passive or static; nor are they
autonomous.

Within this framework patriarchy takes a political as well as an economic form and engenders opposition, but it also generates ideological
constructions of reality as justification for and maintenance of its inherent
material relations of dominance. It is here that hegemonic masculinity
pervades the state and its institutions, regenerating and reconstructing
ideas as well as policies which form a potent defence of the structural
contradictions and alienating processes of patriarchy. While that pervasiveness is to be found overtly in the making, enforcement and application of the law, it is also found covertly in the academic discourses which
prevail within malestream criminology.

Critical criminology sets out to theorize and research the interconnection between marginalization and criminalization, to understand the
relationship between management by consent and rule by coercion.
Authoritarianism is not an alternative state form to liberal democracy;
rather it is the flipside of the same coin. As feminist critiques have
emphasized, hegemonic masculinity might attempt to establish the subordination of women and other masculinities through processes of ideological construction and political management but the threat and reality
of state-legitimated physical violence directly related to sexuality remains
fundamental to patriarchal domination.

This leads to concluding comments concerning possible directions forward. In her examination of contemporary motherhood, sexuality and
men's dominance, Ann Ferguson (1989) presents a socialist–feminist

vision aimed at 'maximising egalitarian and democratic values' involving: the elimination of gender dualism; the creation of democratic parenting; the promotion of sex for pleasure; the promotion of committed sexual relationships; and the guaranteeing of gay and lesbian rights. Central to her project is the 'transcendence of old oppositional gender categories' – masculinity and femininity – and the 'breakdown in the gender division of labour and in the household'. She concludes, 'since roles would no longer be tied to gender or even to all aspects of individuals' interactions, they would not support hierarchical relationships between individuals such as male dominance or compulsory heterosexuality' (1989: 232). As Cynthia Cockburn (1986) states, however, gender dualism is deeply ingrained in personal, social and occupational lives and is strongly related to institutionalized hierarchies. As men's supremacy is social, economic and cultural all men have much to lose in entering the world projected in Ferguson's vision. Cockburn argues that while 'masculinity loses' in the 'escape from gender complementarity' there are major advances to be made in a society based on a 'celebration of multiplicity and individual difference' (1986: 231). This proposes a release from oppression and coercion wrought on women through their subjugation to men's supremacy and from the distortion and dislocation experienced by the supremacists as they struggle to conform to the demands of hegemonic masculinity. Further, it affirms the need to move beyond ways of thinking, acting and responding rooted in the social arrangements and structural relations inherent in gender divisions and compulsory heterosexuality.

Critical criminology requires at its core not only analysis of gender divisions but also of sexuality. The important work of Jeff Hearn (1987) and Bob Connell (1987) on hegemonic masculinity and Arthur Brittan (1989) on masculinism as a dominant ideology has much to offer the debate. In terms of academic practice, the need to identify and combat hegemonic masculinity and homophobia cannot be externalized simply to men's behaviour outside the institution. In the early 1980s David Morgan tackled the twin pillars of 'academic machismo' (the competitive display of masculine skills) and 'male homosociobility' (the processes of discrimination against and exclusion of women). A decade on, the twin pillars remain fixed, as if in concrete. What this confirms is the durability of patriarchal structures. Sadly, it leads to the inevitable conclusion that academic disciplines have realigned with their brother institutions to resist and marginalize feminist critiques. In knowing their enemy, the proponents of malestream criminology, be they of the establishment or of 'new/left realism', have resisted the 'feminist project of reconstructing knowledge so that it no longer reflects exclusively a male social reality' (Naffine, 1987: 127). It is a resistance which has been determined and which has become part of a much wider backlash against feminist research, teaching and practice.

Acknowledgements

Many thanks to Sheila Scraton for her critical comments and support, to Kathryn Chadwick for several years of shared work and to our undergraduate and postgraduate students on the 'gender and sexuality' courses . . . many were women . . . too few were men. Finally, my appreciation to the editors for their patience and encouragement.

3　Foucault, gender and the censure of deviance

Colin Sumner

The insights and silences in the work of Michel Foucault have opened up a space which at the same time they leave conspicuously vacant. That space concerns the gendered character of disciplinary procedures and categories. Foucault raises questions about the origins and content of the modern system of social regulation that are not dealt with in those feminist histories which portray an eternal, unending and undifferentiated dirge of patriarchy;[1] yet he avoided answering them in quite spectacular fashion. Indeed he has been accused of both neglecting gender issues and of relegating women to a minor role in world history: 'a profoundly androcentric writer . . . Foucault's work is not the work of a ladies' man' (Morris, 1988: 26; and see Diamond and Quinby, 1988, in general).

This chapter makes a minor exploration of the space Foucault left behind. It involves a mischievous play rather than a comprehensive review, with the intention merely of clearing some ground for the further development of the sociology of social censure and regulation (see Sumner, 1976; 1979; 1983; 1990). Beginning with an interpretation of Foucault's theory of normalization, it goes on to offer some thoughts on the relation between gender and the censure of deviance. The central theses are (1) that there are such things as master-censures[2] which are central features of hegemonic ideology; (2) that the censure of femininity is still one of them; (3) that social censures are interconnected by their associated historic employment in ideological practices; and (4) that therefore most hegemonic censures of deviance are, at a minimum, coloured at a deep-structural level by the master-censure of femininity, in connection with other master–censures. Underpinning the argument is a conviction that criminological theory has not yet begun to recognize the hegemonic masculinity of its central concepts nor, therefore, to revise its deep-rooted androcentrism. This conviction is compounded by a feeling that the much needed renewal in criminological theory is significantly blocked by the unreconstructed gender character of its orthodoxy, and that developments in men's studies and socialist–feminist analysis can help to dissolve those theoretical blockages.

Normalization and deviation

In *Discipline and Punish* Foucault argues that the carceral archipelago takes the 'penitentiary technique . . . from the penal institutions to the entire social body' (1977: 298). Bad manners, he claims, have been moved into the same disciplinary field as multiple homicide (see also Elias, 1978; 1982; *Theory, Culture and Society* 1987). Nowadays, virtually every social practice is invested with a single technique, that of discipline, a strategy of cost-efficient domination that homogenizes, simplifies, regiments and scientizes an otherwise messy practical world of hungry, passionate and creative human beings. The *grundnorm* of subjection, in the service of capital accumulation (1977: 220–1) and the will to power thus creates a degree of moral unity which, once established, turns each technical infraction of its codes and procedures into a moral deviation and each errant subject into a deviant. Simultaneously, each practical penalization of deviance creates, sustains and maximizes that degree of disciplinary unity. In other words, the evil enemy of the merchant–monarch in the *ancien régime* of the penality of terror has been transformed into the deviant of the bourgeois welfare state, 'who brought with him the multiple danger of disorder, crime and madness' (1977: 300); and with her?

To extend this creatively, or to play inside the Foucauldian pen as he did inside the Nietzschean (see Foucault, 1980: 53–4), we could say that the order of sin is now conjoined with the order of crime. Criminal codes, the norms of the ecclesiastical courts, the disciplining of labour, the protocols of court manners and the general regulation of popular appetites have been gradually synthesized, unified and co-ordinated. But the state has not simply converted virtue into a question and object for social administration and legal regulation (Foucault, 1971: 61); it has also distilled from it a categorical table of deviations which run from treason to bad table manners. The abstract unity of bourgeois–disciplinary power has transformed and moulded the contextuality, complexity and imprecision of the human judgement of immorality into a hierarchy of deviant behaviours.

For raw materials, this labour of punitive signification has drawn upon the older ideological spectres of disorder, crime and madness. Always metaphors of significant and already well-signified fears, these master-censures and their associated moral tales (or narratives) have become deeply imbricated in the disciplinary system and its knowledges, profoundly shaping the criteria of gradation and explanation: 'underlying disciplinary projects the image of the plague stands for all forms of confusion and disorder' (1977: 199). These dominant-ideological but popular master-censures, and the emotions they generate, were, for Foucault (but in my terms), the basic ideological formations inscribed in the codes and procedures of disciplinary power. They provided a passionate impetus for the daily detail of social regulation (Foucault, 1977: 299).

In Foucault's work this whole process I have just outlined is described as normalization, or the permeation of normalizing power into the arteries of social practice; a process whereby the carceral network, with its systems of insertion, distribution, surveillance, observation' is the key support 'of the normalising power', 'the universal reign of the normative' (1977: 304). Hegemonic power is thus consolidated (1977: 208). Normalizing power works through the norm, which is 'a mixture of legality and nature, prescription and constitution' (1977: 304), to produce 'a physics of a relational and multiple power, which has its maximum intensity not in the person of the King, but in the bodies that can be individualized by these relations' (1977: 208). This power of the norm is different from the power of law and analysis should recognize its dominance in modern reality, 'not out of a speculative choice or theoretical preference, but because in fact it is one of the essential traits of Western societies' (1978: 102). But it does not displace law, rather law is subsumed: 'the law operates more and more as a norm . . . the judicial institution is increasingly incorporated into a continuum of apparatuses . . . whose functions are for the most part regulatory' (1978: 144). Discipline became 'co-extensive with the state itself' (1977: 215), but is not confined to state apparatuses and operates across the whole social field, infiltrating, linking and extending other modalities and mechanisms of power. It supports law, by its 'systems of micro-power' (1977: 222), and 'neutralises' counter-power or resistance with the principle of 'mildness–production–profit' rather than the levy of violence (1977: 219).

Normalization involves, then, a combination and generalization of 'panoptic techniques', subsuming other forms of power. In this process the censorious ideological formations and knowledges which feed the will to regulate, are reformed, strengthened and reinforced by their role in the exercise of this new modality of power; indeed new ones arise in the course of regulation itself. The censures thus established, we could say, acquire (1) the authority of detail and the persuasiveness of superficial efficacy; (2) the formal neutrality of a decentred mode of political subjection, no longer dependent on the sovereign; and (3) the political legitimacy of being sanctioned by the burgeoning state power.

In this way a complex composition of hegemonic, and therefore social, censures emerged and, eventually, became the foundation of positivist and administrative forms of criminology. Later still, a sociology of deviance was constructed which took the hegemonic norm as its basemark or yardstick in defining and investigating 'deviations'. The sociology of deviance would have no subject matter to speak of unless it assumed a generalized normative order which specified an extensive table of deviations. Thus, when liberal and radical sociologists finally turned the tables and examined the powers behind the norm, instead of the infractions of the alleged deviant, the central structure of this disciplinary knowledge fell down like a house of cards.

Broad images of disease, the devil, crime and treason had been intellectually converted by the, mainly American, sociology of deviance between 1937 and 1968, into neutral-sounding deviations, allegedly curable by psychiatry, social work and social policy. Later on, in the 1968–75 period, these deviations were sometimes romanticized as resistances, before being finally more realistically reconstructed and reconstituted in the late 1970s and the 1980s as social censures (see Sumner, 1990). But the return of unreason to its constitution in ideology and knowledge as the cut or caesura of a moral–political censure (see Foucault, 1971: ix and 250), the return of censure to its origins, involves an as yet unwritten history of the censure of deviance, well beyond my present competence. Suffice it to note for now that Foucault thought that we now live in societies ridden with the surveillance and discipline of normalizing judgements:

> It must be recognised that one was in the grip of a positive operation that confined madness in a system of rewards and punishments, and included it in the movement of moral consciousness. A passage from a world of Censure to a universe of Judgment.
>
> (1971: 250)

It is also now recognized that the myth of neutral, professional judgement has begun to be exposed by recent radical sociology, as the evaluative cut of moral–ideological censure (see Pearson, 1975; Box, 1983; Sumner, 1983; 1990).

So far, this discussion has taken the form of creative and synthetic interpretation; now let us turn to critique. Normalization, on Foucault's analysis, seems to work as a neat historical trick. It is presented as a strategy which produces a disciplined individual who is normally so unaware of the place of individualization in the general strategies of domination that s/he operates within the illusion of a rationalistic voluntarism, while performing the economic, political, sexual and ideological roles required by sustained capital accumulation and bourgeois hegemony. It is a central concept in Foucault's account of the subjection of the human capacity to a monarchy of legal–rational personality, a capacity whose ultimate truth is supposed to reside, according to a popular ideology, in sexuality and the psycho-analysis of the unconscious, in the recesses of a suppressed unreason; his mimic of Hobbes is striking. In a nice irony, the suppressed half-truth of the human condition (the world of passion, spontaneity and non-rationality) has become, on Foucault's analysis, the whole truth of the permissible other half-truth of humanity (the world of rationality, judgement, conformity and discipline); but without even an advertence to the feminist view of the subjugation of women and femininity as the foundation of the supremacy of men and masculine rationality. Not even a word for the *fraternité* of 1789. Having recently celebrated the bicentenary of the French Revolution, we should reflect on the masculinity of the Enlightenment.

The concept of normalization, in Foucault's analysis, not only produces an apparently gender-neutral, political and economic subjection (cf Pate-man, 1988) and a consciously free, choosing subject (unrestrained it seems by gender), but also a subjection to the 'monarchy of sex' (1978: 159) and a consciously sexual subject:

> We expect our intelligibility to come from what was for many cen-turies thought of as madness . . . over the centuries it (sex) has become more important than our soul, more important almost than our life.
>
> (1978: 156)

Sex became, on Foucault's argument, the illusory key to the intelligibility of a universal subjectivity and a distraction from and condensation of the real polymorphism of human desires (1978: 157; 1986).

It seems clear to me that, at best, Foucault's analysis misses a great opportunity to understand the construction and role of gender categories in the establishment of capitalism, disciplinary power and the modern state. At worst, his work is guilty of a sustained androcentrism and gender-blindness at the deepest level of formation of his theoretical con-cepts. His concept of normalization completely glosses over the role of the censure of women and femininity in the hegemonic ideologies constitut-ing the political and economic fabric of the modern state. At no point during the Enlightenment, or even by the twentieth century, were the notions of right, personality, contract, property and equality ever free from the oppressive limitations of the censure of women and femininity. Nor could the militaristic mechanics of disciplinary power, so important to Foucault's neo-Nietzschean schema, ever be seriously combined, unproblematically, with the historic features of what is known as the feminine; they represent only the method of hegemonic masculinity, its own distinct political tactics. Rousseau once commented, in *Emile*, that

> Woman, who is weak and who sees nothing outside the house, estimates and judges the forces she can put to work to make up for

her weakness, and those forces are men's passions. Her science of mechanics is more powerful than ours; all her levers unsettle the human heart.

(1762, in 1979: 387)

Foucault never seems to see that disciplinary power is based on a military masculinity and, in that it has a major problem with human values and emotion, is thereby brittle and very limited in character; or that an awful masculinity based upon a militaristic orientation to life is a major concomitant of disciplinary power.

Nor could subjection to a 'monarchy of sex' ever be imagined to be anything other than a *male* problem: women have long complained that the problem is not so much men's obsession with sex but rather that the monarch of sex and sexual ideology is a macho male. The formation of the modern subject is a profoundly gendered process, as indeed is the formation of the modern state. Modern social censures and forms of social regulation are fundamentally gendered.

The gender of censure

The androcentric fallacy, which is built into all the mental constructs of Western civilisation, cannot be rectified by simply 'adding women'. What it demands for rectification is a radical restructuring of thought and analysis which once and for all accepts the fact that humanity consists in equal parts of men and women and that the experiences, thoughts, and insights of both sexes must be represented in every generalization that is made about human beings.

(Lerner, 1986: 220)

Foucault's archaeological excavations dug up more than he was aware of, or at least more than he could handle theoretically (or emotionally?). Whether we can do more than clear the dirt off and polish these interesting clues to the construction of our present moral order I do not know; but they certainly provide an opportunity to clarify the working assumptions of my own enquiry into the sociology of censures. In an earlier essay (1983) I had merely implied the relative autonomy of gender division without exploring the issue or emphasizing its importance.

Foucault's argument is that during the seventeenth century virtue became 'an affair of state': 'the laws of the state and the laws of the heart are at last identical' (1971: 61). Madness 'had been sequestered and, in the fortress of confinement, bound to reason, to the rules of morality and their monotonous nights'. 'Here reason reigned in the pure state, in a triumph arranged for it in advance over a frenzied unreason' (1971: 64). But was this identity of the law of state with the laws of the heart a gender-neutral affair?

Foucault clearly implies that it certainly has a specific class content: 'The walls of confinement actually enclose the negative of that moral city of which the bourgeois conscience began to dream in the seventeenth century' (1971: 61). But he seems not to make much of the gender content of his own evidence. To take one interesting example, an observation from 1770, presumably by a doctor:

> Most men are censured, not without reason, for having degenerated in contracting the softness, the habits, and the inclinations of women; there is lacking only a resemblance in bodily constitution. Excessive use of humectants immediately accelerates the metamorphosis and makes the two sexes almost as alike in the physical as in the moral realm. Woe to the human race, if this prejudice extends its reign to the common people; there will be no more plowmen, artisans, soldiers, for they will soon be robbed of the strength and vigour necessary to their profession.
>
>   (la Mesnardiere, quoted in Foucault, 1971: 170)

Foucault's brief comment is that this 'moral therapeutics of the body' (1971: 159) supposed that 'the abuse of hot drinks risks leading to a general feminisation of the human race' (170). Well, yes, but so much more can be said. After all, if Foucault can mock both empiricist and totalizing historiographies with his frequent use of the discourses of apparently minor, unidentified figures of no obvious representativeness, we can use those same sources to question whether Foucault's love of the obscure and unimportant might, ironically, lead him to make molehills out of mountains.

The doctor's statement suggests that by 1770 in France there was a general notion of what masculinity men should display, that a certain kind of masculinity was seen as vital to the role of the lower orders in reproducing the wealth and power of the bourgeoisie and aristocracy and that women do not possess the strength and vigour to sustain the state of the *ancien régime*. Rousseau's *Emile* of 1762 is little different, portraying women as lacking in strength and reason, and therefore as unsuitable for tasks of political society (1979: 357–72, and see Pateman 1988: 96–102); women are said to be compensated with their wit, guile, modesty and beauty. Sadly, statecraft is not seen as requiring such qualities and it is very clear that state power, at that time as now, took a distinctly masculine form. Moreover, our doctor's statement uses the term censure, suggesting that Foucault's assertion that we have moved from a 'a world of Censure to a universe of Judgment' (1971: 250) misses the point that the judgemental world of disciplinary society depends on constant and institutionalized censure, on the penetration of the dominant-ideological formations of censure into every institution of social regulation. Finally, the statement reminds us so clearly of discourses in the following two centuries which specify the censure of inappropriate masculinities in a whole range of social practices, suggesting that some comment linking the masculinity of the nation state with the social censure of homo-sexuality and effeminacy would not have been too bold, and certainly not for such an adventurous philosopher as Foucault. It would have been interesting too, given that the French court was despised by the public for its effeminacy and homosexuality (Greenberg, 1988: 315–20).

In Shakespeare's *Measure for Measure*, written around 1604, Lord Angelo, the temporary and stern governor of the ailing and increasingly criminogenic city state, is described by that mischievous devil Lucio as follows:

> Lord Angelo: a man whose blood,
> Is very snow-broth; one who never feels
> The wanton stings and motions of the sense.
> But doth rebate and blunt his natural edge
> With profits of the mind, study and fast.
>
> (Act II, Scene I)

When he is urged to exercise leniency in sentencing Claudio under an old law punishing fornication (the censure of sexual deviance was severe in Europe during the period 1540–1650: Greenberg, 1988: 312), he replies in true character:

> What know the laws
> That thieves do pass on thieves? 'Tis very pregnant,
> The jewel that we find, we stoop and take it,
> Because we see it; but what we do not see
> We tread upon and never think of it.
> You may not so extenuate his offence
> For I have had such faults; but rather tell me,
> When I that censure him, do so offend,
> Let mine own judgment pattern out my death,
> And nothing come in partial. Sir, he must die.
>
> (Act II, Scene I)

The cold masculinity of the military scholar, judge and ruler metes out a sense-less judgement, devoid of the awareness of the humanity of passion, in its conversion of contextual moral censure into the ruthless universal-ism of consistent but abstract justice. Through Shakespeare's eyes we can see that the truly sense-less violence is that of the state armed with new wealth, military might and scholarly rationality, exhibiting the preferred masculinity in every exercise of its power over questions of virtue. By the twentieth century, however, it is a commonplace to read about the sense-less violence of the 'militant' or the 'terrorist', and to see it portrayed as passionate and subversive with no rational cause. The wheel has turned full circle; now only the rational is seen as sensible, passion is linked with subversion and state violence is rarely viewed as inhuman in its coldness. But even by the late eighteenth century, even before the full emergence of industrial capitalism, the censure of men who had 'contracted the softness, habits and inclinations of women' was becoming part of common sense, part of 'technical' knowledges such as medicine, part of our definition of justice and part of a social policy now in the hands of a rising bourgeoisie.[3]

Foucault had brilliantly observed the suppression of unreason (in *Madness and Civilization*), the rise of military strategies and tactics (in *Discipline and Punish*), and the obsession with sexuality (in the *History of Sexuality* volumes) as the unconscious truths of the rational modern individual without a soul. But what he does *not* do is to notice (1) that the rise of reason, disciplinary power, and sexual obsessiveness (and the loss of the soul) was historically parallel, and probably causally interconnected, with the emergence of the modern conception of the preferred masculinity; (2) that what we think of as rationality, productivity, strength, justice and enlightenment are the soul brothers of a dominant notion of masculinity and are not only deeply imbued with its character but daily express its premises; and (3) that the repression of unreason since the fifteenth century was not only the suppression of passion, the spirit, the soul, madness, crime, disease, childishness and animality but also of what was supposedly feminine. In this movement not only was softness, openness, flexibility, litheness, sensitivity, emotionality, warmth and passivity identified as feminine and censured, but these characteristics also became associated with their bedfellows in unreason, such as mental illness, black culture, and the innocence of the child. How often today are the so-called feminine traits linked in one discourse or another with intimacy, spiritualism, counselling skills, insanity, blackness, the causes of crime (hence the military–masculine regimes of the juvenile reformatory), vulnerability to disease and a closeness to animal nature?

Foucault's silence on the masculine character of the state, social censures and procedures of social regulation is extraordinary: see how little *The Use of Pleasure* (1985) says about the significance of men's domination for the form and direction of the Greek state. There are many other examples from his work, such as the discussion of hysteria in *Madness and Civilization*, which involve the same reticence. Yet how can we understand modern subjectivity without tracing the growth of the gender division and its links with capitalism?

The sheer longevity of the connection between men's domination and the patriarchal character of the state is itself remarkable and suggests that it would be very odd if the constitution of the modern state was not profoundly masculine. It is hard to see, as feminist writers have argued (Pateman, 1988: Chapter 4; Lerner, 1986: Chapter 3; and Mies, 1986: Chapters 1–3), how hegemonic conceptions of right, justice, contract and agency could possibly be understood without an extensive analysis of the effects of men's domination, patriarchy and hegemonic masculinist ideologies. Even if we want to argue against a notion of the eternity of patriarchy, and for the view that there was a transformation of patriarchy into fraternity (or hegemonic masculinity) during the rise of the bourgeoisie, the fundamental point is clear: criminal law and the dominant codes of morality, and therefore also criminology and the sociology of deviance, must be deeply entrenched in the ideological censure of women, femininity and subversive masculinities. The censure of gender is basic to both the formation of gender division and the character of modern criminal law.

Capitalism, normalization and the censure of gender

All this suggests that we move beyond Burstyn's valuable analysis of the masculine principles of state organization (see Burstyn and Smith, 1985; Messerschmidt, 1987: Chapter 2) which sees men's domination in the state as an outcome of economic class inequalities between men and women. It seems more accurate to argue that the state form itself is profoundly masculine in that its fundamental organizing concepts, institutions, procedures and strategies are historically imbued with, and are themselves descriptive of, an ideological notion of masculinity that is hegemonic (over other ideas of masculinity and all femininity); and that this hegemonic masculinity which contributes to the very form of state power is not so much an effect of men's economic power as an overdetermined historical condensation of the economic, political and ideological power of ruling-class men (and those men who follow their lead, actively or passively, in their daily practice: see Rutherford, 1988). In short, the masculine character of the state would not disappear automatically if the unequal sexual division of labour was removed; although clearly the two go together, and economic equality would, eventually, provide changes in state form. On my argument it is just as important to fight for political change, to challenge the hegemonic masculinity of state form, if economic equality is the aim.[4]

Burstyn's conception, while ahead of most male sociological theories of the state on the question of gender, glosses over differences in economic power, political interest and ideological disposition between men of different classes and ethnicities and over the state's perpetual censure of 'deviant' men in order to secure the hegemonic masculinity. I would prefer a view based on Connell's position (1987: 130–1). Burstyn's formulation does not help to explain why the economic power of some men, during a particular historical period, in specific social formations, translates into the kind of rationalistic, militaristic, scientistic, penetrative state power we experience today, with its legitimating philosophies of universalism, rationalism, expansionism and paternalism. In short, her account of state form and legislation seems to be open to the usual range of criticisms against economic–reductionist explanations (see Jessop, 1982).

Nevertheless, it is worth observing that the most sophisticated analysis of state theories, Jessop's book (1982), says virtually nothing about women or gender, except to refer in bizarre fashion to the importance of building 'non-class' elements into the theory, which can only be seen as a reflection of the lamentable understanding of gender issues in male Marxist theory at that time. Apart from the fact that women are not outside class, and occupy some very definite positions in the process of producing and reproducing capital, it seems obvious that gender divison and the reproduction of hegemonic masculinity are vital processes at the heart of the capitalist state.

There is a specificity to the state form in modern societies which is expressed in, and partially determined by, a particular conception of masculinity. Indeed it is a notion of masculinity which had to be constructed and fought for. It is not given in the eternity of power, or in the fact of maleness, but has been developed during a long period of history and is immediately determined by the condensation of economic, political and ideological forces involved in the rise of capitalism and the modern state's historic colonization of popular questions of virtue. It is a historically specific form, one that develops during the formation of modern reason, as part of the obverse of unreason, and is rooted in the economic conditions, political needs and ideological categories of dominant-class men.

Hegemonic masculinity is a positive element, and therefore an integral moment, in the series of ideological censures or cuts which divided reason from unreason (see also Foucault, 1971: xi and x). It is part of a positive movement in thought and political economy, not simply an effect of the negativity of censures. So, while contemporary hegemonic masculinity does seem to have emerged through a series of censures of femininity, feminization and alternative masculinities, as Foucault concluded during his sexuality research, we have to look at the ideological formations, and their supporting practices, within which these censures are lodged (1985: 10–11). It would therefore be wrong to say that the gender constructs were the products of censure. However, this conception does not deny that the censure of femininity and inappropriate masculinity in the developing bourgeois society greatly assisted the realization and institutionalization of hegemonic masculinity (see, for example, Elias, 1978: 184–7). Indeed it seems quite plausible to suppose that this censure is very much part of the state's legal colonization of the realm of virtue and thus an integral part of the contemporary state and its extensive interventions into the social.

In short, my critical readings of Foucault's researches support the idea that the gender constructs, as we know them, develop inside, and along with, the dialectics and lineages of the bourgeois state; and that the state is not just a class state, or even just a male state, but the state of hegemonic masculinity. These ideological formations have roots prior to the beginnings of the bourgeois state and are often condensations of quite independent practical processes. Indeed, they may be substantially prefigured in Judaeo–Christian theology. Nevertheless, I am not convinced that the full consciousness of a masculine/feminine division arises until that point in history, ironically, when the feminine is clearly defined and accepted as a fully equal and parallel gender, probably in court society (see Elias, 1978). Men's domination is one thing; the domination of hegemonic masculinity is another. The gender constructs do seem to be an inextricable part of the growth of the modern state, active determinants of its structure, tactics and procedures. The definition and suppression of the feminine, and of unacceptable masculinities, is part of the historic censure of unreason which is itself a relatively autonomous process much older than, but still intimately connected with, the rise of capitalism and the formation of disciplinary power. As Foucault said when talking about 'the great confinement' of the classical age:

> The law of nations will no longer countenance the disorder of hearts . . . men were confined in cities of pure morality, where the law that should reign in all hearts was to be applied without concession, in the rigorous forms of physical constraint. Morality permitted itself to be administered like trade or economy.
>
> (1971: 60–1)

Indeed men were so confined, but so too were women, and much more in the *longue durée* of the hegemonic masculinity – as the suppressed gender of the new political economy of virtue, a reserve army of housewives and surplus labour whose life-enhancing force was rarely recognized in theories of production (see Mies, 1986), in forms of state and law or in the normative order of disciplinary efficiency. Ultimately, all were confined by the tyrannical censure of femininity.

For Foucault, capitalism and disciplinary power are interdependent:

> In fact, the two processes – the accumulation of men and the accumulation of capital – cannot be separated; it would not have been possible to solve the problem of the accumulation of men without the growth of an apparatus of production capable of both sustaining them and using them; conversely, the techniques that made the cumulative multiplicity of men useful accelerated the accumulation of capital.
>
> (1977: 221)

Again, however, Foucault makes nothing of the gender point discernible here. It was indeed the accumulation of 'men', as 'plowmen, artisans, soldiers' (to quote la Mesnardiere) that sustained the accumulation of capital. The cultivation and acquisition of distinctly masculine men was a vital part of the earlier stages of the capital accumulation process as was the expropriation of women from key positions in production, community medicine, and local politics (Clark, 1982; Pinchbeck, 1981; Balkan *et al.*, 1982; Mies, 1986). Whether the logic of capital necessarily requires a gradual degendering of occupations is a moot point but certainly contemporary Western capitalism seems to permit it to a degree. Equally certainly, I would not want to claim that the censure of femininity is unreservedly functional for capital today.

I am not concerned here to investigate the logical relations between capital and gender. But, clearly, I do not think that they are merely analogous and I want to observe that the normalization process concomitant with capitalist development contains within it the censure of the feminine and of deviant masculinities. This censure, which of course has many instances, is part of the dominant-ideological knowledge that the powerful try to invest in the practices and thus the bodies of subjects. Successful subjection of women thus produces a 'modality of embodiment that is peculiarly feminine', as Bartky points out (1988: 64); but, I would suggest, it also conditions the body movements, language, style, speech and general cultural expressions of both men and women in ways that are in accord with the hegemonic masculinity. That is, it has a bigger impact than mere feminization. It is also true, as Bartky says, that

> Foucault treats the body throughout as if it were one, as if the bodily experiences of men and women did not differ and as if men and women bore the same relationship to the characteristic institutions of modern life.
>
> (1988: 63)

and that women have a distinct experience of capital and disciplinary power (1988: 80). However, it is important to grasp that all this is not just because there are powerful, practical and positive norms of femininity, nor just because women occupy different positions in the social structure of capitalism from men, but also because the dominant gender norm within disciplinary power practices is that of the hegemonic masculinity, which censures both the feminine and alternative masculinities. That norm affects both men and women, producing female subjects who are not just appropriately feminine but also only masculine in hegemonic ways, or at least who are feminine within the limits of hegemonic masculinity, and male subjects who are not just masculine in hegemonic ways but who are also only encouraged to express the allegedly feminine traits in a manner acceptable to the norm of hegemonic masculinity. Thus it is, ironically, that too much masculine expression in women is censured as deviant even though the masculinity they express rarely moves outside the norms of hegemonic masculinity; and that too much feminine expression in men is censured as deviant even though that femininity rarely moves beyond the hegemonic masculinity's specification of what is conventional or true femininity.

Such is the enormous productivity of power: it manages to persuade us that what it censures as deviance is actually deviance from its norms, when in fact the censured activities or demeanours are usually well within the terrain of the dominant norms. This example illustrates well the need for complete transcendence of the whole masculine/feminine binary opposition rather than any simple homosexual inversion of the norm. To celebrate deviance as political resistance when it is no more than creative compliance is to confuse the issue. We should never complacently assume that something is censured because it deviates from the norm; nor, indeed, more perversely, that it is not deviant just because it is censured by authority.

Conclusion

The implications of this analysis are manifold, particularly for the understanding of gender censures. But this is only an exploratory essay, not a comprehensive statement. It is more important to outline certain general conclusions here, before moving into illustrations and details elsewhere. Most notably, my arguments suggest that Foucault's work has systematically ignored the gendered character of disciplinary power in itself and the extent to which the censures of femininity and alternative masculinities have contributed to the formation of modern subjects and to the subjection of modernity. It thus says virtually nothing about one fundamental structural feature of modern censure and social regulation, namely its masculine character.

Like liberal feminism, Foucauldian thought addresses issues of discrimination but not the deeper, structural condition of hegemonic masculinity. The neglect of women in the sociology of deviance is only the tip of the iceberg of its gender-blindness and a critique of that neglect is only a comment on the surface appearances of the discipline. A realistic or historically accurate critique must attend to the gendered character of all censures and the censorious character of the gender constructs.

This essay itself merely scratches the surface of a much deeper argument. It demands further historical evidence and theoretical consideration of the gendered character of the categories of deviance and law. Any criminology which pretends to accuracy or insight must appreciate the depth to which it is structured by the sedimented moral and legal assumptions of patriarchy, sexism and hegemonic masculinity. Moreover, it should recognize the role played by social censures and legal rules in the formation of the categories of gender. Gender does not emerge through the vague consensus of 'socialization', but by the practical definition and oppression of social censure. Modernity would be very different without its simple binary oppositions of masculine/feminine and normal/abnormal. Indeed this essay has suggested, very tentatively, that these two oppositions are strongly interlinked, both in the categories and in their realization, and that their tight overlap and interconnection is very much a result and feature of their conjoined role in the practical construction of the modern capitalist state.

Acknowledgments

I would like to acknowledge the tremendous encouragement of Pat McNeill, various people in my 1988 MPhil. seminar on 'Foucault and social regulation' (notably Rosie Gandolfi, Ruth Jamieson and Bridget Orr), my equivalent 1989 seminar at Simon Fraser University (notably George Pavlich), and my colleagues in Vancouver: John Lowman, Dorothy Chunn, Karlene Faith, Joan Brockman, Dale Philippe, Diana Doherty. Diane Betts, Brian Burtch, Charlie Singer and Simon Verdun-Jones from Simon Fraser University, Brian McClean from UBC and John McLean from the University of Victoria. The essay has benefited greatly from the comments given to me at staff seminars at Simon Fraser, UBC and the University of Victoria.

Notes

1 Not to mention Reich's 'patriarchal authoritarian civilization that goes back thousands of years' (1975: 31). On the other hand, see Carole Pateman's careful commentary on the shifting legal and ideological forms of men's domination for an important corrective to this tendency (Pateman 1988).
2 This development in the concept of social censure owes something to the concept of master status in the work of Everett Hughes and Howard Becker. I have retained the term master because, in the light of my argument, it acquires a new and richer significance. Hughes and Becker did not notice its role as a signifier of the hegemonic masculinity inherent within dominant culture.
3 See Greenberg (1988: 341–2). He argues that the shift towards a more puritan attitude towards male homosexuality and effeminacy in the late eighteenth century is precipitated by the 'bourgeoisification of the aristocracy'.
4 People in the GDR recently have demonstrated the importance of changing political form as a precondition for thoroughgoing economic change, although, no doubt, the drive for political reform is underpinned by major economic problems. There is always a dialectic between economy and politics. Even in underdeveloped societies, such as Tanzania, where there was a strong inclination to claim that democratization was a luxury pursued by Western radicals, unhampered by the need for food, shelter, water, and medicine, there is now a growing realization among socialists that political liberty is a precondition for the ability to fight for better economic conditions (see Sumner 1981 on the importance of civil liberties for Marxist political theory; also Shivji 1985, and Legal Aid Committee 1985, on developments in Tanzania).

4 Reassessing the critique of biologism

Beverley Brown

In the context of feminist discourse, 'biologism' refers to the statement that women have a physically determined nature that makes them inherently different from and inferior to men, mere creatures of their bodily drives and derangements. Biologism is associated with the presumptions that women are inherently maternal, passive and domestic and, at the same time, driven by uterine ailments of excessive or repressed sexuality and tendencies to hysteria and psychological instability. Women's conduct is thus not rational or freely chosen. Rather they are pictured as the puppets of reproductive imperatives and its moon-based phases. In its simple form, biologism posits a 'male' and 'female' nature, each attributed with distinct attributes and modes of conduct. However, biologism means something more than this. The issue is not only the givenness and hierarchy of 'male' and 'female'. Crucially, what is at stake is the way that the categorization of women has come to be located entirely in the realm of nature while men are placed on the other side of the boundary that separates nature from culture, determinism from freedom of will, emotion from reason.

In feminist critiques of criminology, biologism is a central target of attack, seen as a crucial instance of sexism at work in criminological theories about women's relation to crime and the workings of the criminal justice system, linking theories and institutions together in a systematic unity of shared assumptions. Hence many arguments have been mobilized in the name of feminism to demonstrate the errors and invidious effects of this doctrine. It will be suggested here that this focus on biologism has been radically mistargeted.

Perhaps it is important to make clear at the outset that this essay is by no means an attempt to rescue conventional criminology. To argue that positions have been misrepresented is not to defend them. On the contrary, it is to suggest that they have not been sufficiently attacked because they have been systematically misrecognized, forced to fit into the available terms of anti-biological criticism. More urgently, from a feminist perspective, it seems that the critique of biologism has led to an extraordinary effacement of the specificity of the ways that women have actually been dealt with in conventional criminological and legal discourses on women's crime.

Strategic centralization

To construct a critique centred on biologism has many obvious advantages, for this is a target that can be attacked from different standpoints, thus drawing together critical resources from many different fields. The distinction between sex and gender is a commonplace of women's studies. Analyses of sex discrimination in the civil courts, such as Sachs and Wilson's *Sexism and the Law* (1978), lend additional weight by describing how myths of women's biologically inscribed differences have been used to justify denying women equal rights to men.

Such established feminist attacks on biologism meet a ready response within criminology, where critiques of biological positivism are a standard, almost obligatory routine. Virtually every new position that comes along defines its virtues by contrast to the evils of biologism, enacted through a familiar ritual degradation ceremony in which Lombroso is expelled as the illegitimate father of criminology – at least so far as biologism has defined the study and treatment of male lawbreakers. Yet – and here the feminist critique scores a major rhetorical victory – it seems that the study of women has somehow never been blessed by the attentions of all these anti-biologistic developments. According to Heidensohn, 'Far from being swamped by the modern criminological tides which have long washed away biological determinism, these ideas have flourished in their rockpools, amazing examples of survival' (1985: 113).

Hence, in a discipline whose own self-image is so strongly defined in terms of a progression away from biological determinism and towards sociological explanation, women, it is claimed, have been left behind in the pre-sociological era. Criminology thus displays its bias in the all too typical positioning of 'female':'male'/nature:culture. Hence, the tradition of male criminology, as defined by feminist critics, is suitably encapsulated in Lombroso and Ferrero's *The Female Offender* (1895), the Ur-text that unites the discipline in a single line of descent.

Attacking biologism

The feminist critique of biologism tends to move through three stages. First, there is an attack on biologism as ideology; next a demonstration of the problems of accepting criminology as a basic premise of criminological thinking; finally, a critical account of the practical effects of biologism in the sphere of criminal justice and the treatment of women. This attack maintains a formal unity because, at each level, biologism is seen as a set of representations of women. It is this centralized focus on representations – myths, stereotypes, images, propositions, beliefs, assumptions – about women that allows all the different critical resources to be mobilized against the defined target.

Taken first as ideology, biologism is understood as a multiply distorted set of beliefs about women that reflect and maintain a sexist social order. The crucial thing about biologism as ideology is that, although its representations of women are drawn *from* society, it is precisely these social origins that are denied by women's re-presentation in the mirror of nature. Ideology reflects the consequences of social process – women's passivity or domesticity or influence by men – yet, according to biologism, these attributes are a natural and inherent part of 'female' nature, dictated by the species' requirement to reproduce. When such biologistic views, distorted in their sources and in their depiction of women's nature and women's worth, are found in criminological theory or criminal justice institutions, then these authoritative discourses must be condemned for lending their weight to legitimating the status quo.

But, in the feminist critique of biologism, such representations are more than just the cultural baggage of a sexist society. For, when distorted ideological views are found within criminology or the criminal justice system, they are held to have internal consequences. Hence in the second stage of attack, the feminist critique interrogates the dynamics of criminological theory. The central move in this reading is to locate biologism as the logical foundation of all theorizing, the crucial assumption taken in from the outside world which, in turn, makes sense of all internal theoretical debate.

Biologism is thus treated as if it were the fallacious first premise of a universal syllogism, a premise that states a general view on 'female' nature: '*all* women's character and conduct is biologically determined'. Criminological theory may thus be deduced from this premise as a series of applications, the most important being the deduction that women's deviance must necessarily also be determined by a biologically based criminal nature with all the associated implications of irrationality, sexual excess, determinism and pathology, and that this is the explanation criminology offers for women's crime. This rationalistic reconstruction of criminological reasoning also has the important correlative that if a criminologist makes any reference to 'female' biology he may automatically be taken to subscribe to the major biologistic premise and hence all its deduced implications.

Here is a classic example of the syllogistic interpretation:

> Women, in this view, are determined by their biology and their physiology. Their hormones, their reproductive role, inexorably determine their emotionality, unreliability, childishness, deviousness, etc. These factors lead to female crime. Even a superficial examination shows up the contradictions here.
>
> (Heidensohn, 1985: 112)

This syllogistic reading of criminology is a crucial element in the basic economy of the feminist critique, for it allows the representations of women that have already been identified from the ideological stance to find an integral role within criminological thought. The logicism of the critique of assumptions is elegant and simple for it allows the whole of criminological theory to be known simply by understanding its underlying logical assumption. The task of demolition is consequently extremely neat. One can go simply for the fallacious premise itself, thus toppling the whole edifice by undermining its crucial foundations. But, to carry through the attack, systematic demolition of all the conseqences is also attractive and, not surprisingly, the charge of illogic and contradiction is a favourite device, contradictions also being a tell-tale symptom of sexism. Hence the query, 'Why is biology invoked to explain women's crime and not men's?' – the favourite example being, once again, Lombroso and Ferrero's *The Female Offender*, for by the time this book was written it seems that Lombroso had made major concessions towards environmental explanations at least as regards men's crime. Yet, the critics insist, these advantages were not to be conferred on women. A second charge is equally persistent: how can all these criminologists subscribe to biologism, with all its obvious implications, without realizing that biologism massively overpredicts women's crime: if women are so inherently pathological, why is there not more women's crime?

Logical critique is supplemented by the combined resources of women's studies and criminology, beginning with the sex/gender distinction, proceeding through some cautious use of role theory and ending with the battery of internal criminological arguments – I shall not rehearse them all here – that oppose biologism with the concepts of differential societal re-action, labelling, opportunities, socialization and so on. To apply such arguments, at last, to the criminology of women is to cross the symbolic divide that separates the study of men from the study of women.

In the third and final stage of denunciation the feminist critique of biologism is most strongly inspired by predecessor critiques of criminology. Here biologistic representations of 'female' nature will be traced through their conseqences in the criminal justice system. The syllogistic reading is now applied to deduce practical effects. Existing criminology provides many critiques of the medicalizing and pathologizing regimes that, it is often asserted, derive from biological positivism. Positivism is frequently characterized as the contrast between 'bad' and 'mad' and its implied forms of interventions attacked. They moralize by other means. They humiliate the lawbreaker by denying her rationality and choice and insist on portraying her as governed by forces outside her intellectual control. They work to establish a vast legal and para-legal archipelago of surveillance and normative mechanism through social work and psychiatry. Such interventions do not make sense since biological determinism cannot logically lead to intervention but only to therapeutic nihilism. Pathologization also means individualization. Every deviant being is seen as a separate case, isolated from the generality of class or sex oppression, ideationally and institutionally fixed as a specific deviation from the norm to be brought back to normality through correctionalist regimes.

Premonitions of mistargeting

Scepticism about the dangers of critique – and especially the overfocusing on biologism – is not unprecedented in criminology (see Matza, 1964: 24; Cohen, 1981: 229). But, however rhetorically satisfying and apparently revolutionary, such critiques may none the less be partial and evasive. Denouncing biological determinism may license social determinism instead. Attacking general images of human/'female' nature may leave untouched the categories of criminology's construction of crime and criminality. The will to produce a comprehensive denunciation of the target may even lead to an attack on a caricature. Such reflections indicate a dual problem of criminological critiques: on the one hand, the misdescription of the target of attack, on the other hand, the resulting preservation of the past in 'embryonic counter-theories'. What seems to be overlooked in these mistargeted critiques is the basic structuring of criminological discourse, notably the relation between categories of crime and criminality, but also lesser, though endemic, concerns such as the problematic visibility of crime to the gaze of legal officialdom and professional criminologists.

A parallel scepticism about the structure of the feminist critique of criminology has been expressed by Greenwood (1981). Although her remarks were directed at the overall targeting of sexism as the object of attack, they may be applied more specifically to the critique of biologism. Greenwood raised the question of whether a critique of sexism might somehow pass over the underlying criminological theses and concerns and that, consequently, feminism might end up as a sort of laundry service, validating not only the general problematic of conventional criminology but also its specific definitions of issues concerning women, once purged of their sexism. Her line of argument clearly bears a close resemblance to the general doubts that have been expressed within criminology about the dangers of critique. Her prime example – the danger that feminist criminologists might come to resurrect one of the central themes of conventional criminology, namely the association of women and conformity – is, in fact, a key instance of the mistargeting associated with the critique of biologism, as will be argued below.

A final point, perhaps too obvious to mention, is that the whole rhetorical structure of the feminist critique of biologism is predicated upon the assumption that critiques of biologism first elaborated with respect to men can simply be applied to women. While there is a great persuasive force in this image of women left behind in the primaeval slime of biologism, the underlying argument seems to be that the criminology of women is to be understood through a rejected criminology of men, that women are now where men once were – which is a strange and paradoxical denial of one of the basic tenets of the feminist critique, namely, that women have been regarded as the 'other' of criminology, ever and always different from men.

Taken collectively, these scepticisms all suggest that the critique of biologism may rest on some fundamental misperceptions about what traditional criminologists have had to say on the subject of women's relation to crime.

Critical overdeterminations

If the strength of the feminist critique of biologism lies in its capacity to bring together arguments from a wide range of sources, this can also be a weakness. Many of these arguments are pre-packaged, imported either from outside criminology or from criminological critiques of the study of men. Can they simply be uprooted and applied to comprehend and criticize the construction of women within the discourses on crime? Were they foolproof in the first place? There is also the fact that these arguments work in different registers – politico–ideological, internal professional criticisms, sociological analyses of institutions, appeals to fairness and equality. Although biologism offers a satisfying thematic coherence, there is also much potential for sliding between different forms of explanation and never handling any of them decisively in their own terms.

Biologism as ideology

An external critique is not an internal critique. The attack on biologism as ideology may demonstrate very powerfully how statements about women contained in theories or institutions may echo and shore up widespread sexist cultural representations. Academic writers can quite rightly be challenged to consider the wider effects of their work. But this is merely to show that theories or institutions may be *vehicles* for the promotion of ideologies. It is not to understand the theories or institutions as such, nor the significance of such statements within their specific discursive contexts. The significance of biologistic references cannot be read off some generalized understanding of myths on the assumption that representations have invariant and acontextual meanings and simply identifiable effects.

The fallacy of meaning is endemic to the critique of biologism and it shows up particularly strongly as a tendency to conflate the contexts of criminological theory and criminal justice settings, the two being homogenized through their joint subordination to a preconstituted definition of the ideological or cultural meaning of biologistic 'myths'. Thus, it is common to find biologism assumed to have a fixed and pre-given set of connotations (irrationality, pathology, emotionality, etc.) opposed to an equally invariant set of terms headed by 'rationality', the former being associated with women, the latter with men, used to produce simultaneous understandings of criminology and the criminal justice system – as if terms such as 'rationality' could possibly have the same meaning in these two different contexts. Carlen, for example, speaks of the 'myth' that women are not real criminals because they are not perceived, as men are, to be serious and intentional in their acts but mere escapees from their biologically determined social role (1985: 6). Hence it appears that a popular cultural image (a myth) is found in an identical form in criminological theory and the criminal courts. But to be a 'real' criminal in criminological and legal discourse means quite opposite things. It is legal discourse that emphasizes rationality and *mens rea* as the markers of seriousness, concepts that have been opposed as irrelevant by criminologists. Conversely, if women really were regarded as biologically pathological criminals they would be taken very seriously in criminological discourses. Thus, while it is undeniably true that crime is, as Carlen argues, regarded as presumptively masculine in both spheres, this cannot be because of some common *content* ascribed to all men and withheld from all women. Such conflations of meaning between criminology and criminal justice are one of the most common phenomena of the critique of biologism.

The other way to relate ideology to specific contexts is through the idea that representations of women are beliefs that have some sort of *effects* on any area of criminological thought or legal decision-making in which they are found. Distort*ed* ideas have correspondingly distort*ing* consequences. Often, too, these effects of ideology are presented in the langauge of contamination or pollution, as the intrusion of 'profane' social interests. Sachs and Wilson's *Sexism and the Law* (1978) is a good example. But many questions have been raised – particularly in the context of judicial decision-making – about how such ideological beliefs are in fact supposed to produce the claimed effects or whether sexist effects are in fact due to sexist sources.

The strong claim is that biologistic beliefs actually cause outcomes in a predictable and demonstrable way. *Because* judges believe women to be biologically inferior, they treat them differently from men. However, biologistic beliefs can lead to quite different outcomes. In the famous Sophia Jex Blake case discussed by Sachs and Wilson some judges thought that women's biology disqualified them from being doctors, others that it made them especially suited for the profession, while still others thought the real problem to be men and women being taught anatomy in the same room. Or, as Ann Edwards (1989) has argued in a critical review of feminist responses to the chivalry thesis, the 'myth' of men's protectiveness, often associated with biologism, could lead *either* to greater harshness *or* greater leniency.

The weak claim is that biologistic beliefs are *post hoc* justifications for a pre-existing sexist motive that is the real force at work. In this case theoretical or practical choices are not actually determined by biologism but merely rationalized in these terms. However, even this claim has been challenged by Gelsthorpe (1986), this time with respect to a different institutional context, the police. First, she argues that sexist assumptions may be activated largely because they allow other organizational elements to function (for example, the wish to do 'real' police work). Second, she suggests that outcomes such as the differential rate of cautioning for boys and girls may be the result of sex-neutral routines and attitudes interacting with differentially socialized male and female subjects (girls may be more likely than boys to fulfil the requirements of cautioning, such as showing remorse through tears and talk). In neither case can sexist beliefs or attitudes on the part of officials be deemed the essential determinant of outcomes, however sex- or gender-differentiated or ultimately disadvantageous to women the effects of such practices may be.

An even more basic set of problems with critiques of biologism as ideology concerns the image of men's beliefs and interests as an improper intrusion of the external social world into the 'sacred' realms of theoretical or institutional practices. As Kingdom puts it:

> Law's sexist bias is conceptualised as the appearance or expression in the legal sphere of elements deriving from . . . the non-legal sphere. The usual presumption is that these elements intervene in the legal sphere in ways which are in some sense, improper or undesirable.
>
> (1981: 100)

Such 'contamination' accounts thus suggest that law normally has no relation to the social and, further, that, were it not for this unwarranted intrusion, the law would be uncontroversial in its concepts and categories. Even pointing out that the law is also 'contaminated' by class and race bias preserves the same basic theoretical assumptions that Kingdom criticizes, and references to the social 'context' of legal decision-making often function this way too. The same arguments can be made, *mutatis mutandis*, for criminological theory. Any presentation of ideological beliefs as a generically improper intrusion into a specific sphere, be it theoretical or institutional, tends to underwrite an assumption of the otherwise intrinsic propriety of that sphere, reinforcing its given standards and denying its social meanings.

Biologism as logical foundation

Here we come to a very important point, the basis of major misinterpretations of criminological theory. To treat biologistic statements as the logical first premise of a syllogism is to obliterate basic categories of criminological discourse. Criminology cannot be rationalistically reconstructed as a set of deductive derivations from founding premises about human, or women's, nature. It is hardly surprising that criminological theory is found to be contradictory and illogical. Such contradictions, so easily dismissed as symptoms of sexism, are all too often the result of the syllogistic reading technique.

The basic problem with this reading is that it ignores the distinction between crime (criminal acts) and criminality (predisposing factors that lead to crime). This distinction can be illustrated by referring to the example of prostitution and the idea that women's crime is sexual in nature, which is usually taken by feminist critics to mean that prostitutes are motivated by a (biologically determined) sexual criminality. However, this is only one of the available criminological meanings. The other is that women tend to commit sexual offences (crimes, lawbreaking *acts*). This is simply to observe (rightly or wrongly) that of the crimes women commit a large proportion fall into the realm of sexual offences, as legally defined. To say this is not necessarily to have any view about underlying aetiology or motivation (criminality) nor indeed to suggest that there is *any* single type of 'criminality' involved.

The crime/criminality distinction is constitutive of conventional criminological discourse. For positivism, it has two fundamental implications: first, that the way to control the problem of crime was to find the 'real' criminals, that is, those with a fixed predisposition towards lawbreaking and whose crimes therefore sprang from their criminality; second, and correspondingly, that not all lawbreakers were real criminals. The reason why it is necessary to remember this distinction in understanding biological positivism as it constructs the question of women's crime is that it is important to ask precisely *what* it is that is biologically determined.

The difference between a logical and a criminological reading may be illustrated by reference to the most familiar example of biologism, Lombroso and Ferrero's *The Female Offender* (1895). Read with a primary question about the relation of biologism to the positivist perception of the potential relations between crime and criminality, one discovers that the central claim of this book is that women's biological nature gives them a fundamentally different orientation to criminality from men. Women as a group are prediposed to *non*-criminality. They are nature's conformists. Thus if there is an important criminological tradition inaugurated by this famous book, it should be defined as the assertion that women's conformity was the key 'woman question' in traditional criminology (as Greenwood argued, 1981: 79).

While feminist commentators do sometimes recognize the primary orientation of Lombroso and Ferrero's work to the theoretical question of women's conformity (see Smart, 1976: 32), strangely enough, the criminological consequences of this recognition are not followed through. Smart still somehow believes that Lombroso and Ferrero see women's crime as biologically caused, even though this does not make sense in criminological terms and is not, in fact, what their book argues. On the contrary: for, given that women's biological nature is taken to be antithetical to crime, women's lawbreaking (crime) simply cannot be caused biologically since women's biology predisposes them to conformity (noncriminality). While the crimes of men find their source in criminality, the crimes of women *cannot*. Such is the logic of positivism and such indeed is the argument of *The Female Offender*. The bulk of female offenders are mere lawbreakers rather than criminals. Lombroso thus argues that women are not real criminals because, unlike men, they are far less likely to be biologically, 'pathologically', inclined to crime (see Brown, 1986 for a fuller exposition of this text).

Once it has been decided that women are biologically inclined to conformity, the next question Lombroso and Ferrero face is what the causes of women's crime actually are. Clearly, these causes cannot be any biologically innate criminality. (Here is the crucial clash between the logical and the criminological reading.) Hence, women's lawbreaking must fall into the category of *mere* lawbreaking, that is, acts that violate the law but committed by people who are not real criminals: in Lombroso's term, 'occasional offenders'. The crimes of mere lawbreakers spring not from any criminal nature but necessarily from external, non-biological causes such as bad associates, the temptations of big department stores, the failure to find a suitable occupation or, to put it simply, environmental factors. The basic message of *The Female Offender* is that the bulk of women's crime is not and cannot be caused by any biologically based criminality but, on the contrary, must be due to external environmental factors precisely because women are inherently biologically oriented to conformity.

For some reason, feminist accounts of *The Female Offender* seem to discount these arguments about the bulk of women's crime, preferring to concentrate on what is said about the rare and residual category of the 'true' female criminal, thus generalizing to all female lawbreakers what was, in the original text, said about a tiny and atypical minority. Even so, the critique's perception of how this categorization of real female criminals is constructed demonstrates a resolutely acriminological interpretation at work to the last ditch. 'True' female criminals are dubbed, in Lombroso and Ferrero's famous phrase, 'doubly monstrous' because they not only share a criminality as real as that of male criminals but, in order to do so, such women must have overcome their constituted nature as conformist women. Thus, sexist though the phrase may be, it cannot be taken simply as men's reaction to women's deviance. Rather, it expresses the theoretical consequences of positing women as non-criminals – those few who are real criminals must have had to be extra deviant in order to clear the hurdle of conformity. Recognizing the structure of argument here also raises the question of whether this implication is in fact banished by an attack that concentrates solely on its biological underpinnings. Greenwood certainly argued that it is not, suggesting that any criminological account that posits women's conformity – whether biologically determined *or* socially induced through the 'informal mechanisms of control, socialisation and the family' – would have the consequence that 'women who do deviate remain anomalies beyond the bounds of normality' (1981: 79). This question is itself the subject of current debate.

However, the point here is the mistargeting involved in failing to see that the important thing about Lombroso and Ferrero's book is not biological determinism but the positing of women's conformity as the object of criminological analysis. The prevailing, syllogistic, interpretation of what is commonly taken to be the exemplary founding text of male criminology thus seems to be, quite simply, wrong. Once the contextual significance of constitutive categories of criminological discourse is recognized, it is evident that Lombroso and Ferrero do not actually locate the sources of women's crime in any physiological, hormonal, psychological or moon-based causation. Women's biology is not and cannot be the cause of crime. Correspondingly, the charge of illogic disappears. Since biology, for Lombroso and Ferrero, explains women's *non*-criminality, there is no overprediction of women's crime. Nor is the study of women's crime left behind in the floodtides of environmentalism. On the contrary, precisely because women's biology predisposes non-criminality, women, far more than men, are likely to find that positivists explain their acts of lawbreaking in external, non-biological terms.

The syllogistic misinterpretation of this classic text is thus a perfect example of the way that targeting biologism can lead to a total and spectacular misrecognition of the way that the categorization of women has been constructed within existing criminological discourse. The syllogistic reading rests on an elementary refusal to pay attention to the structure of criminological discourse, disregarded in the higher imperialism of philosophical views of human and 'female' nature and presumptively abstract logical forms of human reasoning. However, philosophy's claims to be the queen of the sciences were discounted long ago. Cynically, one could say that the very irrelevance of such grandiloquent attacks makes them harmless. Just as the earlier sceptics warned, there is nothing like critique for keeping conventional criminology's 'business as usual' sign on the door and drumming up new customers.

There is one more major problem with the syllogistic reading that deserves attention. This is the assumed correlative that any writer who refers to biology is assumed to operate from the foundationalist universal premise about women's nature. Otto Pollak is the most obvious victim of this misreading. His notorious book *The Criminality of Women* (1961) was, for the most part, concerned with another recurrent criminological theme, the visibility of crime, and he argued that women's crime went undetected for a series of reasons. One of these reasons was that women had learned to be deceitful because, he alleged, there was a universal male social reaction against menstruation and women, in turn, had compensated for this. Somehow, in the process of feminist critique, Pollak has been transformed into someone who argued that women's criminality was biologically determined. Even overlooking the fact that his remarks on the subject of menstruation were a (rather bad) attempt to use the notion of societal reaction, it is an extraordinary leap to 'deduce' from an argument about the *visibility* of crime a thesis as to its *causes*. Nowhere in his book does Pollak offer any biologistic account of the causes of women's crime. The few comments he makes on the topic of crime causation, which is not the subject of the book, are largely orientated to a denunciation of women's oppression. While one sometimes feels these texts have never been read, it is fairer to attribute such gross misinterpretation to the syllogistic reading.

Philosophy versus criminology

In some ways it seems unfair to criticize feminists for the failures of a reading predicated on biologistic foundationalism. As noted above, it is already widely recognized, outside feminist critiques, that such critiques are generically mistargeted. The misplaced picture of biological positivism as a general theory of human conduct is hardly unique to feminist critics. Even Comtean positivism is sometimes misrepresented as an attempt to *reduce* all human conduct to physical laws and determinations (see Giddens, 1974: 1–2 on this fallacy). However, in criminology the key distinction is really between Comtean positivism, which was an attempt to create a *unified* theory of physical and social knowledge, and late nineteenth-century positivisms, such as sociology, criminology and legal positivism. Sometimes defined as 'neo-Kantian' (Hirst, 1976: 58), these positivisms split away from each other, each posing separate and autonomous objects of knowledge (society, crime/criminality, legal rules) requiring special methods and techniques to understand their object. Whereas Comtean positivism sought deep laws, criminological positivism seeks immediate indicators and factors. It is, as Matza (1964: 5) puts it, 'a superficial science'. Scientific method is invoked as an *analogy*, not a reductionism. Criminological positivism cannot be understood as a general theory of human behaviour. In accepting this pre-packaged critique – in presenting its non-application to women as an emblem of sexism – feminists have been far too trusting.

Biologism and sexual difference

To construe the criminological tradition as unified by its commitment to a biologistic view of women's nature is also to fail to address the underlying question of essentialism, the assumption that there is some general category of 'womanhood' that may function as the basis of explanations. Cousins (1980: 116–17) points to anti-biologism as a particularly evasive form of argument. A universal 'female' essence may be presupposed in terms other than biology and hence to attack theories merely for their biologism is to leave unchallenged the underlying essentialist assumptions of a general unifying character that constitutes 'womanhood'. Following Cousins, Carlen (1985: 7–10), therefore, argues against pursuing either a 'global' (sex- and gender-neutral) study of crime or equally any study predicated on a distinctive 'female orientation to deviance' (and, one would presume, non-deviance). However, while such arguments are very useful in indicating how targeting biologism may miss the underlying problem – and how, thereby, the effects may be carried over into resulting feminist work – they still do not quite address the specificity of the construction of sexual difference within criminology. For, if we keep the example of Lombroso, it is clear that what is involved is not only an essentialist depiction of women, but a distinction between the *generality* ascribed to women's character and the *individuality* attached to the male of the species (see, notably, Lombroso and Ferrero, 1895: 108). The focus on biologism thus distracts attention away from the *asymmetry* of this essentialism, precisely the sort of asymmetry we would have expected a feminist critique to be attuned to recognize.

Biologism and interventionist techniques

The idea that the sentencing and subsequent 'disposal' of women by the criminal justice system can also be deduced from the premise of biologism suffers from the same problems as the syllogistic deduction of criminological theory from a foundation in biology:

1 Not all approaches are, in fact, grounded in biologism.
2 Even where biologism is involved, it may lead to or justify different outcomes.
3 Biologism cannot be isolated as the sole significant element in any organizational context.

One important index of these problems is the fact that there is currently a (well-hidden) conflict within feminist accounts of women's prisons. For many years it has been taken as axiomatic that women's prisons were based on psychiatric or therapeutic principles, both because this was how female offenders were widely perceived in society and because existing critiques of biologism indicated this line of criticism. Carlen protests against the 'myth' that women's prisons are 'hybrids between mental hospitals and some rather saucy St Trinians' (1985: 10). However, she ascribes this belief solely to the realms of popular stereotype rather than taking issue with the fact that, if it is a myth, it is one that has been actively propagated as part of the feminist critique of biologism. Such diplomacy seems an unnecessary obfuscation.

Yet if we return once again to the primal scene of the crime, Italian positivism, we find that neither Lombroso's (1911) recommendations for the treatment of women nor, indeed, his approach more widely, counsel anything like medicalization. As far as women were concerned, they simply did not need any radical intervention since they were basically conformist. What they 'needed' was to be reminded of the coincidence of womanhood and citizenship: he recommended forms of public symbolic humiliation such as head shaving (1911: 406–7). Repellent and sexist as this may be, it is not a medicalizing strategy. In fact, even for male criminals, the dominant positivist strategy was 'elimination' – death, transportation, permanent incarceration, removal from society – for the thesis of the born criminal was precisely that. The association of Lombroso with therapeutic intervention is another example of feminism taking on inadequate pre-existing critiques. All this is not to deny that there was indeed a great pressure on the criminal justice systems of Europe to medicalize crime and recognize less than full responsibility on the part of some lawbreakers, of which women were an often cited example. The irony is that this pressure came from Lombroso's 'virtuous' opponents, the French environmentalists (Nye, 1976).

Clearly, one episode is not a history, even if the episode concerns such a notorious figure as Lombroso whose name is so often used as a substitute for history. This is really the main lesson to be drawn: there is a need for a 'non-deductive' history of practical techniques used with respect to women, a history that neither looks for a general premise about women, criminological or social, that is then 'applied', nor adopts existing critiques of the treatment of men. Deductivism is particularly inappropriate to understanding the formation and use of techniques of social management. It is a form of 'top down', rationalist reading that fails to recognize that the relationship between theories and practices is usually the other way around. The space for a study of the actual 'influences' and historical formation of practices of intervention is closed off.

It is true that some writers, such as Susan Edwards (1981) and Frances Heidensohn (1985), have suggested that traditional criminology may have had very little influence on the way that the courts and other institutions operate. Yet, where such comments might have led to interesting investigation, instead what is suggested is that, sharing the same social source, the 'study and treatment of women' are simply parallel worlds, each separately mimicking and mirroring the underlying social order. This 'parallel worlds' vision thus inscribes an approach that eschews attention to the specificity of contexts and undermines any interest in the interactions between them in favour of similitude and the crudities of social reductionism.

Abstracting the problems

This chapter has sought merely to describe the mistargeting involved in the critique of biologism and has touched upon some of the potential consequences for current feminist work. If the list of problems could be reduced to two basic issues – for clearly there are overlaps between all these instances and causes of mistargeting – they could be called 'foundationalism' and 'borrowing from the boys'.

By 'foundationalism' I mean the attempt to understand theories or institutions as deductions from some general views about women. It has been argued that this style of reading entails a sort of rationalist reconstruction that is ultimately indifferent to its alleged object of analysis. Since, in this case, the object concerns women, this is a surprising form of indifference to find in feminist analysis. Yet foundationalism is deeply embedded in feminist critiques. It is the essence of that form of denunciation that concentrates on *assumptions* about women seeking to bring together ideological, theoretical and institutional analysis in a single cohesive critique. The 'assumption' of this form of critique, in turn, is that all and any discursive constructions of the category of women can be known in advance through a study of its representations of women, taken as an invariant set of meanings and fixed oppositions.

The second, and supplementary, problem is the way that the critique of biologism uses pre-packaged criminological routines and critiques. This borrowing strategy, while rhetorically attractive, also leads to the obliteration of the specificity of women. Further, it means that feminists are involved in recycling not only conventional criminology but rather inadequate critiques of it.

Acknowledgements

I would like to thank Loraine Gelsthorpe and Allison Morris for their useful suggestions in the editing of this piece and also for their general forbearance.

5   Challenging orthodoxies in feminist theory: a black feminist critique

Marcia Rice

Over the past decade feminist criminologists have been challenging stereotypical representations of female offenders. Despite these advances, black women and women from developing countries have been noticeably absent from this discourse. However, in part as a result of a surge of writings by black women (for example, Amos and Parmar, 1984; Carby, 1982; Mama, 1984; Bhavani and Coulson, 1986), there are now attempts to incorporate black women's experiences into feminist writings (Carlen and Worrall, 1987), though few attempt to develop perspectives which take into account race, gender and class simultaneously.

In this chapter I assess the limitations and potential of feminist contributions to these developments. I will focus on feminist criminologists' failure to see that traditional machocentric[1] criminology was constructed on racist as well as sexist ideologies of femininity (and, indeed, of masculinity). I will also show that feminist, just as much as conventional, orthodoxies are based on ethnocentric principles.[2] I will then argue that a broader conceptual framework is necessary which not only acknowledges the triple oppression of race, class and gender but also examines the historical basis of their inter-relationship. Finally I will argue that a black feminist perspective is necessary in order to understand the complexity of the struggles which black women face. I do not intend to present a definitive account of a black feminist perspective, merely one which serves to underline the need to give theoretical consideration to the experiences of black women.

The other dark figure in crime

Traditionally, the phrase the 'dark figure' of crime has been associated with hidden or unreported crime. The term is used here to refer to the way in which black female offenders have been overshadowed by both black men and white women in the criminological literature.[3] Black female offenders are straddled between what I call 'black criminology' (see, for example, the work of Hall *et al.*, 1978; Gilroy, 1982; 1987; Troyna and Cashmore, 1982; Bridges, 1983) which has focused on black men and feminist criminology which is largely concerned with white women. In the next section, I discuss in brief the failings of 'black criminology' and then discuss in more detail my concerns about current feminist criminological writings.

The contribution of 'black criminology'

There is now a significant body of research in Britain which has focused on black men and crime. One of the most popular assertions in conventional wisdom on race and crime is the inherently violent nature of West Indians. Writers such as Gilroy (1987) and Troyna and Cashmore (1982) have disputed this and argue instead that social, political and economic marginalization are of key significance. There is also a considerable amount of research on the experience of black men in the criminal justice system. Studies such as that of Smith and Gray (1983) show that young black men are roughly ten times more likely to be apprehended by the police than their white counterparts. There is also some evidence that black male offenders reach the courts at an earlier stage in their criminal careers (McConville and Baldwin, 1982; Crow, 1987) and are more likely to receive custodial sentences and imprisonment for longer periods than their white counterparts (NACRO, 1989; Crow, 1987).

None of these studies included black women or considered issues of particular relevance for them.[4] For example, concern about the high rates of arrest of black people on the streets does not extend to black women who are harassed by the police on suspicion of soliciting. There can be little justification for this neglect: black women make up over 20 per cent of the prison population, but only around 5 per cent of the general population.

The research which has addressed issues of racial bias in policing and sentencing has targeted particular types of offences and offenders (McConville and Baldwin, 1982; Crow, 1987; NACRO, 1989). The emphasis has been on street crimes and crimes of a predatory and violent nature (Hall *et al.*, 1978; Gilroy, 1982; Troyna and Cashmore, 1982). This discourse has failed to locate black women but, at the same time, has exacerbated the negative image of black men. The seeming invisiblity of black women creates false impressions about the extent and the nature of their involvement in criminal activity although research suggests that they are subjected to similar stereotyping and discriminatory treatment in the criminal justice system as black men (Lewis, 1977; GLC, 1985).

The contribution of feminist criminology

Given the history and theoretical objectives of feminist criminology, one might have assumed that the monolithic, uni-dimensional perspectives employed by traditional theorists would have been abandoned for a more dynamic approach. But, almost without exception, feminist criminological research – from the late 1960s to date – has focused on white female offenders. Pioneering writings by Heidensohn (1968) and Smart (1976) and more recent writings by Carlen and Worrall (1987) and Morris (1987) have all adopted an essentialist position with regards to the construct of 'women' and have paid little attention to the relevance of race. Sexist images of women have been challenged, but racist stereotypes have largely been ignored.

(White) women and crime

Since the 1970s, feminist criminologists have launched a critical attack on male-dominated theoretical premises in criminology. The basic point which they make is that these expositions are not theories of women's crime but stereotypes which perpetuate sexist ideologies of women. Feminists insist that many of the assumptions made about female criminals are incorrect – they are based on middle-class notions of morality and behaviour – and that the focus on biological and social pathologies to explain both crime and conformity is inadequate.

Central to these arguments is the belief that notions such as 'femininity' and 'sexuality' are constructs, not objective givens. But, this said, feminist writers have made little reference to the different cultural experiences and socialization patterns of black women. There is a failure to situate, for example, discussions of sex roles within a structural explanation of the social origins of these roles which are influenced by black women's racial and sexual experiences and their general position in society (Malson, 1983). Gender differences are assumed to be universal, irrespective of race (or class).

This is clearly not so. Despite significant changes in family structures in Britain, the popular representation of the family is the husband/father as the economic supporter of his wife and children and the wife/mother as the full-time domestic worker and child carer. This idealization does not touch on the experiences of black (or working-class) women. It not only excludes them, but distorts the particular gender roles adopted by them (Lewis, 1977; Carby, 1982; Malson, 1983). I provide two examples of this.

First, as a result of economic pressures and cultural distinctions, black women in Britain are more likely than white women to be single and full-time employees on low wages and are less likely to be primarily dependent on a man. Thus, in 1986, 40 per cent of West Indian women worked full-time compared with 20 per cent of white women and 25 per cent of Asian women. Moreover, *Social Trends* (Central Statistical Office, 1988) indicates that most women from ethnic minorities work soon after the birth of their children out of the necessity to provide for their families. Female-headed households are common amongst West Indians; yet the matriarchal family structure (coupled with low rates of marriage and high rates of illegitimacy) is viewed as 'pathological'.

Second, black girls develop early on a particular set of subcultural values which stress strength, independence, resilience and perseverance and which are necessary in the face of a racist and sex-segregated labour market (Riley, 1981; Bryan *et al.*, 1985). However, these qualities, when judged by ethnocentric standards, are viewed as 'unfeminine'. Feminist writers have challenged neither of these steroetypical representations.

(White) women and the criminal justice system

Also since the 1970s a number of feminist researchers have investigated a series of issues pertaining to the discriminatory practices and sexist ideologies present in the criminal justice system. They have covered a range of areas – women as defendants (Edwards, 1984), probationers (Worrall, 1989) and prisoners (Carlen, 1983). While there has been some acknowledgement that black women are not dealt with in the same way as white women (Eaton, 1986; Morris, 1987), no research has been carried out in Britain which compares the sentences of black and white women. This is an important point as a failure to consider the potentially different experiences of black women may invalidate the research findings. Race may be as important as gender, if not more so.

Research into women's imprisonment has covered a range of topics – experiences in prison (Carlen, 1983; O'Dwyer *et al.*, 1987), prison discipline and medical services (Mandaraka-Sheppard, 1986) and post-prison experiences (Wilkinson, 1988). Most of the studies point out that the majority of women are there not because of the seriousness of their offence or their criminal record, but rather as a result of their different and 'unacceptable' lifestyles. Particular emphasis has also been laid on the patriarchal ideologies which attempt to reinforce traditional modes of feminine behaviour on women in prison.

Almost without exception the bulk of the research carried out on women in custody has referred to 'women' (cf GLC, 1985) as a homogeneous category and has ignored the interaction of gender, race and class. For example, there is hardly any recognition of the special problems which black female prisoners encounter during their sentence on remand or after release. There is an assumption that all women are equally dis-advantaged. For example, O'Dwyer, Wilson and Carlen write:

> Women in prison suffer all the same deprivation, indignities and degradations as male prisoners. Additionally they suffer other problems that are specific to them as imprisoned women.
>
> (1987: 178)

This statement is inadequate as it stands: it does not acknowledge the added problems of the isolation of and discrimination against black women. Bryan *et al.* (1985), for example, point to the fact that a higher percentage of black than white women in prison are on prescribed psychotropic drugs. This requires explanation. Furthermore, many black women serving long sentences are not indigenous but are from West Africa and are serving sentences for drugs offences. This group of female prisoners, often awaiting deportation, have special needs; for example, contact is usually severed with their families and there are problems of communication.

Feminist criminologists have paid more attention to race in research on women's victimization. Hall (1985), for example, found that black women were much more likely to be assaulted than white women because black women's economic situation tends to exacerbate their vulnerability, particularly as they work unsocial hours and rely on public transport. But while feminists have readily acknowledged that sexism is an important explanatory factor in the physical and sexual assault of any woman, they have been slow to see that racism is a further precipitating factor in attacks on black women. One black woman in Hall's survey sums up the significance of this:

> There's a particular fear of white men that Black girls grow up with. We know they think we're hot, sexual animals, that we're always available. It goes back to slavery. What they think about us sexually is part of the racism.
>
> (1985: 48)

There is another point to be made here. Some feminist criminologists, in arguing for longer sentences for offences against women, have ignored the discriminatory impact this is likely to have on black (and working-class) men.

Feminist research methods

Feminist theories have prided themselves on developing a method of in-quiry which reconsiders the relationship between the researcher and the subject (McRobbie, 1982). Therefore, most of the research done by feminists has used methods which allow some participation by subjects in the re-search process. However, despite claims by feminists to be representing the subjective experiences of *all* women, much of the research has yet to prove its relevance to black women. In hooks's words:

> White women who dominate feminist discourse today rarely question whether or not their perspective on women's reality is true to the lived experience of women as a collective group.
>
> (1984: 3)

Feminist theorists have assumed that, as women, they were qualified to make assertions and generalizations on the grounds that all women's experiences are reducible to gender. However, as McRobbie pointed out in a different (class) context:

> No matter how much our past personal experience figures and feeds into the research programme, we can't possibly assume that it necessarily corresponds in any way to that of the research subjects.
>
> (1982: 52)

This must apply even more so when the researchers are white, middle-class feminists. Ramazanoglu makes clear the reasons for this:

> [They] can live in communities where marriage is unnecessary . . . can choose to avoid families, have the power to counter some of the effects of patriarchy, [can] exercise considerable control over reproduction and their own bodies, [and] are far removed from the experiences of the majority of women. They are unusual in the extent of the choices they can exercise, and in the lack of contradictions in their personal lives – in short, they are highly privileged.
>
> (1986: 85–6)

In sum, feminist criminologists have developed a theoretical approach which emphasizes the significance of patriarchal oppression and sexist ideological practices. The main problem with this is that, in assuming a universal dimension of men's power, this approach has ignored the fact that race significantly affects black women's experiences in the home, in the labour market, of crime and in the criminal justice system.

Ethnocentrism and feminist theory

Black women, like most other women, experience some degree of sexual oppression. However, this fails to acknowledge the complexity of gender considerations and the significance of other social taboos such as ethnicity and economic marginality. Kate Millett defined patriarchy as 'a set of social relations which has a material base in which there are hierarchical relations between men and solidarity among them which enables them in turn to dominate women' (1970: 25). This unqualified focus on men's domination does not allow for the historical specificity of patriarchy which has meant that oppression is not experienced in the same way by all women or expressed by all men (Davis, 1981; Anthias and Davis-Yuval, 1983; Mama, 1984; hooks, 1989).

To take the first point. While accepting that relationships between black men and black women are likely to be as sexually oppressive as those experienced by white women, the historical experiences of black women compound their situation and produce a more complex mesh of struggles both within and outside the family. The experiences of black women as chattels under slavery and colonialism has meant that social relations were often mediated and bound up with economic as much as sexual reproduction. Thus, to understand the unique oppression of black women, we need to consider their experiences as black *people*.

We need to note also that black women do not comprise a homogeneous group, although the majority share a similar class position. Black women are further subdivided in terms of ethnicity. For example, there are differences in histories and experiences between Afro–American, Afro–Caribbean and Asian women (Anthias and Davis-Yuval, 1983). Finally, the relationship between black women and black men is not necessarily analogous to relationships between white women and white men; black women experience sexual and patriarchal oppression by black men but at the same time struggle alongside them against racial oppression (Davis, 1981; hooks, 1982).

With respect to the second point, the hierarchical relationship on which patriarchal oppression is premised assumes that black men naturally occupy a similar economically privileged position to white men. However, in Western industrialized countries black men have been socially and politically disadvantaged to an extent which has limited their power both in the family and in society in general.

One of the consequences of the employment structure in capitalist countries has been reliance on the labour of black women which has reduced their dependency on black men. This has contributed to the complex social and patriarchal relations in which black women are involved and stands in contradiction to the conception of the family which predominantly white feminist academics have endorsed. The traditional model of the family is based on ethnocentric ideals of the dependent married women with a male patriarchal head of the household. Black women's relationship to the family is then presented as deviant or pathological. This is reiterated in discussions of the black family in feminist theory where the dominance of black women in the family is portrayed as both a cause for consternation and an explanation for structural weakness.

An example is the work of Shulamith Firestone (1981) whose theories are based on the ethnocentric assumption that black women's experiences of racism can be understood simply as an extension of sexism (see Simons

(1979) for a critique). She denies the significance and impact which the added dimension of racial oppression has for black women. However, the testimony of black women bears witness to the complex interaction of sexist and racist forms of oppression occurring simultaneously. To quote Bryan *et al.*:

> Our relationship with men – both Black and white – has meant that in addition to racism, Black women have had to confront a form of sexism and sexual abuse which is unique to us. But it is impossible to separate our understanding of sexism in our community from its context in a racist society because popular acceptance of racist stereotypes of Black women, Black men and Black juveniles not only compound our sexual oppression but have also become internalised.
>
> (1985: 212)

Nor does Firestone's thesis acknowledge the status hierarchy which exists between black and white women. Hooks explains that white women may be victimized by sexism, but racism enables them to act as exploiters and oppressors of black women (and men):

> Black women are in an unusual position for not only are we collectively at the bottom of the occupational ladder, but the overall social status is lower than that of any other group. Occupying such a position we bear the brunt of sexist, racist and classist oppression. Racist stereotypes of the strong, superhuman black woman are operative myths in the minds of many white women, allowing them to ignore the extent to which black women are likely to be victimised in this society and the role white women play in the maintenance and perpetuation of that victimisation.
>
> (1984: 14)

Thus it is not just or simply that black women are subject to 'more' disadvantage than white women. Their oppression is of a qualitatively different kind. Women's experiences of oppression in social or patriarchal relations cannot be reduced to those of white middle-class women. Ethnocentric feminist analyses are not adequate. In areas as diverse as women's employment (Barrett, 1980; Beechey and Whitelegg, 1986), the family (Barrett and McIntosh, 1982) and crime (Smart, 1976; Carlen, 1983; Heidensohn, 1985; Morris, 1987), the history of racism and its implications have been ignored. The significance of this intellectual exclusion or marginalization is far reaching. Joseph (1981: 95) has pointed out that to speak of women, all women categorically, is to perpetuate white supremacy because it is white women to whom the comments are addressed and for whom they are most appropriate. Barrett and McIntosh recognize this: 'Our work has spoken from an unacknowledged but ethnically specific position: its apparently universal applicability has been specious' (1985: 25). They appreciated the need for such work to be over-hauled and re-examined in order to remove ethnocentricism.

Towards a broader framework

Since neither feminist criminologies nor black criminology adequately account for the crimes of black women – the former focuses exclusively on gender and the latter on race – one has to look beyond these perspectives for a more comprehensive understanding. This is not an easy task; it demands a more sensitive and complex set of analytical tools for understanding race and gender relations than currently exists (Brittan and Maynard, 1984).

There are various possible reformulations. First, if the problem is defined in terms of ethnocentricity, then the remedy could be a reconceptualization of the basic notions employed by feminist criminologists. For example, the category of 'women' and characterizations of 'femininity' and 'masculinity' could be constructed in ways which acknowledge black women's experiences (and black men's).[5] The ideology of 'femininity' as it is usually portrayed lends support to the view that women have low crime rates and that women's crimes are trivial and insignificant (Carlen, 1985; Carlen and Worrall, 1987). Neither of these statements is necessarily true of black women.

Second, feminists could simply insert references to black women without altering their underlying theoretical premises. But ethnocentrism is not a 'problem' which can be eradicated simply by grafting black women onto the conceptal framework. Nor do black women want to be grafted on to feminism in a tokenistic manner (Carby, 1982: 232). Black feminists have argued that, by focusing primarily on patriarchal oppression and by not fully considering the significance of race and racism, feminist theory has oversimplified the position of black women who experience the triple oppression of racism, patriarchy and class discrimination. They have argued also that the racism in economic, social and political institutions must be confronted and theories based on cultural pluralism must be developed.

Third – and this is the approach I advocate – the remedy could be to develop a perspective which is both situational and interactive (Bourne, 1984). By this is meant an approach which recognizes that race, class and gender are ideological constructs which overlap and take on particular significances at particular periods in history and which require three levels of analysis: the macro (which involves examination of historical, economic and political influences), the middle-range (which involves consideration of cultural ideologies) and the micro (which includes identification of geographical location, age and other demographic factors).

One of the central elements in developing a black feminist perspective is the development of black consciousness and 'recognising that black women and white women have different histories and different relationships to present (and past) struggles in Britain and internationally' (Bhavani and Coulson, 1986: 82). Black feminists are therefore interested in describing the ways in which racism not only divides but draws together gender identities and how gender is experienced through racism. This particular discourse locates racism as central to feminist theory and practice. Thus a viable black feminist perspective would give full consideration to *all* women. In the words of Smith, a black American feminist:

> Feminism is the political theory and practice that struggles to free *all* women: women of colour, working class women, poor women, disabled women, lesbians, old women – as well as white economically privileged heterosexual women. Anything less than this vision of total freedom is not feminism, but merely female self aggrandizement.
>
> (1982: 49) (my emphasis)[6]

Taking this wider approach, research would not simply address two race/gender groups (that is, black men and white women) but would include black women and white men (Smith and Stewart, 1983). Thus research into the effects of racism would explore whether or not this is experienced differently by black men and black women and research into the effects of sexism would explore whether or not this is experienced differently by white and black women. It would not assume that the experiences of each group were the same.

A black feminist perspective

By focusing primarily on gender and patriarchy, feminists have been constrained by their own limiting definitions. This stance, as I have shown, omits consideration of the complex process of oppression experienced by women (Brittan and Maynard, 1984). The histories of racism and sexism have meant that, as each social group cuts across racial, ethnic, sex and class lines, experiences vary as to degrees of discrimination and oppression. The forms and intensity of oppression are shaped by relationships between the oppressor and the oppressed and these are constantly renegotiated, reconstructed and re-established in their relative positions. My point is that oppression cannot be conceptualized in abstract and global ethnocentric terms such as patriarchy, but has to be seen as a set of dynamic relations based on concrete and specific situations.

Historically, the struggles of black men and white women have not always signified the liberation of the entire social group which they were representing, that is, black *people* and *all* women. As bell hooks succinctly states:

> White women and black men have it both ways. Black men may be victimised by racism but sexism allows them to act as exploiters and

oppressors. White women may be victimised by sexism but racism enables them to act as exploiters and oppressors of black people. Both groups have led liberation movements that favour their interests and support the continued oppression of other groups. Black male sexism has undermined struggles to eradicate racism just as white female racism undermines feminist struggle.

(1984: 14–15)

Black feminist politics was constructed out of a disillusionment with the peripheral treatment of black women by black liberation and feminist movements. In Britain, for example, black women committed to improving the quality of life of black women in particular and of black people in general have organized activities around such issues as immigration, employment, housing and education policy (Zhana, 1989). One of the distinguishing features of their work is their definition of feminism. A traditional definition is centred on advocacy of the political, economic and social equality of the sexes. Many black feminists believe this to be inadequate and propose an alternative framework.

Black feminists have been engaged in a process of extending the parameters of conventional definitions of feminism which are alien to many of them into a movement which is more relevant to their experiences (Davis, 1981; hooks, 1984; 1989). For the majority of black women, feminism is not just about equal rights for women but involves a much broader commitment to eradicating oppression in all its forms as it affects the lives of men and women. This approach recognizes the similar economic pressures from the state on black people in developed countries and on those suffering from imperialist oppression.

Drawing on this experience, black feminists in Britain and elsewhere have attempted to develop a theoretical perspective which recognizes the constraints of a racially structured, patriarchal capitalism (Bhavani and Coulson, 1986: 89). The emphasis is on the pervasiveness of racism in economic, social and political institutions through which black women's and black men's oppression is manifested (Bryan *et al.*, 1985). The inclusion of men in a black feminist perspective is based on the realization that the liberation of women through challenges to patriarchal structures cannot be successful unless *all* repressive ideologies and practices are eradicated. Black women have added to the potential power of feminism as they have explored wider collective struggles against imperialism and racism (Hull *et al.*, 1982; hooks, 1984; 1989). What these women have demonstrated is the possibility of a liberating feminist theory capable of being translated into practice.

Conclusion

If feminist criminologists wish to take account of black women's criminality then they must think carefully about the framework which they are using to analyse women's involvement in crime. Feminists must not include black women solely to add an extra edge to the victimization or offending patterns of women. Black women do not represent a homogeneous group and, as such, should not be grouped together and referred to as a common 'other'. Finally, the issues relevant for black women are applicable to the social, economic and political development of all. In essence, then, I would suggest:

1 Theories of black women's criminality should not be based on ethnocentric models or racist stereotypes which construct an inaccurate picture and which ignore important differences between female offenders.
2 Criminology should avoid the use of universal, unspecified categories of 'women' and 'blacks' in theoretical discussions and in research. Homogeneity cannot be assumed.
3 The significance of race and racism must be seen as integral to any analysis of (women's) criminality. There is insufficient research which analyses how gender roles and differential opportunity structures are affected by racism as well as sexism and which considers the implications of this for female offenders.
4 Comparative studies, on the basis of race, sex and class, should be carried out to determine how black and white women (and men) are dealt with in the criminal justice system.
5 Following the sentiments of Smart (1976: 85), studies of (women's) offending should be situated in the wider political, economic and social sphere.
6 The experiences of (black) women should not be investigated in a manner which separates the researcher from the subject. There should be a dynamic exchange which involves participation and consultation at all stages in the research process.

Notes

1 The term 'machocentric' describes a discourse which is male-centred. It represents 'masculinity' as the primary defining characteristic and as qualitatively different from 'femininity', but it is more extreme than the normal usage of masculinity as aggression is central to it. Thus researchers such as Gilroy (1982 and 1987) employ a machocentric perspective when focusing on black men and on particular types of crime with an aggressive imagery – 'black street crime' – to the exclusion of other types of criminal involvement.
2 This concept was coined by Sumner (1906) and was used to criticize sociologists and anthropologists who often imported narrow culturalist assumptions drawn from their own social milieu into their research. According to Troyna and Cashmore 'it refers to a view of the world in which one's self or one's group is at the centre of things: a failure to take into account the perspectives of others' (1982: 45).

3 Brown (1986) employs a similar characterization of women as dark figures in criminology.

4 There are some American theories which purport to explain black women's crimes. Vedder and Somerville (1970), for example, attribute their crime to dilemmas of self-identity, negative feminine narcissism and general physical characteristics. They quote from Mary Harrinton Hall in support of this:

> The black girl is, in fact, the antithesis of American beauty. However loved she may be by her mother, family and community, she has no real basis of feminine attractiveness on which to build a sound feminine narcissism. When to her physical unattractiveness is added a discouraging, depreciating mother–family–community environment, there is a damaged self-concept and an impairment of her feminine narcissism which will have profound consequences for her character development.
>
> (1970: 159)

This explanation of black women's criminality is obviously based on a racist and sexist construction of beauty.

5 Eichler (1980: 120) makes the point that 'masculine' and 'feminine' should only be used as labels for empirically established configurations of variables which are differentiated by sex and never generally as valid descriptions (cf Malson, 1983; Naffine, 1985).

6 This view is echoed by white feminists, Barrett and McIntosh: 'It is not the exclusive responsibility of black women to develop an analysis of the inter-relation of class, race and gender; we see this project as that of white women too (1985: 26).

6 Feminist approaches to criminology or postmodern woman meets atavistic man

Carol Smart

Some ten years ago it was *de rigueur* to start any paper on this topic with a reference to the dearth of material in the field. Now it is difficult to keep up with the production of papers and books. On the face of it this might seem a good thing but on closer inspection we might begin to have some doubts since it is usually quality rather than quantity that counts. This is not to imply that there has not been a substantial amount of good work; rather it might be that valuable energies have been misdirected. In this chapter, I want to explore schematically how feminist work in this field has developed and some of the problems that have been encountered. But first it is necessary to give some consideration to criminology – the atavistic man of my title. I shall argue that the core enterprise of criminology is problematic, that feminists' attempts to alter criminology have only succeeded in revitalizing a problematic enterprise, and that, as feminist theory is increasingly engaging with and generating postmodern ideas, the relevance of criminology to feminist thought diminishes.

It should be stressed of course that this is not exactly a novel exercise. Criminology seems to be *the* enterprise that many scholars desert or reject (Hirst, 1975; Bankowski *et al.*, 1977). However, these notable rejections of criminology were based on a particular reading of Marx which led to the conclusion that Marxism and criminology were fundamentally incompatible. I am not interested in treating a text as a means of focusing and restricting thought and so I shall not be appealing to a feminist orthodoxy with which criminology is incompatible. Rather I shall draw attention to the rich variety of feminist scholarship at large when compared to the limited horizons of feminist criminology. I see criminology as something of a siding for feminist thought, with feminist criminologists risking something of a marginalized existence – marginal to criminology and to feminism.

The problem of criminology

The appliance of science

It is a story that has been told many times (although most effectively in *The New Criminology* (Taylor *et al.*, 1973)) that criminology is an applied discipline which searches for the causes of crime in order to eradicate the problem. Admittedly, criminology as a subject embraces much more than this. For example, it tends to focus also on the operations of the criminal justice system, the relationship between the police and communities or systems of punishment. However, such topics fit just as easily under the rubric of the sociology of law or even philosophy. What is unique about criminology, indeed its defining characteristic, is the central question of the *causes* of crime and the ultimate focus of the 'offender' rather than on mechanisms of discipline and regulation which go beyond the limits of the field of crime. It is this defining characteristic with which I wish to take issue here. Arguably, it is this which creates a kind of vortex in this area of intellectual endeavour. It is the ultimate question against which criminology is judged. Can the causes of crime be identified and explained? Moreover, once identified, can they be modified?

Criminologies of the traditional schools have been unashamedly interventionist in aim if not always in practice. This goal was criticized by the radical criminologists of the 1970s for being oppressive, conservative and narrowly partisan (that is, on the side of the state and/or powerful). Moreover, the radicals argued that the traditional criminologists had, in any case, got their theories wrong. Crime, it was argued, could not be explained by chromosomal imbalance, hereditary factors, working-class membership, racial difference, intelligence and so on. So, among the many errors of traditional criminology, the two main ones to be identified were an inherent conservatism and inadequate theorization. The repudiation of these errors was condensed into the most critically damning term of abuse – positivist. To be positivist embodied everything that was bad. Positivism, like functionalism, had to be sought out, exposed and eliminated. Now, in some respects I would agree with this; but the problem we face is whether critical criminologies or the more recent left realist criminologies have transcended the problem of positivism or whether they have merely projected it on to their political opponents while assuming that they themselves are untainted.

I would argue that positivism is misconstrued if its main problem is seen as its connection to a conservative politics or a biological determinism

The problem of positivism is arguably less transparent than this and lies in the basic presumption that we can establish a verifiable knowledge or truth about events: in particular, that we can establish a causal explanation which will in turn provide us with objective methods for intervening in the events defined as problematic. Given this formulation, positivism may be, at the level of political orientation, either socialist or reactionary. The problem of positivism is, therefore, not redeemed by the espousal of left politics. Positivism poses an epistemological problem; it is not a simple problem of party membership.

It is this problem of epistemology which has begun to attract the attention of feminist scholarship (the postmodern woman of my title). Feminism is now raising significant questions about the status and power of knowledge (Weedon, 1987; Harding, 1986) and formulating challenges to modes of totalizing or grand theorizing which impose a uniformity of perspective and ignore the immense diversity of subjectivities of women and men. This has in turn led to a questioning of whether 'scientific' work can ever provide a basis for intervention as positivism would presuppose. This is not to argue that intervention is inevitably undesirable or impossible, but rather to challenge the modernist assumption that, once we have the theory ('master' narrative (Kellner, 1988)) which will explain all forms of social behaviour, we will also know what to do and that the rightness of this 'doing' will be verifiable and transparent.

The continuing search for the theory, the cause and the solution

It is useful to concentrate on the work of Jock Young as a main exponent of left realism in criminology. His work is particularly significant because, unlike many other left thinkers, he has remained inside criminology and, while acknowledging many of the problems of his earlier stance in critical criminology, has sustained a commitment to the core element of the subject. That is to say he addresses the question of the causes of crime and the associated problems of attempting to devise policies to reduce crime. For example, he states:

> It is time for us to *compete* in policy terms . . . the major task of radical criminology is to seek a solution to the problem of crime and that of a socialist policy is to substantially reduce the crime rate.
>
> (1986: 28, emphasis in the original)

This is compelling stuff but it is precisely what I want to argue is problematic about the new forms of radical criminology for feminism. It might be useful initially to outline Young's position before highlighting some of the problems it poses.

As part of his call for a left realist criminology, Young (1986) constructs a version of the recent history of post-war criminology. He sees it as a series of crises and failures (and in this respect we are at one). He points to the positivist heritage of post-war criminology in Britain which, in his account, amounts to a faith in medicine and cure and/or a reliance on biologically determinist explanations of crime. He sees the influence of North American criminology in a positive light (for example, Cohen, 1955; Cloward and Ohlin, 1961; Matza, 1969) and then turns to the work of the 'new criminologists' in Britain who constructed a political paradigm in which to reappraise criminal behaviour. He is, however, critical of the idealism of this work and interprets it as the 'seedbed' of more radical work to come rather than a real challenge to mainstream orthodoxy or an adequate account in and of itself.

The failures of the criminological enterprise overall which Young identifies are twofold. The first is the failure 'really' to explain criminal behaviour. The theories are always flawed either ontologically or politically. The second is the failure to solve the problem of crime or even to stem its rise. These are not two separate failures, however, as the failure to stop crime is 'proof' of the failure of the theories to explain the causes of crime. Young argues:

> All of the factors which should have led to a drop in delinquency if mainstream criminology were even half-correct, were being ameliorated and yet precisely the opposite effect was occurring.
>
> (1986: 5–6)

It is through this linkage between theory and policy that the positivism of the left realists comes to light. The problem is not that there is a commitment to reducing the misery to which crime is often wedded, nor is the problem that socialists (and feminists) want policies which are less punitive and oppressive. The problem is that science is held to have the answer if only it is scientific enough. Here is revealed the faith in the totalizing theory, the 'master' narrative which will eventually – when sufficient scales have fallen from our eyes or sufficient connections have been made – allow us to see things for what they really are.

To return to Young's story, we pick up the unfolding of criminology at the point of intervention by the new criminologists. Young points out that while this intervention may have excited the academic criminologists there was simultaneously another revolution in mainstream criminology. This revolution was the transformation of traditional criminology from a discipline concerned with causes and cures to one concerned with administrative efficiency and methods of containment. Young argues that mainstream criminology has given up the search for causes, the goal of the meta-narrative of criminal causation. It has gone wholeheartedly over to the state and merely provides techniques of control and manipulation. Again it is important to highlight the linkages in Young's argument. On the one hand, he is critical of what he calls administrative criminology because it has become (even more transparently?) an extension of the state (or a disciplinary mechanism). But the reason for this is identified as the abandonment of the search for the causes (a search which was, according to Young, in any case misdirected). The thesis, therefore, is that to abandon the search for the causes is to become prey to reactionary forces. This, it seems to me, is to ignore completely the debates which have been going on within sociology and cultural theory about the problems of grand and totalizing theories. And such ideas are coming not from the right but precisely from the subjects which such theoretical enterprises have subjugated, that is, lesbians and gays, black women and men, Asian women and men, feminists and so on. I shall briefly consider aspects of this debate before returning to the specific problem of feminism in criminology.

The debate over postmodernism

There is now a considerable literature on postmodernism and a number of scholars are particularly concerned to explore the consequences of this development for sociology (Bauman, 1988; Smart, 1988; Kellner, 1988) and for feminism (Fraser and Nicholson, 1988; Weedon, 1987; Harding, 1986). The concept of postmodernism derives from outside the social sciences, from the fields of architecture and art (Rose, 1988). Bauman (1988) argues that we should not assume that postmodernism is simply another word for post-industrialism or post-capitalism. It has a specific meaning and a specific significance, especially for a discipline like sociology (and by extension criminology), one which challenges the very existence of such an enterprise. Postmodernism refers to a mode of thinking which threatens to overturn the basic premises of modernism within which sociology has been nurtured.

Briefly, the modern age has been identified by Foucault (1973) as beginning at the start of the nineteenth century. The rise of modernity marks the eclipsing of Classical thought and, most importantly, heralds the centring of the conception of 'man' as the knowing actor who is author of his own actions and knowledge (that is, the liberal subject) and who simultaneously becomes the object of (human) scientific enquiry. Modernism is, however, more than the moment in which the human subject is constituted and transformed. It is a world view, a way of seeing and interpreting, a science which holds the promise that it can reveal the truth about human behaviour. The human sciences, at the moment of constituting the human subject, make her knowable – a site of investigation. What secrets there are will succumb to better knowledge, more rigorous methodologies, or more accurate typologizing. Implicit in the modernist paradigm is the idea that there is progress. What we do not know now, we will know tomorrow. It presumes that it is only a matter of time before science can explain all from the broad sweep of societal change to the motiviations of the child molester. And because progress is presumed to be good and inevitable, science inevitably serves progress. Knowledge becomes nothing if it is not knowledge for something. Knowledge must be applied or applicable – even if we do not know how to apply it now, there is the hope that one day we will find a use for it (space travel did after all justify itself for we do now have non-stick frying pans).

Modernity has now become associated with some of the most deep-seated intellectual problems of the end of the twentieth century. It is seen as synonymous with racism, sexism, Euro-centredness and the attempt to reduce cultural and sexual differences to one dominant set of values and knowledge. Modernism is the intellectual mode of Western thought which has been identified as male or phallogocentric (for example, by Gilligan, 1982 and Duchen, 1986) and as white or Eurocentric (for example, by Dixon, 1976 and Harding, 1987). It is also seen as an exhausted mode, one which has failed to live up to its promise and which is losing credibility. As Bauman argues:

> Nobody but the most rabid of the diehards believes today that the western mode of life, either the actual one or one idealized ('utopianized') in the intellectual mode has more than a sporting chance of ever becoming universal . . . The search for the universal standards has suddenly become gratuitous . . . Impracticality erodes interest. The task of establishing universal standards of truth, morality, taste does not seem that much important.
>
> (1988: 220–1)

Clinging to modernist thought, in this account, is not only antediluvian; it is also politically suspect. It presumes that sociology (which for brevity's sake I shall take to include criminology in this section) as a way of knowing the world is superior, more objective, more truthful than other knowledges. However, it is easier said than done to shake off the grip of a way of knowing which is almost all one knows. In turn, this reflects a dilemma which has always plagued sociology. If we say we do not know (in the modernist sense) then we seem to be succumbing to the forces of the right who have always said we knew nothing – or, at least, that we were good for nothing.

The irony is, as Bauman (1988) points out, that we are damned if we do and also if we do not. He points to the way in which sociology has little choice but to recognize the failure of its originating paradigm. On the one hand, doubts cannot be wished away and we cannot pretend that sociology produces the goods that the post-war welfare state required of it. On the other hand, governments already know this. We cannot keep it a secret. State funding of sociological research is already much reduced and what will be funded is narrowly restricted to meet governmental aims. It may have been possible in the past to claim that more money was necessary or that a larger study was imperative before conclusions could be drawn but now we know (and they know) that conclusions, in the sense of final definitive statements, cannot be drawn. The point is whether we argue that all the studies that have been carried out to date have been inadequate or whether we reappraise the very idea that we will find solutions. Young, for example, is scathing about a major study carried out on 400 schoolboys by West (1969). He points out that this was one of the largest and most expensive pieces of criminological work to be carried out in Britain. Yet, he argues disparagingly, it could only come up with a link between delinquency and poverty and no real causes. For Young the problem is the intellectual bankruptcy of the positivist paradigm. From where I stand he is right, but, as I shall argue below, the problem is that he locates himself inside exactly the same paradigm.

The vortex that is criminology

It is, then, interesting that Young acknowledges many of the problems outlined above, although he does not do so from a postmodern stance. Rather he is situated inside the modernist problematic itself. He acknowledges that mainstrean criminology has given up the search for causes and the 'master' narrative. He also recognizes the power of governments to diminish an academic enterprise which they no longer have use for. Hence, to keep their jobs, criminologists have had to give up promising the solutions and knuckle down to oiling the wheels. He is rightly critical of this, but, rather than seeing the broad implications of this development, these criminolog*ists* are depicted as capitalist lackeys while criminolog*y* as an enterprise can be saved from such political impurity by a reassertion of a modernist faith. While applauding Young's resistance to the logic of the market which has infected much of criminology (and sociology), I am doubtful that a backward looking, almost nostalgic, *cri de coeur* for the theory that will answer everything is very convincing. Yet Young can see nothing positive in challenging the modernist mode of thought; he only sees capitulation. The way to resist is apparently to proclaim that suffering is real and that we still need a 'scientific' solution for it.

In so doing Young claims the moral high ground for the realists, since to contradict the intellectual content of the argument appears to be a denial of misery and a negation of the very constituencies for whom he now speaks. So, let me make it plain that the challenge to modernist thought, with its positivist overtones which are apparent in criminology, does not entail a denial of poverty, inequality, repression, racism, sexual violence and so on. Rather it denies that the intellectual can divine the answer to these through the demand for more scientific activity and bigger and better theories.

The problem which faces criminology is not insignificant, however, and, arguably, its dilemma is even more fundamental than that facing sociology. The whole *raison d'être* of criminology is that it addresses crime. It categorizes a vast range of activities and treats them as if they were all subject to the same laws – whether laws of human behaviour, genetic inheritance, economic rationality, development or the like. The argument within criminology has always been between those who give primacy to one form of explanation rather than another. The thing that criminology cannot do is deconstruct crime. It cannot locate rape or child sexual abuse in the domain of sexuality or theft in the domain of economic activity or drug use in the domain of health. To do so would be to abandon criminology to sociology; but more importantly it would involve abandoning the idea of a unified problem which requires a unified response – at least, at the theoretical level. However, left realist criminology does not seem prepared for this: see, for example, Young, 1986: 27–8.

Feminist intervention into criminology

I have argued that the core enterprise of criminology is profoundly problematic. However, it is important to acknowledge that it is not just criminology which is inevitably challenged by the more general reappraisal of modernist thinking. My argument is not that criminology alone is vulnerable to the question of whether or not such a knowledge project is tenable. But criminology does occupy a particularly significant position in this debate because both traditional and realist criminological thinking are especially wedded to the positivist paradigm of modernism. This makes it particularly important for feminist work to challenge the core of criminology and to avoid isolation from some of the major theoretical and political questions which are engaging feminist scholarship elsewhere. It might, therefore, be useful to consider schematically a range of feminist contributions to criminology to see the extent to which feminism has resisted or succumbed to the vortex.

Feminist empiricism

Sandra Harding (1986 and 1987) has provided a useful conceptual framework for mapping the development of feminist thought in the social sciences. She refers to feminist empiricism, standpoint feminism and postmodern feminism. By feminist empiricism she means that work which has criticized the claims to objectivity made by mainstream social science. Feminist empiricism points out that what has passed for science is in fact the world perceived from the perspective of men, what looks like objectivity is really sexism and that the kinds of questions social science has traditionally asked have systematically excluded women and the interests of women. Feminist empiricism, therefore, claims that a truly objective science would not be androcentric but would take account of both genders. What is required under this model is that social scientists live up to their proclaimed codes of objectivity. Under this schema, empirical practice is critiqued but empiricism remains intact. Such a perspective is not particularly threatening to the established order. It facilitates the study of female offenders to fill the gaps in existing know-ledge; men can go on studying men and the relevances of men as long as they acknowledge that it is men and not humanity they are addressing.

In criminology there has been a growth in the study of female offenders (for example, Carlen, 1988; Heidensohn, 1985; Eaton, 1986). It would be unjust to suggest that these have merely followed the basic tenets of mainstream empirical work, but a motivating element in all of these has been to do studies on women. But, as Dorothy Smith pointed out in 1973, to direct research at women without revising traditional assumptions about methodology and epistemology can result in making women a mere addendum to the main project of studying men. It also leaves un-challenged the way men are studied.

Harding sees a radical potential in feminist empiricism, however. She argues that the fact that feminists identify different areas for study (for example, wife abuse rather than delinquency) has brought a whole range of new issues on to the agenda. It is also the case that feminists who subscribe to empiricism have challenged the way we arrive at the goal of objective knowledge. Hence different kinds of methods are espoused, note is taken of the power relationship between researcher and re-searched and so on (Stanley and Wise, 1983). The move towards ethno-graphic research is an example of this (although this is not, of course, peculiar to feminist work).

It is perhaps important at this stage to differentiate between empiricism and empirical work. Harding's categories refer to epistemological stances rather than practices (although the two are not unrelated). Empiricism is a stance which proclaims the possibility of objective and true knowledge which can be arrived at and tested against clearly identified procedures. Mainstream criminology, having followed these tenets, claimed to have discovered valid truths about women's criminal behaviour (and, of course, men's). The initial reaction of feminism to this claim was to rein-terpret this truth as a patriarchal lie. It was argued that the methods used had been tainted with bias and so the outcome was inevitably faulty (Smart, 1986). This left open the presumption that the methods could be retained if the biases were removed because the ideal of a true or real science was posited as the alternative to the biased one.

Empirical research does not have to be attached to empiricism, however. To engage with women, to interview them, to document their oral histories, to participate with them, does not automatically mean that one upholds the ideal of empiricism. To be critical of empiricism is not to reject empirical work *per se*. However, some of the empirical studies, generated under the goal of collecting more knowledge about women, which feminist empiricism engendered presented a different sort of problem for the project of a feminist criminology.

This problem was the thorny question of discrimination. The early feminist contributions did not only challenge the objectivity of criminological thought; they challenged the idea of an objective judiciary and criminal justice system. Hence there grew up a major preoccupation with revealing the truth or otherwise of equality before the law in a range of empirical studies. Some studies seemed to find that the police or courts treated women and girls more leniently than men and boys. Others found the opposite. Then there were discoveries that much depended on the nature of the offence or the length of previous record or whether the offender was married or not (see, for example, Farrington and Morris, 1983). As Gelsthorpe (1986) has pointed out, the search for straightforward sexism was more difficult than anyone imagined at first. It was, of course, a false trail in as much as it was anticipated that forms of oppression (whether sexual or racial or other) could be identified in a few simple criteria which could then be established (or not) in following a ritual procedure. So in this respect the (with the benefit of hindsight) overly simplistic approach of early feminist work in this field has created an obstacle to further developments.

The other drawback to this type of research is the one which has been highlighted by MacKinnon (1987). She argues that any approach which focuses on equality and inequality always presumes that the norm is men. Hence studies of the criminal justice system always compare the treatment of women with men and men remain the standard against which all are judged. This has led to two problems. The first arouses a facile, yet widespread, reaction that if one has the audacity to compare women to men in circumstances where men are more favourably treated, then in those instances where they are treated less favourably one must, *ipso facto*, also be requiring the standard of treatment for women to be reduced. Hence, in comparing how the courts treat men and women, the response is inevitably the threat that if women want equality they must have it in full and so some feminists want women to be sent in their droves to dirty, violent and overcrowded prisons for long periods of time. This is what Lahey (1985) has called 'equality with a vengeance'.[1]

The second problem goes beyond the transparent difficulties of treating women as if they were men to the level of the symbolic. Basically the equality paradigm always reaffirms the centrality of men. Men continue to constitute the norm, the unproblematic, the natural social actor. Women are thus always seen as interlopers into a world already organized by others. This has been well established in areas like employment

law where the equality argument has been seen unintentionally to reproduce men as the ideal employees, with women struggling to make the
grade (Kenney, 1986). Underlying such an approach in any case is the
presumption that law is fundamentally a neutral object inside a liberal
regime, thus wholly misconstruing the nature of power and the power of
law (Smart, 1989). Law does not stand outside gender relations and ad-
judicate upon them. Law is part of these relations and is always already
gendered in its principles and practices. We cannot separate out one
practice – called discrimination – and ask for it to cease to be gendered as
it would be a meaningless request. This is not to say we cannot object to
certain principles and practices but we need to think carefully before we
continue to sustain a conceptual framework which either prioritizes men
as the norm, or assumes that genderlessness (or gender-blindness) is
either possible or desirable.

Standpoint feminism

The second category identified by Harding is standpoint feminism. The
epistemological basis of this form of feminist knowledge is experience.
However, not just any experience is deemed to be equally valuable or
valid. *Feminist* experience is achieved through a struggle against oppression; it is, therefore, argued to be more complete and less distorted than
the perspective of the ruling group of men. A feminist standpoint then is
not just the experience of women, but of women *reflexively* engaged in
struggle (intellectual and political). In this process it is argued that a more
accurate or fuller version of reality is achieved. This stance does not
divide knowledge from values and politics but sees knowledge arising
from engagement.

Arguably, standpoint feminism does not feature strongly in feminist
criminology except in quite specific areas of concern like rape, sexual
assault and wife abuse. It is undoubtedly the influence of feminists
engaged at a political level with these forms of oppression that has begun
to transform some areas of criminological thinking. Hence the work of
Rape Crisis Centres (for example, London Rape Crisis Centre, 1984) has
been vital in proffering an alternative 'truth' about rape and women's
experience of the criminal justice system. However, as far as mainstream
criminology is concerned we should perhaps not be too optimistic about
this since the accounts provided by such organizations have only been
partially accepted and, even then, as a consequence of substantiation by
more orthodox accounts (Blair, 1985; Chambers and Millar, 1983).

Taking experience as a starting point and testing ground has only made
a partial entry into criminology and, interestingly, where it has entered
has been in the domain of left realism. It is here we find the resort to
experience (that is, women's experience of crime) a constant referent and

justification. Women's fear of rape and violence is used in this context to argue that rape and violence must be treated as serious problems. The question that this poses is whether we now have a feminist realist criminology or whether left realism (and consequently criminology as a whole) has been revitalized by the energies and concerns of a politically active women's movement. If we consider texts like *Well Founded Fear* (Hanmer and Saunders, 1984) or *Leaving Violent Men* (Binney *et al.*, 1981), we find that the motivating drive is the desire to let women's experiences be told. These experiences are not meant to stand alongside the experiences of the police or violent men; they represent the expression of subjugation which will replace the dominant account. Hanmer and Saunders outline methodological procedures for tapping into this experience and produce what Harding has referred to as a 'successor science'. As she argues, 'the adoption of this standpoint is fundamentally a moral and political act of commitment to understanding the world from the perspective of the socially subjugated' (1986: 149). In fact, it goes beyond this as the researchers, as feminists, also inhabit the world of the socially subjugated. It is not an act of empathy as such but a shared knowledge.

The real issue remains unresolved, however. For while feminist work is generating another sort of knowledge (for example, other ways of accounting for violence), feminist work which fits under the umbrella of left realist criminology does not embrace the full scope of what Young has called for (see, for example, Gregory, 1986).[2] This is because standpoint feminism has not taken masculinity as a focus of investigation. Precisely because standpoint feminism in this area has arisen from a grassroots concern to protect women and to reveal the victimization of women, it has not been sympathetic to the study of masculinity(ies). Indeed, it would argue that we have heard enough from that quarter and that any attempt by feminists to turn their attention away from women is to neglect the very real problems that women still face. So the feminist realists (if we can use this term for the sake of argument) are on quite a different trajectory from the left realists. It may be convenient to the left to support the work of feminists in this area but it is unclear to me where this unholy 'alliance' is going analytically. Like the protracted debate about the marriage of Marxism and feminism, we may find that this alliance ends in annulment.

Feminist postmodernism

It would be a mistake to depict feminist postmodernism as the third stage or synthesis of feminist empiricism and standpoint feminism. Feminist postmodernism does not try to resolve the problems of other positions; rather it starts from a different place and proceeds in other directions. Much postmodern analysis is rooted in philosophy and aesthetics (Rorty,

1985; Lyotard, 1986; Fekete, 1988) but in the case of feminism it started in political practice. It began with the separate demises of sisterhood and of Marxism.

By the demise of sisterhood, I mean the realization that women were not all white, middle class and of Anglo-Saxon, Protestant extract. Feminism resisted this realization by invoking notions of womanhood as a core essence to unite women (under the leadership of the said white, middle-class and Protestant women). However, black feminists, lesbian feminists, Third World feminists, aboriginal feminists and many others simply refused to swallow the story. To put it simply, they knew power when they saw it exercised. Feminism had to abandon its early framework and to start to look for other ways of thinking which did not subjugate other subjectivities. But at the same time, feminism came to recognize that individual women did not have unitary selves. Debates over sexuality, pornography and desire began to undo the idea of the true self and gave way to notions of fractured subjectivities. These developments were much influenced by the work of Foucault and psychoanalytic theory but they cannot be dismissed simply as a 'fad' because the recognition of the inadequacy of the feminist paradigm was not imposed by the intellectuals but arose out of a series of painful struggles for understanding combined with a progressive political stance.

The other key element in this development was the demise of Marxism as a rigorously policed grid of analysis, adherence to which had meant the promise of the total explanation or master narrative. Again, feminist practice revealed the inadequacy of the grand theoretical project of Marxism quite early in the second wave. But the struggle to retain the paradigm lasted much longer. None the less it is now realized that we cannot keep adding bits of Marxist orthodoxy to try to explain all the awkward silences. While many Marxian values may be retained, the idea and the promise of the totalizing theory have gradually loosened their grip.

The core element of feminist postmodernism is the rejection of the one reality which arises from 'the falsely universalizing perspective of the master' (Harding, 1987: 188). But unlike standpoint feminism it does not seek to impose a different unitary reality. Rather it refers to subjugated knowledges, which tell different stories and have different specificities. Thus the aim of feminism ceases to be the establishment of the feminist truth and becomes the deconstruction of truth and analysis of the power effects which claims to truth entail. So there is a shift away from treating knowledge as ultimately objective or, at least, the final standard and hence able to reveal the concealed truth, towards recognizing that knowledge is part of power and that power is ubiquitous. Feminist knowledge, therefore, becomes part of a multiplicity of resistances. Take, for example, feminist interventions in the area of rape. This is an area which I have explored in detail elsewhere (Smart, 1989) but for the sake of this discussion I wish to rely on the work of Woodhull (1988). Woodhull, in an article on sexuality and Foucault, argues against a traditional feminist mode of explanation for rape. She concentrates on Brownmiller's (1975) approach which seeks to explain rape in terms of the physiological differences between men and women. Woodhull's argument is that in explaining rape in this way, Brownmiller puts sex and biology outside the social, as preceding all power relations. What is missing is an understanding of how sexual difference and the meanings of different bits of bodies are constructed. Woodhull argues:

> If we are seriously to come to terms with rape, we must explain how the vagina comes to be coded – and experienced – as a place of emptiness and vulnerability, the penis as a weapon, and intercourse as violation, rather than naturalize these processes through references to 'basic' physiology.

> (1988: 171)

So it becomes a concern of feminism to explore how women's bodies have become saturated with (hetero)sex, how codes of sexualized meaning are reproduced and sustained and to begin (or continue) the deconstruction of these meanings.

This is just one example of how postmodernism is influencing feminist practice (for others, see Diamond and Quinby, 1988; Jardine, 1985; Weedon, 1987; Fraser and Nicholson, 1988) and it is clear that the ramifications of the epistemological crisis of modernism are far from being fully mapped or exhaustively considered as yet. We are in no position to judge what shapes feminism will take in the next decade or so. However, it might be interesting to consider, albeit prematurely, what all this means for criminology.

Concluding remarks

It is a feature of postmodernism that questions posed within a modernist frame are turned about. So, for a long time, we have been asking 'what does feminism have to contribute to criminology (or sociology)?'. Feminism has been knocking at the door of established disciplines hoping to be let in on equal terms. These established disciplines have largely looked down their noses (metaphorically speaking) and found feminism wanting. Feminism has been required to become more objective, more substantive, more scientific, more anything before a grudging entry could be granted. But now the established disciplines are themselves looking rather insecure (Bauman, 1988) and, as the door is opening, we must ask whether feminism really does want to enter.

Perhaps it is now apt to rephrase the traditional question to read 'what has criminology got to offer feminism?' Feminism is now a broadly based scholarship and political practice. Its concerns range from questions of philosophy to representations to engagement; it is, therefore, no longer in the supplicant position of an Olivia Twist. On the contrary, we have already seen that a lot of feminist work has revitalized radical criminology. It might be that criminology needs feminism more than the converse. Of course, many criminologists, especially the traditional variety, will find this preposterous; but perhaps they had better look to who their students are and who their students are reading.

It is clear that if mainstream criminology remains unchanged it will follow the path that Young has outlined into greater and greater complicity with mechanisms of discipline. However, the path of radical criminology seems wedded to the modernist enterprise and is, as yet, unaffected by the epistemological sea changes which have touched feminism and other discourses. Under such circumstances, it is very hard to see what criminology has to offer to feminism.

Notes

1 I have argued against equality feminism elsewhere (Smart, 1989). However, my criticism is that equality feminism misunderstands the nature of the law and the state and naively asks for equal treatment on the assumption that it will improve things. Evidence indicates that equality legislation only improves things for men (MacKinnon, 1987; Fudge, 1989).
2 Jeanne Gregory's paper in the Matthews and Young (1986) collection is an interesting example of what I mean here. Located alongside Young's call for a re-emphasis on criminology and deviance is Gregory's paper which starts within a criminological perspective but moves rapidly outside this field as she progresses on to a discussion of the future direction of feminist work.

PART 2

The transformative experience in feminist research: from practice to theory

---

'I know what you're thinking about,' said Tweedledum: 'but it isn't so, nohow.'
'Contrariwise,' continued Tweedledee, 'if it was so, it might be; and if it were so, it would be: but as it isn't, it ain't. That's logic.'

(Lewis Caroll 1871, *Through The Looking-Glass*)

How do we recognize an example of feminist research? Are there certain essential characteristics that mark 'x' as a feminist and 'y' as a non-feminist piece of work? Can we say, for example, that research by or on women is feminist, that the research of self-declared feminists is feminist or that the essence of feminism lies in interpretation or content? Does the placing of women's experiences, ideas, achievements and visions at the centre of a piece of research make that work feminist?

These questions are not open to easy solutions. Research by or on women cannot be taken to be synonymous with 'feminist research'. Equally, an examination of authorial intention raises more questions than answers. Sometimes research conceived with the most laudable political motives can prove ultimately lame and unconvincing. Conversely, research by people with no particular sympathy for feminism may provide a rich vein for feminist thought and action. A useful way of exploring the difference between feminist and non-feminist research is to examine a specific example in which considerable research has been carried out. One such area is violence against women.

Conventional approaches to the study of wife-battering have revolved around such questions as 'What particular psychopathology leads to violence?', 'Is violence within the family related to violence within wider society?', 'Why does violence run in families?', 'What did the victim do to precipitate the violence?' and 'Why did she stay?' Conventional research has, therefore, concentrated on the offender, the effects of the mass media, the psychodynamics of families and interpersonal behaviour within the home, especially the behaviour of the victim. Psychologists have aimed to understand wife-battering through examination of the characteristics of the batterers (primarily men) and psychodynamic researchers have focused on personality traits, psychopathology or mental illness (Roy, 1977; 1982; Gayford, 1975). Social learning theorists have studied, *inter alia*, the presence of violence in individuals' extended families and women's helplessness when they perceive a lack of control over their environment.

In contrast, conventional sociological approaches have focused on social structural factors which lead to wife abuse (Finkelhor *et al.*, 1983; Gelles, 1983). Some sociologists, for example, have examined patterns of wife abuse in relation to class, education, race and religion. The assumption here is that particular structural arrangements within families produce stress and conflict and lead to violence. Other sociologists have explored cultural norms and values to explain men's prerogative to batter their wives.

Research methods in this sphere of activity have included quantitative surveys, structured questionnaires with pre-categorized responses, clinical observation, experimental tests, matching techniques, personality inventories, multifactorial questionnaires and statistical sampling based on those who have been arrested, imprisoned or hospitalized because of their violent behaviour.

Feminist writers have already presented a critique of conventional research findings: see Russell, 1982; Adams, 1988; Rosewater, 1988 for a full discussion and also, in brief, the introduction to Part 3. Our concern here is with the general approaches and specific research methods used. In contrast to conventional researchers, feminist researchers have asked different questions: rather than asking 'why do women stay?', for example, feminists ask 'what factors inhibit women's opportunity to leave violent men?' Also, exploring how battered women are different from non-battered women implies that something is wrong with these women which leads to the violence. Feminists try to understand what all women share within the institution of marriage (Wardell, Gillespie and Leffler, 1983) and in their interactions with men.

Different questions, of course, involve different methodologies and feminist researchers have abandoned many of the positivistic, quantitative methods conventionally used in favour of qualitative, open-ended questionnaires and interview schedules, allowing women to speak for themselves about their experiences as victims. This is not to suggest that quantitative research is not utilized, far from it: quantitative approaches produce important background data (who abuses whom, for instance). Interview methodologies and case histories would provide only a very partial picture here (Yllö, 1988). The important point is that feminist researchers use a multiplicity of methods to explore wife-battering in a way which both provides accurate information on the extent and seriousness of battering and which examines what violence means to women; how, for example, they make sense of, define and experience a wide range of physical and sexual force used against them by men. Feminist researchers are also concerned to evaluate their research methods and to distinguish the effects of questions and interpretations of any 'findings'. Self-awareness and self-criticism are the hallmarks of feminist methodologies.

Feminist approaches in this sphere thus attempt to make women's experience visible and to challenge current explanatory frameworks about wife abuse (Edwards, 1985). Feminist researchers also explore what violence means to them – they reflect on their own feelings about the research and the research process; they do not see those being researched as research 'objects', but as participants. Liz Kelly (1988) and in her essay in this volume, for example, is explicit about her identity as a woman, as a researcher and as a political activist and how this influenced her choice of methodology.

Significantly, feminist research in this area is often 'action research': that is, the research is linked very directly to action. Sometimes this occurs incidentally, putting women in touch with lawyers, Women's Aid Refuges, and counsellors, for example. At other times, the research has involved a local group of women and researchers and the whole research group functions as a support group. Jalna Hanmer and Sheila Saunders (1984) carried out a community study of violence against women, drawing on the experiences of women in a neighbourhood in Leeds, to show both the importance of small-scale research of this nature and how it might be done. Their book, *Well Founded Fear*, demonstrates very clearly that good research can be done by non-academics and with little, if any, funding. Feminist research in this area thus provided information which challenges popular conceptions of violence and of 'appropriate' legal and criminal justice system responses to it. The research also has practical implications in that information can be used to force authorities to provide better legal protections as well as more and better social and housing provision for women who want to leave their violent partners. All of these methodological issues are explored further in the four essays in this section.

Reference to research on wife-battering is helpful in highlighting the impact of feminism, but we need to consider also its potential relevance more generally. What difference would a feminist approach make to the study of police decision-making or to environmental criminology, for example? It would probably involve a clear focus on women and girls, a sensitive approach to interviewing, greater involvement with the research subjects and so on. Theory might also be allowed to emerge from the research findings instead of being seen as a crucial determinant of the research design. Rather than relying on some large-scale statistical monitoring of all the factors which might influence their decision-making, police officers, for example, might be asked to tell the story of how they make their decisions. And in the case of environmental criminology, the focus might be on ethnographic work which allows people to describe the effect of the environment on their lives, their experiences of crime and their motivations to commit crime. These are the kinds of differences a feminist approach might make but we cannot be more precise than this. The important point to make is that there is no one definition of 'feminist' research, merely a host of methodological preferences.

Loraine Gelsthorpe, Liz Kelly and Annie Hudson in their contributions all distinguish themselves from conventional approaches and methodologies and explore at a personal level how the various elements of a feminist approach have transformed their individual research experiences. Each of these writers reflects on her research experiences and on some of the challenges presented by feminism and its core principles of relating research to practice: engaging with 'the researched', recognizing their subjectivity in a non-hierarchical way, and using sensitive research methods which maximize opportunities to reflect more accurately the experiences of 'the researched'. Above all, each of these contributions is testimony to the principle of viewing one's own involvement as both problematic and valid and of recording the subjective experiences of doing research, for these experiences underpin the creation of knowledge.

In the final paper in this part, Maureen Cain develops a new and exciting framework for these experiences by providing a new conception of feminist standpoint epistemology. Feminist research produces a search for reformulations of knowledge rather than a test of fixed formulae; but there remains the question of why anyone should accept these. Personal reflexivity goes some way to resolving the issue; indeed, one of the essential ingredients of feminist approaches is that theorizing has to begin with the researcher's own experience. There is no other knowable place to begin. But comprehension of knowledge production demands more than sharing as best one can the process of coming to know; one has to be able to distinguish 'good and useful knowledge' from 'less good and useful knowledge'. The knowledge claims of science, of course, can be viewed as deeply suspicious (Feyerabend, 1975; 1978; Popper, 1963) and Maureen Cain thus takes the issue of accountability further by describing how the choice between science and unscience can be transcended. She outlines some ingredients for a 'successor science' and indicates how theoretical congruence might be achieved in committed research. Thus personal reflexivity becomes linked with theoretical reflexivity.

7　Feminist methodologies in criminology: a new approach or old wine in new bottles?

Loraine Gelsthorpe

What does it mean to label research as feminist research? There is no single, definitive answer and writers and researchers have seen various elements as the essentials of a feminist approach. These include the choice of topic, the aims of the research, the research process and the role of 'the researched'; but my main concern in this chapter is with the potential impact of feminist approaches for criminological research. I describe some of the ways in which a feminist approach helped 'transform' some prison research I was involved in between 1985 and 1987 and the difference such an approach *might* have made to some other pieces of research since, had external constraints and inherited methodologies allowed. Finally, I describe some current research in which I do have more control over the aims, objectives, research design and so on and in this I discuss the issue of whether or not feminist research is merely 'good' research under a new name – old wine in new bottles.

What is feminist research?

This question has been the subject of much discussion in recent years (Clegg, 1975; Kelly, 1978; Stanley and Wise, 1979; 1983; Roberts, 1981; Spender, 1981; McRobbie, 1982; Bowles and Duelli Klein, 1983; Jaggar, 1983a and 1983b; Harding and Hintikka, 1983; Itzin, 1984; Kay, 1985; Cook and Fonow, 1986; Cain, 1986a). Four major themes emerge from these discussions, which also illuminate some of the dilemmas and pitfalls of adopting a specifically feminist method or of choosing to label particular methodological preferences as feminist.

The first concerns the choice of topic. As Renate Duelli Klein claims, 'the "what" to investigate must come prior to the decision of "how" to go about doing research' (1983: 88). For most this has meant choosing topics which are relevant or sympathetic to women and to the women's movement. In essence, it has meant choosing topics which it is hoped will contribute to ending the oppression of women, that is, topics which have both political and practical import (Mies, 1983).[1]

The concern to 'make women visible' has also led to the suggestion that feminist research must be 'on, by and for women' (Stanley and Wise, 1983: 17–21). Some writers, however, have found this dictum problematical and Maureen Cain (1986a), for instance, argues that none of these three criteria is adequate as a test. She writes that 'a more valid test would interpret the social and political character of these "by, on and for" relationships, rather than treating the criteria themselves as empirical givens' (1986a: 255). Clearly, a socio–political analysis of this sort would make it possible to determine 'how, why and when' the 'by, on, and for' criteria for feminist scholarship could be usefully applied. This is essential in the field of criminology, for so much of the system revolves around men: it is mainly men who are labelled offenders, mainly men who police offenders, mainly men who sentence offenders (although it should be noted that in fact there are about as many female as male magistrates), and mainly men who are imprisoned. Maureen Cain (1986a) and Loraine Gelsthorpe and Allison Morris (1988) are thus among those who argue that men cannot be excluded from the enterprise. However, involving men does not necessarily mean conceding the whole terrain. Cain rationalizes men's involvement on the basis that feminist criteria are satisfied if those researched remain active and gendered subjects. Thus her revised version of the 'on, by, and for' dictum demands only that the subjectivity of those investigated should be taken into account.

The second theme concerns process. There is the by now familiar debate about the merits and demerits of qualitative and quantitative research, styles of interviewing and so on (Glaser and Strauss, 1967). Some writers further suggest that quantitative methods are inconsistent with feminist values, have an objective appearance and, therefore, have no place in feminist methodologies. Both Shulamit Reinharz (1979) and Evelyn Fox Keller (1980), for example, are keen to emphasize a preference for qualitative work and suggest that it better reflects the nature of human and, therefore, women's experiences. Indeed, they argue that quantitative methods cannot convey an in depth understanding of, or feeling for, those being researched and that they often ignore sex and gender differences or look at them without considering other mediating variables. However, the problem is perhaps not quantification itself but insensitive quantification. Some of the difficulties can be corrected (Eichler, 1988). Thus qualitative methods can be used in devising questionnaires for quantitative surveys (Hunt, 1986). Within criminology, large-scale quantitative surveys can be an important means of gaining an overall picture of events. The British Crime Surveys (Hough and Mayhew, 1983 and 1985; Mayhew *et al.*, 1989), for example, were primarily based on quantitative methods of data collection. Though initially criticized because of insensitive questioning, the surveys were refined to deal more sensitively with questions of sexual harassment and abuse. While there is always scope for further refinements, the surveys nevertheless provide important background data for feminist, as well as for other, researchers (Worrall and Pease, 1986).

Paradigms for traditional interviewing practice create problems for feminist researchers (and for research subjects). Ann Oakley (1981), for instance, argues that conventional methods of interviewing (whereby the process is seen as a one-way process, where researchers allocate 'the researched' an objectified function as data and where interviews are seen as having no personal meaning in terms of social interaction) invalidate women's subjective experiences as women and as people. She dismisses 'masculinist paradigms' of interviewing (and thus the masculinist view of social reality) in favour of an approach which acknowledges the subjectivity of the researcher and the researched and which exposes the notion of 'unbiased, objective interviews as myth'. Others in the field have endorsed this view (Bowles and Duelli Klein, 1983).

The third theme which can be discerned is that of the related issue of power and control. Liz Stanley and Sue Wise, among others, reject the traditional relationship between the researcher and the researched:

> It is obscene because it treats people as mere objects, there for the researcher to do research 'on'. Treating people as objects – sex objects or research objects – is morally unjustifiable.
>
> (1983: 170)

Many have found a solution to this by adopting an interactive methodology which means that the principle of a hierarchical relationship between interviewer and interviewee is not adhered to and, as Robert Rapoport and Rhona Rapoport put it, 'an attempt is made to generate a collaborative approach to the research which engages both the interviewer and respondent in a joint enterprise'. Thus rather than minimizing the personal involvement of the interviewer the approach relies on forming a relationship between interviewer and interviewee 'as an important element in achieving the quality of the information . . . required' (1976: 31).

Nancy Kleiber and Linda Light (1978) provide an example of this in their description of research carried out on, within and for the Vancouver Women's Health Collective. In essence, the people who were the 'subjects/objects' of the research helped to choose the methods used, to identify objectives and were closely involved in the interpretation of the results and in the use of these in changing the operational practices of the Health Collective. In a sense, this is tantamount to action research (and thus satisfies the requirement that feminist research should have political and practical import). Action research, of course, is not new; what is new is the conscious decision to share skills. The approach adopted in this research signifies recognition of the fact that the researched have power and knowledge which researchers need, and the power to withhold it.

Would we, indeed, should we, allow 'the researched' to have the last word? In practice, of course, research methodologies are often negotiated with those who are the subjects; but how far we are prepared to reject the traditional relationship between researcher and researched is another matter and not one which is easily resolved in a simple commitment to 'egalitarian research'. Few of us have absolute control over what we do. There are funding agencies to consider, research committees to appease, financial and time constraints to note.

There is another difficulty, too. The dismantling of power differentials between women is one thing; that between female researchers and men who are 'researched' is potentially quite another. While an 'interactive methodology' may have obvious value in research on, by, and for women, it is possible to envisage situations where men are the research subjects where such an interactive approach might be difficult to implement because of the attitudes of the men involved. This is simply to reiterate Cain's proposal that the 'on, by and for' criteria must be interpreted in a social and political context.

There is also a problem in that one cannot, and should not, assume that women who participate in other women's research necessarily share their politics (Acker *et al.*, 1983). There is a need for sensitivity; 'egalitarian research' cannot be adopted as a new orthodoxy. It is possible to imagine a situation where the researcher's interpretation is not only different from but potentially threatening and disruptive to the subject's world view. It may be, too, that the researched do not want to play the game this way. Joan Acker *et al.* describe a situation in which the women who were the subject of the research questioned the inclusion of life histories and extended quotes and urged the researchers to include more analysis. Thus the democratization of the research process is not necessarily easy or clear cut.

The work of Fiona Poland (1985) and Hilary Barker (1986) provides further illustration of the difficulties. Indeed, Barker suggests that we are in danger of creating a 'false-equality trap' whereby feminists negate their own possession of knowledge and skills in order to minimize differences between women. Thus hierarchies of skill superimpose upon the suppositions of sisterhood. But this does not mean that moves towards democratization have to be thrown out. The important point in this third theme is that hierarchical relationships are not denied but questioned. Feminist researchers do not regard it as reasonable to adopt a purely exploitative attitude to interviewees as sources of data. It may mean 'negotiating' the research focus and methods (depending on who is being researched, what the subject matter is and what the research objectives are). It may also mean being honest about the research – answering all questions about it as fully as required – and answering personal questions, too. (Ann Oakley (1981) gives a vivid account of the dilemmas which conventional, textbook paradigms of interviewing create.) The researched have a perfect right to ask questions and they have a right to reasonable answers which signify respect for them as people. In this way feminist researchers do at least approach *some* of the issues of power and control.

Finally, feminist research is characterized by a concern to record the subjective experiences of doing research. As Stanley and Wise point out:

> Whether we like it or not, researchers remain human beings complete with all the usual assembly of feelings, failings, and moods. And all of these things influence how we feel and understand what is going on. Our consciousness is always the medium through which the research occurs; there is no method or technique of doing research other than through the medium of the researcher.
>
> (1983: 157)

Helen Roberts (1981) uses the concept of 'reflexivity' to describe the process through which feminist researchers locate themselves within their work. Indeed, this is seen as integral to a feminist approach to research. Of course, the concern to be open and honest about the research process and our part in it sometimes leads to accusations of a lack of objectivity but it is precisely this notion of 'objectivity' which feminist researchers aim to question and hold up to scrutiny. A rejection of the notion of 'objectivity' does not mean a rejection of a concern for being accurate (Du Bois, 1983). Other writers have expressed the importance of reflexivity rather differently. Stanley and Wise (1983), for example, write that 'the personal is political' and that experience must be prioritized – not only for the researched, but for the researcher too. As Angela McRobbie has pointed out, feminists doing research both draw on, and are constantly reminded of, their own experiences: 'Feminism forces us to locate our own autobiographies and our experience inside the questions we might ask' (1982: 52). This does not mean, of course, that our experience cannot inform our work on men. What is crucial is that feminist researchers explore the nature of their own experience (of women or men) and do not dismiss it as irrelevant.

There are other themes which are implicit in those which I have out-lined. Feminist research is seen to be anti-positivist; it involves a link between beliefs, life and research; it is opposed to what is sometimes termed 'decorticated' theory – theory which is essentially speculative, concerned with abstractions and does not reflect knowledge grounded in lived experience. In contrast, feminist research is concerned with theory which arises out of experience. Further, in feminist research perspectives conventional 'value free' research is replaced by conscious partiality. (See Reinharz, 1979, for a fuller discussion.)

While none of these four areas of debate is new what *is* new is the unequivocal commitment to women (whether directly or indirectly) which is expressed through the adoption of some of these strategies and which entitles feminists to label their inquiry a feminist inquiry. In sum, then, a feminist approach to research or a feminist methodology usually involves a focus on socially significant problems; feminist researchers typically become involved with the research subjects; they also aim to record the impact of the research on themselves. They disclaim any pretensions to 'value free' research and set out to make explicit their own values. They also aim to evaluate the usefulness of their research; this usually means engaging in direct discussion with the 'user com-munity' as opposed to the 'scholarly community' (Reinharz, 1979). Fem-inist research *can* involve men, and can mean research on men, for men and by men, though this remains a matter of debate (Cain, 1986a; Morgan, 1981). In practice feminist research usually indicates a prefer-ence for small-scale qualitative work, though again, this is open to discussion.[2]

The challenge to traditional criminology

It is easy to see the difference that feminist approaches make to a subject like violence against women (see the introduction to this Part). It is perhaps less easy to see some of their wider applications. The following discussion describes some of my research experiences during the past few years to illustrate the point that feminist research is often a case of *trans-forming* conventional approaches to research.

'Transforming' research: a project on prisons

This research came about as part of the Economic and Social Research Council initiative on crime and the criminal justice system. The (male) director of the project employed two researchers (on a contract basis for a period of three years) to carry out qualitative and quantitative research on 'the concept of humane containment in a context of security and control' in a representative sample of prisons.

The research proposal made no mention of gender issues. However, the project director did consciously set out to employ at least one woman for the fieldwork and, in fact, both fieldworkers were women. The research study itself involved five prisons: Gartree, Nottingham, Ashwell, Featherstone and Winson Green, and we also carried out some pilot work in Stafford prison. We spent a period of three to four months in each prison, four days a week, though the days varied to try to cover every aspect of the regime and we maintained contact with the prisons, and individual prisoners, for much longer.

The research methodology was wide ranging and included questionnaires for prisoners and staff to complete, individual interviews, group discussions, observation, time-sampling and monitoring of shifts, menus, ethnic representation in 'good' prison jobs (in the kitchens and gardens), educational provision and opportunities and so on. It also involved discussions with senior management at a regional and national level as well as an examination of policy documents, assessment of staffing levels, analysis of medical records (to identify staff absenteeism and health problems) and a description of disciplinary procedures.

While the director had overall control of the project, the actual research process was open to negotiation. The first few months of the research saw many revisions and refinements to the 'data collection instruments' – questionnaires, interview schedules and so on. Also, despite the fact that the original proposal made no mention of gender issues, these did have some consequences for the nature and structure of the research. This was not necessarily the result of any 'feminist input' but was a reflection of the fact that the two female researchers encountered a whole range of difficulties which were peculiar to them as women. Our male colleague did not experience the research in the same way.

The extent to which experience, age, sex and ethnicity influences the field researcher's role is often underplayed, if not ignored, in more traditional approaches to research which do not ask how far personal biography and experience influence the research role, what the significance of age is on field relations, what it is like to be a woman/man doing research in a male/female setting, or how a white/black researcher works in a research situation involving blacks/whites. Yet these are all important questions. In my research diary (which was hard to distinguish from a personal diary since I was concerned to record my experiences and interactions within the prison, rather than record so called 'objective observations'), I noted a number of points which were relevant to the influence of (my) gender, age and race.

One of my first experiences working in the prison was to realize, with some force, that I, and my female colleague, were quite out of place. We were incongruous in the nearly all-male environment. The only other women in the prisons were secretaries or probation officers. There was a female assistant governor in Birmingham but her position was rather unusual because she was also a union representative and in some sense considered a pseudo man because of this. It is not that she was labelled as such, but rather that she was accepted as 'one of the boys', albeit one of the management boys, because of her union interests. Indeed, she explained to us that this position gained her both respect and acceptance within the prison. Having no such kudos we were regarded with great suspicion. Prison officers frequently commented, 'What's a nice girl like you doing in a place like this?' or stressed that 'This is not a place for ladies'.

Suspicion of us as women, of course, was hard to distinguish from suspicion of us as researchers. Some officers thought it particularly devious of the government to employ 'women as spies'. Despite our protestations that we were not working for the government some individual officers remained hard to convince.

During our initial visits to the prisons we were normally cast in the role of casual visitors – often mistaken for trainee governors, representatives of the board of visitors or magistrates spending a day in prison as part of their training. Our induction period in each prison, however, marked the beginning of more intensive work within the prison and it was during this time that our research roles became blurred. Management insisted on announcing us as Dr Gelsthorpe and Dr McDermott, even though we asked them not to. My feeling at this time was that the intention behind this was to try and secure co-operation through our perceived status. Inevitably, it was assumed that we were medical doctors or psychiatrists (some of the visiting doctors were female). One incident which illustrates the confusion is where an officer in Stafford prison assumed that we would want to interview all those on his wing who were 'strange' or disturbed', and he duly selected prisoners for us on this basis.[3]

Where we managed to disclaim the awkward prefixes to our names we were often cast in the role of students in a way that our male colleague, a professor, was not. We were respectively in our 30s, 40s and 50s. Being the youngest in the research team meant that it was assumed that I was the others' assistant and my decisions were sometimes questioned because of this. It was assumed that I had no authority to make decisions.

The term 'researcher' itself created some confusion in that it was often taken to mean 'psychological tester' (again, the staff and prisoners *were* familiar with female psychologists). However, the 'observation' part of our role was widely and, apparently, clearly understood. We presented ourselves as observers of the prison who wished to learn what went on, where it went on and how staff and prisoners felt about it.

This being so, it still did not mean that we were welcomed. Indeed, we experienced considerable 'testing out'. Having said that we wanted to consider every aspect of the regime in each prison – daytime, night-time and so on, prison staff asked us to be there from 6.30 a.m. until 10 p.m. and then back again at 6.30 a.m. to see if we were 'man' enough to take it. This was not simply because we were female, of course, but it was an indication of their suspicion and resentment of our intrusion. Although we said we were there to learn we were often regarded as 'experts' who were there to spy and then 'tell them how to do the jobs they had been doing for umpteen years'.

Acceptance in the prison environment was slow and painful. It partly came through the role foisted upon us. The more we talked with both staff and prisoners the more we gained a reputation as 'good listeners'. Prisoners were often desperate for someone to talk to and, in essence, we became 'counsellors'. It is hard to negate the influence of our gender in this since our male colleague had very different experiences when he visited the prisons. Whereas our 'interviews' more often than not became 'conversations' – partly through our approach and partly through the fact that the long, structured interview schedule proved to be impracticable – his did not. Interestingly, our male colleague felt excluded from the research to some degree. This was in part a reflection of the fact that his role meant that he spent less time in the prisons. But it also reflected a difference in approach. As a research team we experienced some tension because of our perceived 'overinvolvement' and the implication that the men only talked to us because we were female.

Finally, my recorded reflections on the research experience included responses to both racism and sexism. Racist and sexist comments in the prison were prevalent. But while racist comments divided the male staff and prisoners, sexist comments united them in a way which transcended the unequal power relationship between them and emphasized the fundamental power differential between men and women. If nothing else, they could share jokes about us, pass comments on the way we dressed and award us marks on our perceived attractiveness (or otherwise).

How, then, was the research transformed? At what point did 'feminism' or feminist concerns enter the research process? We did not have control over the choice of topic or over the methodology, though we had some influence over the latter. Our discussions about methodology were influenced by feminist preferences, by our experiences as female researchers and by our sense of what was 'good research'; but it is hard to distinguish between these factors or to weigh up their relative importance. Combined, however, they did influence our approach to the research and there were specific consequences for both the nature and structure of the research, particularly for the style of interviewing and the content of discussions. Our respective 'feminist perspectives' increased our awareness of gender issues within the prison; but not everything about the way we worked can be put down to some abstract or theoretical feminist stance. I cannot separate a feminist and a non-feminist me. Therefore, the way in which I conducted the research had as much to do with my collective experiences – as a researcher, as a woman, as someone with a particular history – as well as to any specific elements of feminism. Thus, although I may attempt to record my experience of the research – to make clear my values, choices and so on – the choices are not always conscious or politicized. Awareness of gender issues is much more diffuse.

Where my feminist commitment was apparent – quite consciously – was in a concern not to view those we spoke with as research 'objects' or 'mere informants'. Although our conversations with the prisoners involved an unequal balance of power – our clothes, tape recorders and freedom to walk around and out of the prison gave us authority, much as we tried to resist it – our vulnerability as women enabled us to share the men's vulnerability as prisoners at least to some extent.[4] And we gained acceptance by wholeheartedly adopting the role ascribed to us – as counsellors – making ourselves more vulnerable as a condition of that acceptance. While feminist researchers might applaud this, honesty compels me to acknowledge that we did it to gain acceptance *for ourselves* as much as for the prisoners. It would be dishonest to describe it as a wholly 'feminist' move. We were uncomfortable in the prisons, out of place and finding it hard to achieve acceptance to the point where prisoners would talk to us freely and not say the kind of things they thought we wanted to hear. The role of counsellor provided a chance to make the experience more meaningful for us as well as for them.

A more overt feminist commitment arose in our refusal to restrict conversations to the research questions and we frequently abandoned formal interviews altogether in the face of someone's distress or concern to express a particular point. Distress and concern to express a particular viewpoint were valuable indicators of a prisoner's experience of imprisonment. Structured and semi-structured interview schedules were obstacles to attempting to understand that experience. Indeed, at times, between us, we identified the questions which were important to the prisoner. More importantly, we tried to include in our discussions with the men, whether prisoners or prison officers, some reference to the impact of their life in prison on their partners, wives and children.

We also attempted, though not always successfully, to meet both women visiting men in prison and the partners of prison officers, in order to learn from them directly something of *their* prison experiences. Thus we tried to gain some insights into the meaning of imprisonment for the women who served out the men's sentences or worked out their men's shifts at home, for these experiences affected men's experience of prison life.

I am not suggesting that this was the 'right' approach. The point is that as feminist women we felt it inappropriate to deny women's experiences in a project designed to focus on men and their experiences. Gender awareness meant that we had to analyse men in relation to women as well as in relation to other men and, in the research process at least, if not in the reporting of the research,[5] to include something of women's experiences. The general consensus of the research team was that feminism had in these ways added an important dimension to the project.

The potential impact of feminism

I have been involved in five other pieces of research since 1987. Three of them lie directly within the field of criminology. Between March 1987 and February 1989 I was the field researcher on a project designed to measure the impact of the Crown Prosecution Service on juvenile justice.[6] I am currently involved in research on racism and sexism in social inquiry reports[7] and on defendants' experiences in an arrears (fine enforcement) court.[8] I now discuss each of these.

In the first example I look back to see what difference a feminist approach or methodology might have made to the research. In the second I consider the potential for changing the methodology which I have inherited with the project. In the third, I record some of my experiences in a project which tries to meet some of the requirements of feminist research.

The impact of the Crown Prosecution Service on juvenile justice

The aim of this research was to look at the impact of the Crown Prosecution Service in general and of 'juvenile specialists' within the service in particular on a range of juvenile justice issues. Would the introduction of the Crown Prosecution Service lead to an 'ironing out' of existing discrimination in decision-making, for instance? There has been much criticism of the police in recent years because of varying police force policies and practices which lead to 'selective' justice and to 'justice by geography' (Morris and Giller, 1987; Giller and Tutt, 1987).

Fieldwork in South Yorkshire and Cheshire began in September and October 1987 respectively. All juvenile crime referrals to the police were recorded for a period of one calendar month. The research methodology was essentially to collect background data (some thirty variables) on all cases referred and to record subsequent police decisions. In those cases referred to the CPS with a recommendation for prosecution further details were recorded and the crown prosecutors' decisions as to whether or not to proceed to court were documented.

The research also included more qualitative data collection methods – interviews, for example, with police officers and crown prosecutors to try and understand how they came to make the decisions they made, and with senior police and CPS officials to try and understand official policy and how this influenced decision-making on the ground. This was an important part of the research: how to make sense of crown prosecutors' 'operational philosophies' and professional ideologies, how to characterize their decision-making, how to tease out those factors which prompted them to confirm or to reject police recommendations for prosecution.

The fieldwork was not without difficulty, however, and modifications had to be made to the methodology. Discussions and interviews, for instance, had to be of a more general nature than I desired and I had to attempt to cull decisions from the general mish-mash of case papers, scrutinizing every slip of paper for throwaway comments and clues as to the reasons for choosing a particular course of action. It also meant that periods of recording data – attending meetings, sitting around in police and CPS offices examining files or waiting to see people – became periods of intense observation: again, searching for clues as to how decision-makers went about the daily business of decision-making. 'Dead time' was utilized; it was used constructively to record occurrences, comments and, crucially, apparent discrepancies between what was being said and what had been written. Additionally, I used a series of case studies as a focus for discussion and as a way of getting the police and prosecutors to define the determining characteristics of particular kinds of cases.

To some extent this research was also 'transformed' by conscious and unconscious influences, some of which related directly to me, my experience, my gender and my preferences for particular courses of action. But looking back and considering now how I might have made the research more overtly 'feminist' there are four key possibilities. Firstly, I might have focused exclusively on girls. This could be justifiable in feminist terms but my view is that the response of the criminal justice system is problematic where boys, as well as girls, are concerned. Looking at the differences in their treatment can help us understand the underlying philosophies which motivate criminal justice system professionals and practitioners and agents in allied agencies to act in one way and not another. The system is sexist, but that sexism works both ways. To focus exclusively on girls would be to abandon boys to their fate (Gelsthorpe, 1985b; 1989). I consider a 'feminist' focus here to mean a focus on 'gender', not an exclusive focus on women and girls.

Secondly, I might have abandoned the large-scale monitoring of cases in favour of a small-scale ethnographic project examining, for example, how crown prosecutors make decisions – the difference between theory, policy and practice. But with the dilemmas of abandoning quantitative research well-rehearsed (Jayaratne, 1983; Hunt, 1986), the exclusive focus on qualitative work would have left a large gap in the research. In a sense, I needed an overall picture of decision-making in order to tease out why the police and the crown prosecutors made the decisions they did. I needed to know that relatively few girls were prosecuted, that girls were more likely to be given a second caution, that girls who commit offences involving violence were more likely to be dealt with than their male counterparts and so on *before* I could focus on responses to them in terms of crown prosecutors' decisions. But it is true that a focus on particular police officers and crown prosecutors, and an in-depth study of their organizational life, would have given me a more comprehensive and possibly more coherent understanding of the exigencies of practice which influence their decision-making.

Thirdly, I might have included some discussion of the impact of the Crown Prosecution Service on defendants. Some consumers were included in the analysis – social service department representatives, intermediate treatment officers and others involved in local juvenile justice systems, for example. But defendants themselves were formally excluded. A relevant (feminist) question here might have been whether or not it makes any difference to someone to be dealt with by the police or by the CPS.

Fourthly, the research might have been linked more directly to participants. I might have used initial discussions with the police and crown prosecutors to work out what *they* needed me to look into, what *they* perceived to be problematic, what *they* would find most helpful and so on. Our discussions of this nature were with headquarters staff rather than the decision-makers on the ground. A small-scale study of just one or two offices would have facilitated responsiveness to their concerns. Indeed, there are more possibilities for research being 'shared' research when it is on this scale.

I did, however, make strenuous efforts to share my thinking and findings throughout the project, particularly at its conclusion, though there were constraints on my ability to do this fully arising from the large-scale nature of the project and from the hierarchical structure of the agencies with whom we were working. In seeking to make the research relevant and responsive to those involved, however, I was not wearing a specifically feminist hat, merely a hat which told me that this was 'good practice'.

An examination of the role of gender and ethnicity in the writing and interpretation of social inquiry reports

There have been relatively few studies which have systematically analysed the differential influences of gender and ethnicity in the preparation, interpretation and impact of social inquiry reports. Moreover, the findings of those studies that have been undertaken (for example, White-house, 1983; Pym and Lines, 1987; Voakes and Fowler, 1989; Mair, 1986; McConville and Baldwin, 1982) remain limited by small samples and are sometimes inconclusive. I inherited this project at a point where negotiations with the relevant agencies were almost complete and the methodology fixed as part of these negotiations. Data collection instruments, draft interview schedules and so on had all been produced. The main aim is to focus on two court areas – in London and Birmingham – and to collect data on all offenders 17 years old and above, charged with indictable or triable-either-way offences, who appear in selected magistrates' courts over a three- to four-month period. Recorded details on defendants include ethnic origin, sex, age, employment status, housing situation, education, number of dependants, charge, plea, previous sentences, contacts with the probation service, the probation service's recommendation and final sentence. Using pairwise matching techniques these variables will then be compared across ethnic group and gender.[9]

The methodology also includes a content analysis of social inquiry reports written during the same three- to four-month period. The aim here is to consider the ways in which gender and ethnicity are presented. Further, the methodology includes interviews (of a semi-structured nature) with probation officers which are designed to determine what factors shape the content of their social inquiry reports (SIRs) and to assess whether or not officers see particular defendants as a low or high priority in probation practice. The interviews also touch on perceptions of the influence of ethnicity and gender in the writing of reports and the making of recommendations and on general perceptions of law-breaking patterns across ethnic groups and between men and women. Magistrates will also be interviewed with the intention of assessing their perceptions of the role and importance of SIRs, general perceptions of lawbreaking across ethnic groups and between men and women, perceptions of the 'usefulness' of SIRs – and what they consider to be the key variables which influence their sentencing decision.

What potential was there, then, for a specifically 'feminist' input? This is hard to answer given the usual constraints. Ideally one might have pursued an approach which gave more weight to defendants and *their* perceptions of sexism and racism ('classism' and 'ageism', too, perhaps). What appears racist or sexist to me (as a white, middle-class academic) might be completely wide of the mark when compared with the experiences of defendants. Moreover, I have never been a defendant. I have never been in the vulnerable position of having social inquiry reports written about me.

Again, an alternative approach might have been to abandon large-scale monitoring in favour of a small-scale qualitative study – for example, an organizational analysis in which the interaction of defendants and probation officers was examined, along with the interaction of probation officers and magistrates, defendants and magistrates and all three together (as well as the influence of others – the court clerk, ushers, solicitors, social workers and so on). Race and gender cannot be separated from the influence of appearance, demeanour and the organizational influences which aid or inhibit magistrates, probation officers and others in making sense of their ascribed roles. Nor can these factors be separated from the exigencies of practice in busy probation offices and court-rooms.

The research could also have been shaped and used to advocate the position of the defendant. Is the 'expert' view necessarily an accurate view, for instance (given that probation officers, along with other criminal justice system agents, try to work out 'what kind of case they are dealing with' and that there is a tendency to use a kind of perceptual shorthand to make this task both easier and more meaningful (Giller and Morris, 1981))? Thus the research might have become action research, designed to provide specific groups of defendants with the information they needed to show that the role of professionals was not always helpful; indeed, that their contributions could be deeply prejudicial.

Research in an arrears court

This research project concerns defendants who are appearing in an arrears court for non-payment of fines, legal aid contributions, compensation and the like. The research, carried out jointly with Allison Morris, is small scale (because of funding and time constraints) and is designed to describe the age, sex, ethnicity and circumstances of those in default, to examine the methods of enforcement used by the court and to report on defendants' perspectives. Our main purpose is to try and understand defendants' responses to the initial fine, the reasons for non-payment and defendants' reactions to subsequent court action. The methodology includes abstraction of details from records, observation in the courtroom and interviews with defendants.

Our suspicions, but not hypotheses, are that the decisions which are made reflect a whole host of factors which are not immediately attributable to the non-payment of the fine alone. It is already apparent from our field-work, for example, that magistrates believe that defendants who owe money to the court should be in work, should not have cars (unless they are absolutely vital for getting to work), should not drink or smoke or pursue any 'extravagant' hobbies, should be prepared to put themselves in debt elsewhere in order to pay the court and, above all, should respect the court and always turn up when told to do so. Thus housing and employment difficulties, battles with the DSS (DHSS), difficulties in managing limited resources, confusing relationships which leave partners in debt, the sheer panic and fear of court action and other debts which paralyse some defendants so they cannot ask for more time to pay, for different payment arrangements, or cannot even turn up to the court, are glossed over in the overall objective of getting the defendant, the 'wrong-doer', to pay his or her penalty.

Moreover, defendants appear to be 'punished' for breaking these 'rules'. Thus some defendants are asked to come back weekly to report on the success of job interviews or are made the subject of warrants of suspended committal to prison if it is felt that they are not trying hard enough to find a job. Others who failed to appear on a particular previous date are told to come back at some future date, despite the fact that they are now working and would lose wages by taking the day off. This is not to imply that magistrates are never sympathetic, but rather to suggest that the issues are more complicated than appears to be the case; everyone gets caught up in the purpose and business of the court and the 'voice' of the defendant is rarely heard.

Is the research 'feminist' in intention and design? Certainly we became interested in the project in the first place because we noticed that a greater proportion of women appeared in the arrears court than in the magistrates' court itself and this raised questions in our minds about the fining of female defendants. This in turn, however, raised more general questions about the fining of low income defendants. We do aim to provide an opportunity for defendants to speak – both directly by listening to them and indirectly in our analysis of the research findings. But we learned very early that this was not enough. Many of the defendants needed advice and asked us for it. Now, although it always seems an inadequate response, we are at least equipped with information to give to defendants should they say that they would like legal advice or advice on money matters (or if they appear to need help in this way from what they say to us).

As far as the research process itself is concerned we have not felt able simply to gain information and then walk away. We have found it difficult to talk to defendants about their financial and personal circumstances – it has seemed intrusive and insensitive and so our approach has been hesitant and uncertain. Interviews have also been abandoned, when it has seemed that the pressure is too great or the distress (in the case of defendants in the police cells at the court) is unbearable, in favour of offering support or putting pressure on courtroom officials to arrange immediate contact for the defendant with the duty solicitor. The research also has practical and political import; we aim to discuss the findings with the magistrates who sit in the arrears court. We hope thereby to make things better for future defendants. In some ways, then, our research conforms to some of the feminist research principles outlined above. Those we speak with are not 'mere informants'; the research experience is one we share though we acknowledge that it can never be the same for them and us.

Conclusion

This may be a rather unusual approach to a discussion about feminist methodologies and perspectives in criminology. I began by thinking that I would discuss the relative merits and deficiencies of certain feminist approaches but it became clear that what I most wanted to convey was something of my working experiences and reflections on research methodologies. I have found this reflexivity one of the most helpful contributions of a feminist approach. While it feels vulnerable to write in this way it does demonstrate a key feminist principle: viewing the researcher's involvement in and experiences of the research as both problematic and valid.

But my purpose in writing in this way was twofold. I also wanted to convey something of the difficulty of distinguishing between feminist research and simply 'good' research. Is feminist research merely 'old wine in new bottles'? If we accept that feminist research can be carried out with men as the focus (and carried out by men) then it may be that we are left with 'good' research. I do not believe that it is as important for feminists to try to lay sole claim to 'good research' as it is to challenge the supremacy of more conventional methods and approaches.

Acknowledgements

I would like to thank Allison Morris and Jane Morris for their helpful comments on earlier drafts of this chapter.

Notes

1 This is an area in which many researchers fail, but there are studies, particularly on women as victims, which are linked with political action. See Jalna Hanmer and Sheila Saunders (1984) for example.
2 Sandra Harding's (1987) discussion is important here as she helps clarify feminist characteristics of research. She does this by drawing distinctions between feminist method, methodology and epistemological issues but her analysis lies beyond the scope of this general discussion.
3 The prisoners we spoke with were largely self selected. We resisted interviewing on the basis of statistical sampling.
4 We took a principled decision not to carry keys in all but one of the prisons although we were repeatedly offered them. Movement around Featherstone Prison would have been impossible without keys; trying to hide the fact that we had them became a major preoccupation each day and we never lost the discomfort of their possession and, hence, our power.
5 The researchers have produced a number of papers to date (see, for example, Roy King and Kathy McDermott 1989) but none of these has made specific reference to gender issues.
6 The main report was published in May 1989. See Loraine Gelsthorpe, Henri Giller and Norman Tutt (1989) and Gelsthorpe and Giller (1990).

7 This research is funded by the Home Office and is due to be completed in March 1991.
8 This is a small project based on a sample of defendants who appeared in an arrears court in September 1989.
9 Pairwise matching techniques in this instance involve the matching of black, Asian and white defendants on a range of variables such as age, sex, charge, number of previous convictions and most serious previous sentence.

8 Journeying in reverse: possibilities and problems in feminist research on sexual violence

Liz Kelly

My 'career' as a researcher has, thus far and in certain respects, been a mirror image of that which Shulamit Reinharz (1979) documents in her challenging account *On Becoming a Social Scientist*. She moved from positivism through more open methods to feminism and a methodology which she calls 'experiential analysis'. I began from feminism and a certainty about creating a 'feminist methodology' and am now involved in using the very research method I (and many others, not exclusively feminists) have been most critical of – the large-scale self-report questionnaire. This short piece is a reflection on this journey in reverse and a contribution to the debates on feminist research and methodology.

The starting point for any discussion of feminist research must be to ask what is feminism? For me, it is a belief that women are oppressed and a commitment to ending that oppression. This allows for differences in women's experience of oppression, in theoretical perspectives and therefore in practical solutions. It none the less provides a minimal framework within which debate, challenge, connection and coalition can take place. Thus feminist research investigates aspects of women's oppression while seeking at the same time to be part of the struggle against it.

In order to investigate women's oppression it has been necessary to question previous constructions of knowledge about women – that is, to challenge 'malestream' thought. From the liberal notion of 'adding women in', feminist researchers and theorists have shifted to the more radical position of taking an explicitly 'feminist standpoint' in their work (Harding, 1987). The basic tenet of a feminist standpoint is that it is a way of looking at the world – from the standpoint of women. Leaving aside for the moment the vexed question of which women, what this seeks to achieve is knowledge created from women's points of view. On the surface, this seems simple enough but, given that most knowledge has been created from men's point of view and that women as well as men have been encouraged to accept this knowledge as having a universal applicability, women can, and often do, see the world through men's eyes. I will discuss later the implications of this for research. Feminists are also increasingly committed to developing a standpoint which, reflecting the debates and challenges within and to feminism outside academia, recognizes and takes account of the compounding oppressions many women experience. The integration of compounding oppressions, the ways in which they determine options and experiences as a woman, is essential if we are to understand the complex and interlocking structures of oppression in order that women's liberation can be achieved for *all* women.

These shifts in feminist theory and practice have been reflected in the ways in which feminists have conducted research – rather than producing work *on* women we now seek to produce work *for* women. A slightly different emphasis, which a number of feminists have put forward, is research *with* women. While research 'for' women need not necessarily have women as its subjects, research 'on' and 'with' women does, by definition. Thus, some conceptualizations of feminist research restrict the questions that can be asked and who they should be asked of. Face to face interviews, with women, have become the paradigmatic method used by feminist social researchers. The remainder of this essay focuses on the problems and possibilities for feminist social researchers and draws on my own research practice in the area of sexual violence.

Journey Part 1

The first project I worked on was my PhD, which formed the basis for *Surviving Sexual Violence*. I believed that feminist research was research *for* and *with* women. I drew on what I had learnt in seven years of activism in the women's liberation movement and the questions I wanted to ask were ones that grew out of my work in a women's refuge, being involved in establishing a rape crisis line and political campaigning locally and nationally. Some of what I knew then from working with and for women has since been transformed into academic knowledge as more researchers have reached similar conclusions, albeit through different routes at times.

The most obvious illustration of differences between conventional and feminist approaches to research concerns the questions we ask and how we ask them. One of the main focuses of second wave Western feminist activism was how men's violence was consistently hidden, minimized, redefined. Not only did this make it difficult for women to speak about what had happened to them (what feminists have called 'silencing') but it also made even defining events as abuse or violence problematic (what feminists have called 'naming'). Thus investigating how common sexual violence was in women's lives in ways which challenged, rather than simply reproduced, the silencing and the limited definitions has required detailed attention to language and to the issues of whether or not our questions presume shared definitions. For example, asking 'have you ever been raped?' will produce different responses from asking 'have you ever been forced to have sex?': the former will fail to uncover the extent of coercive heterosex which women experience but do not define as rape.

The form of the questions asked can to some extent overcome the problem of presuming shared meanings; but where the topic of investigation is one which asks participants to recall painful events other factors may prevent disclosure. Where an experience carries negative cultural meanings (for example, shame and self-blame), establishing a context in which it is possible to tell about distressing events becomes an important facet of research methodology. Feminists have, therefore, tended to opt for face to face interviews as the preferred research method and it is now accepted within the international research community that this method produces the most accurate findings, at least in relation to prevalence (Finkelhor, 1986). It is also feminist researchers who have begun to explore, and take responsibility for, the potential impact of participating in research which requires recalling disturbing memories.

What I have said so far suggests that these shifts in methodology were primarily pragmatic, directed at increasing the validity of findings. My methodology did reflect these concerns but the choices also stemmed from a belief that enabling women to speak easily about what had happened to them, reflect on their experiences and discuss issues relating to sexual violence more generally could be positive for them. Face to face interviews allowed for the possibility of talking through any distress. While the majority of the 60 women I interviewed said that it had been a positive experience to participate, I do not know what the 13 women who did not take part in the second interview, during which we discussed the impact of the interview and read their transcript, felt. Several of the women whom I met twice continued to be troubled by issues raised by their participation and I remained a source of support for some time after the research was over. I probably learnt as much, if not more, from this continued interaction as I did from the research interviews themselves; but this none the less raises complex questions about the role of the researcher.

Not all interviewers, feminist or otherwise, are prepared, willing or able to offer this kind of ongoing support. This leads me to at least question the unproblematic endorsement of face to face interviews. While they undoubtedly offer the potential for more accurate findings and for reflecting the complexity of experiential knowledge, they also raise the possible problem of bringing to the surface distressing experiences which were previously suppressed. What responsibility do we have as researchers for dealing with this? Might an impersonal questionnaire allow participants more control over their emotions and memories? While I have no easy answers to these questions, they are ones which feminist researchers must address. At the very least, where our work involves human subjects, investigating the impact of participating in research must become a necessary part of every project's methodology.

Having moved into the area of ethics, the other issue which preoccupied me during the project was how to involve women in the project itself. It is no accident that feminist researchers have questioned the use of people as 'objects' of research, since women are continually 'objectified' in Western culture. But is simply calling women 'subjects' an adequate feminist response? It is the issue of *power* which underpins the ways in which researchers relate to the researched. Power, and the lack of it, operates at a number of levels in research. Researchers can retain the power to set the research agenda, to determine where and how it is conducted, to remain aloof, separate ('objective') and to interpret and control the outcome. All that remains within the power of the researched in the traditional model is to refuse to participate at all or to refuse to answer certain questions or deliberately answer them dishonestly.

Feminists have attempted to redress the balance – opting for more open forms of research, discussing issues, answering questions and being flexible about where research is conducted (see, for example, Oakley, 1987; Kelly, 1988). One of the basic criticisms of questionnaires is that they set the research agenda in advance and offer no possibility for dialogue. Feminist researchers have tried to treat women involved in research as 'subjects', as experts on their own lives, worthy of respect and honesty. Democratizing the outcome of research – treating the researched as participants in a joint venture – is, however, another matter. It is relatively easy to change the style of interviews, quite another to share interpretation, analysis and writing up. One of the few honest accounts of an attempt to share power at the later stages of a research project demonstrates the complex issues involved, not least the women participant's expectations that it should be the researchers who developed an overview and analysis (Acker, Barry and Esseveld, 1983).

The model of social research with women which comes closest to a feminist ideal of sharing power is 'participatory research' (Maguire, 1987). Patricia Maguire defines participatory research as having 'the explicit intention of collectively investigating reality in order to transform it' (1987: 4). Although she accepts that until recently this method has had an 'androcentric filter' she sets out a framework for a specifically feminist participatory research practice.

The second half of her book documents a 'project conducted with a multi-cultural group of formerly battered women in Gallop, New Mexico' (1987: 134). One aim of the study was to explore how women coped when they left the local shelter (refuge). Women were contacted and inter- viewed individually but half way through the project the participants formed a group which was to be support for themselves and a way of reaching women in their communities. What Maguire encouraged and facilitated was thus much more than a support group; one of the out- comes of the group was that the ex-residents presented their ideas about policies and practices in the local shelter and suggested areas of change.

My attempts to involve women in the research process fell short of this ideal. While I tried to check my interpretation of the women's accounts and give something back to them – by offering time to talk through issues which had come up, by giving them a copy of their transcripts and time to reflect on them – this was not a collective endeavour. While some of the women's understandings shifted during the research I did not attempt to encourage them to take part in collective transformative action. Maguire's work illustrates that research in which women are full participants and which has a central aim of enabling them to collectively challenge oppres- sion can be undertaken.

Journey Part 2

The second project I was involved with concerned a piece of funded research for a local authority (McGibbon, Cooper and Kelly, 1989). It was not research 'on' women, nor was it solely 'with' women but we saw it as research 'for' women. Our brief was to investigate services in Ham- mersmith and Fulham for women who had experienced, or were cur- rently experiencing, violence from male partners. While the research findings would, we hoped, benefit women, the study itself focused on agency policy and practice.

With only eight months in which to carry out the research, one full-time researcher and a small budget, we had to devise a strategy which ob- tained the greatest amount of information from the widest sources. We also attempted, within these constraints, to include aspects of action research in our methodology. Firstly, we used interviews as a way of raising issues workers might not have thought about – particularly whether or not they were operating with stereotypes about violence against women and whether or not they understood the ways in which compounding oppressions might affect women's ability to seek help and the kinds of support they might require. (We asked explicit questions about black and ethnic minority women, elderly women, women with disabilities and lesbians.) We hoped that this would not only provide us with information on workers' ability to respond appropriately but would also raise issues which they would think about and discuss with colleagues. Secondly, we passed on information about available services to groups and individuals who were not aware of them throughout the fieldwork rather than waiting until the final report was written. Thirdly, in our interim report, instead of just offering a statement of 'work in progress', we included initial policy recommendations. We were therefore involved in ongoing policy discussions and were able to witness change taking place during the second half of the project.

We have described our research strategy as a 'multi-methodological' approach. We sought out all policy documents (few in number!) and conducted interviews with housing workers, social workers, community groups, workers and residents in the local refuges and the local police. We sent questionnaires to local solicitors, training officers and community groups – again the questionnaires were designed not only to elicit data but also to raise the issue and explore possibilities for future development work in the borough.

Since we knew from previous research that most women who are being abused do not go to refuges (partly because they believe that there would be no room for them but also because not all women know about them and some who do choose other escape routes), we wanted to reach a broad sample of women in the borough to ask about their experiences of violence, what agencies, if any, they had contacted, and what services they would like to see locally. We were also interested in comparing what women who had not been abused thought they would do if faced with violence with what women who had been abused actually did. To achieve this we adapted the method used by Amy Manchershaw (1988), of asking women attending doctors' surgeries to fill in an anonymous questionnaire.[1] Interestingly, over 50 per cent of the women who completed it took away with them the list of support services we had attached.

This project clearly involved a more distanced methodology than that in my previous research. What it did produce, however, was a response from a large and more representative group of women. We were able to explore the range of women's experiences of violence in relationships, the complexity of the ways in which they coped and sought support and what services women wanted.

Unlike traditional academic research, where the research report is seldom read and the implications of the findings seldom extend beyond the research community, we were required to draw up practical recommendations (that is, recommendations which did not have huge resource implications) for the local council to implement. The final report contains 73 recommendations. Six months after the completion of the project a number of them have been implemented and others are under consideration. The recommendations covered general council policy; the special needs of black and ethnic minority women, older women, women with disabilities and lesbians; housing policy and practice; social services; refuges; law and law enforcement, and the voluntary sector. Already, the need for information and training has begun to be addressed and a working group within the housing department has investigated the implications of changing the currently restrictive interpretation of housing legislation and adopted a more open policy. In fact, before the project was completed our suggestion that a 'women only' bed and breakfast hotel be established in the borough had already been achieved.

This experience of research raises issues about how studying women's oppression and 'transforming reality' can take place in different ways, and the variety of roles that research and researchers can play. This research did not focus on direct contact with women as 'research subjects'; nevertheless, the research questions elicited evidence to support the borough's commitment to tackle issues relating to violence against women within the home. The researchers have subsequently been involved in developing an information pack and a training programme.

Journey Part 3

My interest in methodology and the influence it has on research findings, coupled with the absence of a carefully conducted study of the prevalence of child sexual abuse in Britain, subsequently led to an application for funding to explore both these issues simultaneously. The original application sought to compare findings from a self-report questionnaire and in-depth interviews but, for complex reasons, only the self-report questionnaire part of the project is currently funded. Certain research questions, important to feminists, can only be answered where relatively large numbers, and a cross-section of the population, participate in the study. Answering the question 'how common is child sexual abuse' has implications for social policy and I hope that the research will provide data which will shed some light on competing explanations as to why it happens as well as on many other critical questions. We will also be asking young people what kind of responses they would want from those in a position to help, and their views on current debates about policy in relation to child sexual abuse. Additionally, we shall seek their views on the questionnaire itself, what it felt like filling it in and how it could be improved.

The current challenge to the research team working on this exploratory study is how to construct a questionnaire which asks questions without presuming shared meaning, which enables young people to fill it in without getting distressed, and how to conduct the research so that support is available for anyone who, as a consequence of participating, needs it.

Our strategy has been to find further education colleges where there are staff and support services interested in developing services for young people who have been abused. We intend to work with them prior to conducting the surveys and to link up with local support services outside the college. We hope that spending three days in each institution will mean that we can facilitate these connections and enable both staff and support services to work with local young people after the surveys are completed.

Crossroads or different routes?

What I have learnt on my journey so far is that there are certain issues which have to be dealt with whatever method you use. I no longer believe that there is only one way to do research as a feminist. I have moved from a methodological purism to wanting to explore and develop methodologies appropriate to the research question/s. The question you are seeking to answer (or are funded to answer) will point to using certain methods. The issue is then how to apply a feminist standpoint to that method or combination of methods. Can all research methodologies be transformed? What are the limits, problems and possibilities that differing methodologies offer us as feminists? We can only answer these questions by attempting to use as wide a variety of methods as we can and by reflecting on what they enabled and what they prevented.

Feminism is a politics of discovery, critique and transformation. While certain research methods (participatory research especially) embody all three features throughout, others focus on discovery and/or critique during the research and transformation is the anticipated outcome of the completed project. Both are valid ways of doing feminist social research.

Notes

1 We subsequently amended our method of contact to try to reach a larger number of black and ethnic minority women. There were some difficulties in doing this and we describe these in the final report (McGibbon, Cooper and Kelly, 1989).

9 'Elusive subjects': researching young women in trouble

Annie Hudson

My relationship with research about young women in trouble has just about turned full circle. As a newly qualified social worker in the mid-1970s I was struck by the way in which young women in trouble got a raw deal from welfare agencies. Perceived as 'hard to work with', having little political capital (unlike young male offenders or children at risk of abuse) and labelled in highly pejorative ways ('manipulative', 'uncontrollable', 'promiscuous' and so on), these social services users had low priority. For most of the 1980s I was a lecturer in social work and involved in various forms of research and consultancy work about 'troublesome' young women. My role thus shifted from being a participant in the state's care/control machinery to becoming a more distanced inquirer. Now, as I write this, I am employed as a first line manager in a social services department and so once again I am part of the state apparatus of which I have previously been critical. Such turnabouts in role might be regarded by some as creating bias and confusion in intellectual analysis. Others are better placed to judge whether or not that is the case for me. My hope and belief is that such changes have enabled me to engage more directly than many researchers with the complexities and nuances of the issues involved.

My intentions in this chapter are twofold. First, I demonstrate, through reference to my research, that researching 'troublesome' young women (aged 13 to 18 years) demands qualitatively different questions from those concerning young men in trouble since the behaviours which bring young women to the attention of state-sponsored agencies, such as social services departments and the courts, are distinctly different from those leading to the referral of young men (Hudson, 1989; Casburn, 1979; Campbell, 1981). Equally gender demarcated are the ideologies implicit in the state's responses. Consequently, those research methodologies used to analyse decision-making processes relating to male offenders are of limited validity, if not redundant, when young women are the research subjects.

My second objective is to elucidate some of the methodological processes that have underpinned the development of my analysis of 'troublesome' young women; I am particularly concerned to illustrate how my subjectivity has shaped this. Theoretical paradigms have undoubtedly had a considerable influence but this has been in a reciprocal and ever-changing relationship to my personal values and experiences. As Mies (1983) has pointed out, it is important that feminist researchers state their conscious partiality; this is qualitatively different from uncritical subjectivity. As an ex-social worker, as a feminist, as a white middle-class woman and as an academic I know that I have an investment in certain ideas rather than others. To pretend that these have not shaped what I have asked, 'seen' and interpreted would be dishonest and reneging on my responsibilities as a feminist researcher.

Defining the subjects: who are 'troublesome' young women?

As a practising social worker I was conscious of the lack of specific resources for the needs of young women referred to my agency and, indeed, of any appreciation that they might have particular needs relating to their age, gender, race and class. As a researcher, it gradually became apparent that this was in some measure due to the elusiveness of their identity as a social group and their lack of 'fit' with pre-existing social science categories.

The somewhat ambiguous place of dissident or 'troublesome' young women in social policy and the sociology of deviance has not, however, necessarily inhibited journalists, social workers and social scientists from investing amounts of (not infrequently vicarious) interest in their deeds, particularly when there is a whiff of sexuality about them. The juxtaposition of images of young women's vulnerability and adolescent sexuality taps general social anxieties about 'teenage girls' (promiscuity, teenage pregnancy, general breakdown of our moral fabric, the dissolution of family life and so on).

That said, conventional social science inquiry has not constituted 'troublesome' young women as a group who have merited the status of 'real' deviants, though during the past decade or so there has been much more research on young female offenders (see, for example, Campbell, 1981; Hudson, B., 1985). However, to equate 'troublesome' young women with young female offenders conceals the far greater number of young women who never fall foul of the criminal law but who are nevertheless brought into the ambit of the state system. Most of these attract the attention of state welfare professionals because of tensions or discord in their familial and interpersonal relationships. The sorts of behaviour that may warrant such attention include staying out late at night, 'associating' with 'disreputable' men, being thought to be at risk of prostitution, 'promiscuity' and pregnancy, 'moodiness' and 'uncommunicativeness', depression, verbal aggression and defiance. It is, in short, behaviour which confronts and challenges dominant notions of how young women 'should be' and which makes them susceptible to the rather all-embracing and vague label of 'troublesome'. The more consternation and anxiety generated by such behaviour the greater the likelihood that such young women will get pulled into the intricate web of welfare experts and social intervention. Statutory social work's somewhat contradictory functions of care and control can then begin to weave an ambiguous tapestry in the lives of such young women.

The central role of the family in these young women's welfare career further distinguishes them from their male counterparts. The more that parents feel unable to cope with or curtail their daughters' perceived waywardness and the greater the force of their pressure for 'something to be done', the greater the likelihood of state intervention. Consequently many young women enter care not through the courts but by way of a voluntary reception into care. Others do appear before the juvenile court but usually because the local authority has applied for a care order on the grounds that the young woman is either 'beyond parental control' or 'in moral danger'.[1]

It was with these young women that I was primarily concerned as a researcher: young women who constitute a problem because of their seemingly individualized 'troubles' rather than because of their actions against others. In many respects these were young women who failed to meet the criterion of 'proper' deviants because their actions seemed to be incomprehensible, irrational and symptomatic of individual pathology rather than conscious rebellion and resistance to social injustice or convention.

The research questions

Three core questions preoccupied me when, in the early 1980s, I commenced research into decision-making processes relating to young women in trouble. First, I was interested in how gendered constructions and expectations of adolescence shape both definitions of, and responses to, behaviour which contradicts those norms. That young women and young men generally behave differently from one another cannot be disputed; their responses to stress, inequality and their material conditions are manifestly related to race, class, sexual identity as well as gender. Young women, for example, are four times as likely to attempt suicide as young men (Kerfoot, 1988). On the other hand, they are less likely to engage in criminal activities.

Second, and this formed the kernel of the empirical research which I conducted (see below), I wanted to investigate how normative ideas about 'appropriate' adolescent femininity shaped the decision-making process affecting young women referred to social services departments. I did not start from a position which saw social work as simply the state's 'iron fist in a velvet glove'. For some young women the need and wish to escape from their families renders state care a desirable alternative, though it is frequently not of the quality which it could and should be.

Finally, I wanted to engage in more than a mere critique of the system and its self-evident inequities; I was equally concerned to consider alternative strategies. My background in social work meant that I had an investment in having an impact (albeit possibly a minimal one) on welfare professionals and the state system itself. Working in women's groups had provided me with experiential as well as intellectual evidence of the possibility of developing prefigurative social relations (Rowbotham *et al.*, 1979). It is obviously naive to believe that racism, sexism and class inequalities can or will magically disappear; but we should not allow ourselves to get hooked into a spiral of fatalism and pessimism that denies the possibility of changing practice here and now (Hudson, A., 1985).

Methodological issues

The images of young male delinquents constructed by many contemporary sociologists has been of romantic, almost swashbuckling heroes (see Heidensohn, 1985 for a critique). Subcultural perspectives, for example, have portrayed young male offenders as rational, exciting and often politically conscious rebels. Such a stance is comprehensible in the context of breaking away from positivistic portrayals of young offenders as 'pathetic victims' of their hapless family circumstances. But such perspectives can also deny the highly personalized brutalization which ensues from constant conflict with the criminal justice system (Cohen, 1985); incarceration in Her Majesty's penal establishments is hardly a liberating experience.

I had no intention of beating the 'boys' at their own game; direct experience of working with young women 'in trouble' had certainly impressed upon me their personal and collective resources. Many young women have considerable insight into their personal predicament and are all too aware of the social inequalities which underpin their lives (Griffin, 1985; Lees, 1986). But to depict 'troublesome' young women as heroines resisting the hegemonic power of the family, sexuality and the state would have presented an inappropriately sanitized and skewed picture. Many of these young women would be the first to say that they are very unhappy (their words, not mine) and that they want their lives to change. *They* know only too well what it feels like to have been at the receiving end of abuse, rejection and loss of control.

The 'formal' research which I undertook in the early 1980s was not on any kind of grandiose scale. Indeed, so powerful are messages about the characteristics of 'real' research that I find, even now, that I am hesitant to describe what I did as 'real' research. Apart from a social science statistics course on my undergruadate degree (which I failed) I had had little formal research training and when I started out I was, with hindsight, somewhat unclear about what I wanted to explore and how. The empirical research involved no number crunching, much 'borrowing' from the ideas of others and a lot of *ad hoc* hypothesizing.

My primary concern in the empirical research (conducted in 1982–3) was to focus on the decision-making processes inside social services departments and to explore, in particular, how social workers' values and assessments of the circumstances of young women shaped decisions relating to their young female clients. The empirical research was thus orientated towards the agents of social intervention rather than towards articulating the voices of the young women themselves.

I chose to examine a random sample of 45 cases on the caseloads of two inner-city area social services teams in a metropolitan borough in the North of England. I read through the files in order to identify patterns in the welfare careers of the young women. I then interviewed their current social workers (and their respective managers) using a semi-structured questionnaire. The data thereby gathered represented the formal empirical component of my study.[2]

Fitting together these two components of the research jigsaw was complex and challenging, not least because the perceptions and assessments conveyed by social workers in the files were often at considerable variance with those of the current social worker I interviewed. One case file, for example, had recorded that a young woman was 'promiscuous'; in contrast, her current social worker verbally commented that she had only (*sic*) ever had one 'steady boyfriend'. Such disjunctions demonstrated vividly the elasticity of many of the terms used to describe the behaviour of young women in trouble.

Reading through the files was a long and sometimes tedious process, waiting for the all too rare moment when a research 'gem' hit me between the eyes. There were some exciting moments, too, however. The interviews with social workers often took off in unexpected directions; for example, some of the interviewees (particularly women) used the interview to let off steam about the informal, but none the less powerful, workings of the system. And several talked candidly about the gendered dynamics of their agencies and how their attempts to set up 'girls only' groups had met with patronizing jokes ('we know you only talk about sex in those groups') and general undermining of their efforts by some of their colleagues and managers.

My initial preoccupation had been with young women *qua* their gender and, to a lesser extent, their class position. By the early 1980s, however, when the research was first conceived my consciousness of the impact of race and racism on different groups of young women had begun to be raised through political activity rather than through reading (Ahmed, 1986; Bryan *et al.*, 1985). I had, therefore, specifically chosen social services offices serving multiracial geographical communities (Asian, Afro-Caribbean and white). As a white woman it has been much harder to recognize and engage with the subtleties of racism than sexism and, even now, as I move towards the end of completing 'the book' about the research (Hudson, forthcoming), I still return to the original data and identify new issues. It was relatively recently, for example, when reading *There Ain't No Black in the Union Jack* (Gilroy, 1987) that I began to make links between the commentary on white British fears of miscegenation during the 1950s and the social anxieties and 'dangers' precipitated in the 1980s by white working-class young women's relationships with black male youth. Similarly, the relative invisibility of Asian young women (as compared with either Afro-Caribbean or white young women) in admission-to-care figures can also be interpreted as indicative of racist stereotypes that Asian young women are 'too subjugated' to be 'trouble-some'. Consequently, many of their specific needs are often overlooked by welfare agencies (Ahmed, 1986).

Experiential knowledge as much as formal inquiry and theory was, however, influential in the development of the research. With good cause, feminists have been highly critical of traditional researchers' methods (from positivists to Marxists) and their claims to objectivity and rationality (Roberts, 1981; Stanley and Wise, 1983). The researcher can never escape the subtle and not-so-subtle influence of her or his values, beliefs and experiences. No doubt one of the reasons why I enjoyed working with young women as a social worker, and equally why I chose to do research in this area, was because some of their experiences and voices echoed those of my own steps towards womanhood (confusions about sexuality, non-communicativeness with my parents, feelings of never being understood and so on). But I also had to keep hold constantly of the fact that my whiteness and middle-classness made for profound structural differences.

Feminists have brought experience back into social science metho-dology through their emphasis on both its value and legitimacy (Bowles and Duelli Klein, 1983; Stanley and Wise, 1983; and elsewhere in this volume). Experience is not an inferior form of knowledge, despite the challenge it presents to conventional research norms that focus on subjects as if they have no relationship to the inquirer and as if their experiences can be boxed in neatly labelled compartments ('sexually abused', 'manipulative', 'from a malfunctioning family'). Experience, then, is more than anecdote; it constitutes a starting point for scholarly analysis and critique. Throughout the research I was involved in a number of activities which had a profound bearing on my analysis.

For example, as the 'scandal' of child sexual abuse gradually hit the public eye in the mid-1980s, I became involved in a women's support group for incest survivors. This was not an activity I undertook wearing my hat of 'university lecturer'. However, its influence on my research was powerful. Political and emotional engagement with the issue of child sexual abuse enabled me to make much more sense of some young women's requests for admission to care, their running away from home and many other attempts to 'escape' from their families (including overdosing and slashing their wrists). Yet state professionals such as social workers often misread these signals so that behaviour which is perhaps connected to sexual abuse is reinterpreted as an index of individual pathology or failure.

Direct experience of groupwork with young women (several of whom were already in care and all of whom were referred by social workers) similarly demonstrated how the assignment of the 'sick' role to young women in trouble reinforces the power of the professional expert at the expense of young women finding their own solutions. The theme of pathologizing deviant women is one that emerges again and again in feminist critiques of traditional paradigms about women's deviance (Carlen, 1985; Hutter and Williams, 1981). My contacts with young women who had been sexually abused reinforced my beliefs that, given appropriate conditions, they can both support one another and use such experiences to empower themselves.

Consultancy and training work with a number of social work agencies provided me with opportunities to test out and develop some of the emergent hypotheses in my research. One of these was the centrality of sexually-related concerns. It seemed to me that young women's sexuality functioned as a barometer for testing whether or not a particular young woman would develop into a 'normal woman' (Hudson, 1989) and that the label of 'promiscuity' was used in a shifting and almost always unsubstantiated way. Discussions in training workshops provided more substance to these hypotheses; social workers and allied professionals talked extensively about the almost unlimited discretion they had in making such judgements. This was, many pointed out, in stark contrast to the much closer monitoring of the content of social inquiry reports for (predominantly male) juvenile offenders.

Consultancy and training activities also helped me to keep my 'feet on the ground'. It is easy for the distanced and supposedly uninvolved researcher to criticize the work of large welfare organizations such as social services. The task of translating the critique into new methods of practice, particularly in an era of ever-diminishing resources, is much more daunting. How, for example, should a social worker respond when faced with parents who refuse to have their 14-year-old daughter at home, when she has made attempts on her life, or has repeatedly stayed out all night without them knowing where she is? Conventional researchers can analyse and criticize both the systems which generate the situation and those which are supposed to respond to it; but they do not have to work within the intense emotional atmosphere which characterizes such crises in the lives of young women and their families.

Throughout the period of undertaking the research, therefore, I was having to attempt to match my findings and critique with some of the realities faced by social workers. This was a constructive and two-way process. On the one hand, my ideas and reflections provided some people with a slightly different way of viewing and making sense of their work with young women or helped them to legitimate what they had already thought out for themselves. On the other hand, consultancy and training work actively fed into the research process, particularly in terms of the identification of service development strategies. It is easy to talk about the importance of empowerment for young women. But how can such a laudable principle best be translated into direct and daily practice when the law and departmental procedures constrain and inhibit both young women and young men from having a real say in their lives? Practitioners and young women themselves, however, were able to offer practical suggestions such as the use of social education and groupwork to allow them to have access not only to different activities but also to different patterns of 'feminine' behaviour; see also Mountain, 1988.

The influences on my research process have thus been diverse and far from conventional. I have not commented extensively here on my theoretical framework and premises. Theory did provide me with a conceptual framework on which to hang the research data, in its myriad forms. But more striking is the unexpected ways in which theory has been influential. For example, the (re)discovery of Bernstein's (1977) work on invisible pedagogies was almost coincidental but provoked me, in the later stages of the project, to revise some of my initial analysis. Notwithstanding his focus on the educational system, his ideas enabled me to decipher some of the very personalized and implicit, rather than explicit, systems of social policing of working-class and black young women. The elusiveness of such systems of social control creates inevitable confusion and ambiguity for young women. They are expected to demonstrate both an active interest in heterosexuality and moral 'competency' and decency.

Young men, in contrast, are only very rarely controlled through a focus on their sexual behaviour.

Life nearer to the social work coal-face does mean that it is much harder to find energy and the time to set ideas down on paper, yet almost daily there is some new piece of data to absorb and digest. Perhaps there are no definitive answers to the types of questions raised in the feminist endeavour. That is the nature of feminist research: constantly searching for answers and coming up with new and different sets of questions.

Notes

1 During the period of the research young women were received into care because of their parents' requests under section 2 of the Child Care Act, 1980. Young women who were admitted to care through the courts on the grounds that they were either 'in moral danger' or 'beyond the control of his (*sic*) parents' did so under section 1(2) of the Children and Young Persons Act, 1969. Following, *inter alia*, inquiries into the deaths of Jasmine Beckford, Kimberley Carlisle and Tyra Henry and into the events in Cleveland, 1987, the Children Act, 1989, has repealed most earlier child care legislation. This Act comes into force in whole in October 1991. Children will no longer be referred to the courts as being 'in moral danger'. However, referral on the basis of being 'beyond parental control' is retained and it is likely that girls who are currently viewed as being 'in moral danger' will continue to be referred to the courts under this heading.
2 For a published account of the research, see Hudson, 1989. A more comprehensive account is to be published in *'Troublesome Girls': Adolescence, Femininity and the State*.

10 Realist philosophy and standpoint epistemologies or feminist criminology as a successor science[1]

Maureen Cain

Neither criminology nor feminism offered the first standpoint epistemology. I believe that Antonio Gramsci (1972: especially 316) did that, although who was first does not matter. In criminology the question of whose side we are on has been around for more than twenty years (Becker, 1967) and, in a discipline which takes processes of societal inclusion and exclusion as its subject matter, decisions about the good and the bad, knowledge that there are at least two sides to every story, constantly threatens to erupt through the well-papered cracks of the discursive surface.

This chapter considers recent feminist standpoint epistemologies and feminist criticisms of them. I then explore the constituent ingredients of successor science: the disjunction between ontology and epistemology and the historicity of knowledge, the reclamation of theory, the new conception of standpoint and the concept of theoretical reflexivity. After that, in an interim section, the critique is reappraised in the light of the new theory. In the conclusion the threads are drawn together so that parts of the outline of a successor science become clear. Here, too, are explored the implications of the project for a feminist criminology.

Feminist standpoint epistemologies

Harding (1986) has ably pulled together and summarized the work of feminist standpoint epistemologists (see also Cain, 1987). In this section, therefore, I will explore only the work of Nancy Hartsock (1983) who stands as an exemplar of the approach.

*Bodies, roles, and double vision: the standpoint epistemology of
Nancy Hartsock*

Like most feminist methodologists Hartsock, in my view, sets up something of a straw man, literally, of the traditional reseacher. But the straw person serves his proper purpose. He establishes for Hartsock what the feminist methodologist is definitely not. The straw man is concerned with establishing absolute truth claims; he achieves this by the monotonic application of a single allowed mode of reasoning; he aims to abstract knowledge formulations which objectify those investigated and which are indifferent to their own understandings of their experiences. He is concerned with separating rather than unifying and prefers dualistic, zero-sum forms for the separations he achieves; he is unemotional and detached, which leaves him in full control of those investigated; this hierarchic relationship is also maintained within the research teams he establishes. We achieve unity as feminists around the fact that we don't like him. For all that he stands for something real.

Hartsock makes the agument that women's bodies and women's life spaces make it easier for them to overcome the dualism between truth and falsity, subject and object, controller and controlled and, she might have added, feeling and detachment. This overcoming is easier for women than for men. It is easier because their subordinate position gives them access to two worlds. In living they are forced to participate both in their own life world *and* in that of the dominant group. This is an essential survival strategy. Thus women become aware of the complexity of social life and of the socially constructed nature of the world. Men do not have occasion to achieve this double vision in the course of their daily routines.

Secondly, and more concretely, Hartsock argues that in the course of domestic life, in cooking, cleaning and child rearing, women are routinely engaged in the production of use values. This applies whether or not they are also engaged in waged labour. So women are pulled away from the abstractions and objectifications of capital and they have more choice and control over whether they use concrete or abstracted modes of thought. (I am slightly distorting Hartsock here because I do not believe she disapproves of all abstract thought.)

Thirdly, women's bodily boundaries are continually being invaded or blurred. The particular examples of this which Hartsock gives are childbirth, pregnancy, coitus and menstrual flow. This, too, means that they are less concerned with separation and with dualistic thinking than are men.

Lastly, Hartsock argues, women are typically involved in processes of change and growth, in voluntarily reducing their control so that others may grow. Their success is measured in terms of how well others – their children – manage without them. This means that women's everday thinking cannot be hierarchic, although it must be responsible. The dualistic choice is daily revealed as a nonsense so that it is easier for women to be anti-hierarchic.

Women are not only better situated to overcome dualistic thinking and hierarchic patterns of relationships than men: they need to develop these alternatives in order to give expression to their experiences. So the standpoint of women is epistemologically privileged: it is a standpoint from which it is easier to understand more and better. Even so, Hartsock is aware that working from the standpoint of women demands a political choice. The life space is facilitative; the standpoint is chosen. Hers is not a determinism. If women simply could not help knowing better we would have a dual knowledge system not a dominant and subjugated one.

Standpoint epistemologies: a critique

Hartsock's sophisticated analysis had the advantage of building on the work of earlier standpoint epistemologists such as Smith (1980) and Jaggar (1983a and 1983b). In the same way, I had the opportunity of assessing her contribution before developing my own (Cain, 1986a) discussion of what a feminist standpoint might entail for criminologists. In this section, therefore, I add my appraisal of Hartsock's work to the assessments of Harding (1986; 1987) and Smart (this volume), before arguing for a particular approach to standpoint epistemologies.

Because it so explicitly seeks to avoid determinism, Hartsock's argument is a very strong one. There are, however, two difficulties with it. In the first place, a lurking essentialism can be identified in her third argument. While accepting Midgley's (1988) point that more philosophical work needs to be done on 'natural' sex differences, I jib at Hartsock's argument here – even on biological grounds. Does semen not leave men's bodies as menstrual blood leaves women's bodies? Does not coitus involve a *mutual* 'blurring' of bodily boundaries? To see only the woman's bodily boundary as blurred is to accept, perhaps, men's definition of the difference between penetration and reception. But it is as easy to see the relation as a joining – a concept which gives primacy to neither of the bodies involved but rather sees both as equally 'blurred'.

Hartsock's other three points are concerned with the social position of women and I find them both plausible and closely fitting my own experience. But there are risks inherent in the first of these arguments too, for one corollary might be that if women stopped being subordinate they would lose their double vision. Their philosophy and their research work might become worse as a result. The points about involvement in production of use values and child rearing have more encouraging corollaries carrying a clear political message. If women abandon their involvement in these two kinds of activities in order to become more like untransformed men then their research will become worse. If, however, people of both sexes become involved in child rearing and the production of use values then women's research will stay the same and that of men will improve.

Harding makes the important point (1987: 187) that all the feminist epistemologies we have should be regarded as 'transitional epistemologies'. They should not be construed as finished products but as efforts which inform an ongoing practical struggle. This shapes our practice of criticism: the object of it is now to see what can be learned from the efforts of others. Scoring points off each other would at the least imply that we were competing for position in an already finished world. Not so.

Her critical discussion of standpoint epistemologies is, therefore, undertaken in this pedagogical spirit. Their value, she says (1986: 162), is that they question the argument that the social identity of the observer is irrelevant to the results, the belief that bias can be eliminated by the ritualistic application of technique, and the idea that political commitment reduces objectivity. On the other hand, some important issues are exposed and left unresolved:

1 A focus on women's world view supports men's notion that women are all the same. Women are different from one another and each woman also has multiple (or fractured) identities, any one of which might arguably provide a 'standpoint' for knowledge.
2 Harding argues that 'women's different reality . . . is also less than the reality we want, is not the only alternative reality, and is disappearing' (1986: 176). Even if women's reality were unitary, would we want it to be the only basis for knowledge production?
3 Comparative analysis suggests that purported women's and men's world views are ethno- and culturo-centric constructs. African men, Harding argues, have many similarities in their thinking to European women.
4 Harding also asks whether or not we really mean that if we can find the most repressed group of all their way of seeing is potentially the most true (1986: 191).

None the less Harding remains open minded. Successor science projects may be the best weapon women have in their engagement with men's knowledge; moreover, she argues (1986: 247) that at this stage in the struggle successor science projects and postmodernist deconstructive efforts require each other's success. As I have argued elsewhere (Cain, 1989; 1990), a strategy for reconstruction is also necessary for a transgressive feminist criminology.

Smart (this volume) points out an additional problem with standpoint feminism, namely, that it has ignored masculinity. Whatever the theoretical arguments, in focusing on women's experiences of oppression standpoint feminists have tended to write of an essential woman, not one in a reciprocally constructive relationship with 'maleness', a concept including both men and men's powers and talk. Not all standpoint epistemologists have done this (see, for example, Stanley and Wise, 1983; Cain, 1986a), but the point is well taken that within criminology those who have studied women's experiences have (with notable exceptions such as Kersten, 1989) tended not to problematize masculinity.

For a successor science

Ingredients of an argument

In this section I argue that it is indeed possible to develop a successor science, although it may be helpful to escape the connotations of the term science and the clouds of meaning which it trails. In an earlier attempt to construct some guidelines for a successor science I referred to that which we aim to produce quite simply as 'good quality knowledge' (Cain, 1987). This preferred term connotes a discerning consumer and announces the fact that, however it is authenticated, the knowledge produced should not be accepted uncritically.

Key ingredients of this are, first, the Bhaskarian notion of the disjunction between ontology and epistemology, from which I elaborate a particular account of the historicity of knowledge (see Cain, 1986a; 1986b; 1987). A second crucial ingredient is an alternative meaning and justification for theory. I spend rather longer on this because I have not written about it before. Thirdly, I elaborate a conception of standpoint which is not vulnerable to the Harding–Smart critique. I re-present the concept as I developed it in 1986 (Cain, 1986a), elaborating it where necessary to take account of the way the debate has developed. I leave to a later section two major questions of the relevance of all this for criminological work and of how good quality knowledge can be recognized or distinguished from knowledge of a poorer quality.

The disjunction between ontology and epistemology

Bhaskar (1971/89) makes the fundamental point that the construction of an ontology in which the reality of objects is independent of knowledge and in which objects can therefore impact directly upon people in no way amounts to a claim that objects in the world can be directly apprehended. Death, floods and relationships of class and gender might be such objects. Similarly, while the realist position must leave open the possibility of correct understanding, there is no way at all that people can ever be sure that they have got things right. Death, floods and relationships of class and gender might be figments of our imagination, false constructions with which we constitute and make sense of our existences. To say that there are realities which exist whether we think about them or not is not to say that we can ever be sure that our knowledges correspond to any or all of them. We do have to make some kind of sense of our bumps up against unthought about reality, though.

Bhaskar borrows the grammatical term 'intransitive' to describe these realities. Once people think about them, however, the realities may become transitive, changed by the ways in which people are thinking about them and relating to them. Patterns of relationships between people are realities which are particularly sensitive to this process, though it seems to be the case that 'nature' has also been changed as a result of being conceived as a passive state for men (*sic*) to 'master' or work upon (Gross and Averill, 1983).

The postulated existence of intransitive, unthought about realities demands a methodology appropriate to their 'discovery', as Bhaskar calls it. Criminologists as well as other social scientists are constrained by these methodological requirements (Cain, 1987). However, there are a number of reasons why knowledge, with whatever care we treat it, can never be certain. I choose to characterize this uncertainty as the *historicity* of knowledge (Cain, 1986a; 1987). Knowledge is historically specific rather than timelessly true because the relationships and human understandings which the sociologist investigates are themselves historical, that is, constantly changing. The larger the scope of the configuration of relationships that we are describing the slower, by and large, will be the rate of change. Thus we can still usefully 'identify' a configuration of relationships called 'class', although particular class relationships have been changing dramatically throughout the twentieth century. But even our most general concepts are liable to become totally obsolete given time.

Apart from the fact that we study shifting objects, we simply cannot find a non-historical or a non-social place from which to do our knowing. There are two reasons for this. In the first place we can only 'know' with discourses historically and culturally available to us: see E.H. Carr (1961) on this issue. Secondly, and here we reconnect with the feminist standpoint epistemologists, we are all located within a (changing) web or configuration of relationships. We all have relationships with other people and we speak each from our own unique site in a complex configuration of interrelated people. In this sense, there are as many knowledges as there are people. And it is to deal with precisely this point that the standpoint epistemologies have been developed. Before returning to them, however, and to criminology, we have the other key ingredients of my version of the realist alternative to consider.

Theorization and humility

Feminists have become increasingly hostile to theory. In the first place, women have been 'misthought' so often, told how they ought to think and feel and be in order to be women, and all this psychic oppression has been justified in the name of theory. More recently, women have discovered that they were also oppressing each other by trying to encapsulate all the rich variety of womanhood in one theory, with one alternative set of needs and feelings and one political direction. A triumph of the 1980s has been that women have concerned themselves with differences from each other and with fractured identities, while maintaining a still recognizable women's movement. The identification of differences has led to sophistication, not schism. We should be proud. But all this has led women to see theory as a weapon of the opposition. I disagree.

Theory is a discursive means for constituting, distinguishing and explaining phenomena. As such, it is culture bound. So when a realist, or this realist, talks about theory she is knowingly speaking from within the historical epistemology described above. She is making a set of culture-bound statements which cannot be proved right in the short term and which are doomed to inevitable obsolescence. She is making them from her own unique site in a configuration of relationships. So let us take all that for granted and enquire briefly what is the difference between theory and any old set of explanatory remarks.

Following Gramsci again I argue that theory is a special kind of knowledge because of the self-consciousness with which it is formulated. Theoretical knowledge is made up of concepts, the relationships between which are logical and therefore public. Because of this, theoretical knowledge is easier to share than other knowledges. Logic too may be culturally specific but the self-conscious awareness of its character by its proponents, the fact that they have a theory of how they are theorizing, makes it easier to transmit it with a confidence that it will be received in a way which is near enough the same for all practical purposes. Knowledge with such a form can therefore be called objective. For the same reasons, theoretical knowledges are easier to defend than less elaborated or common-sense knowledge. Thirdly, and again for the same reasons, theoretical knowledges are more persuasive than other forms of knowledge.

In a movement with strong political objectives, like feminism, these are convincing arguments for giving one's knowledge a theoretical, that is to say an 'objective', form. It is politically important to be able to hold one's knowledge product up to view, to assess it, to communicate it beyond the boundaries of an immediate empathetic group. The pitfall here is to forget that the objectivized knowledge was created for a purpose, from a site and so on. Feminist thought, however, is sufficiently sophisticated to contain both objectivized knowledge and knowledge scepticism and so, for the time being, to attain the best of both worlds.

Apart from the form of theory, there is the question of what theory does. A major plank of realism, starting from Keat and Urry (1975), has been to substitute the notion of mechanism for the empiricist concern with constant conjunction when considering causality. In this view the job of theory is to indicate how underlying realities make surface realities happen. A social mechanism, however, leads to just those 'one way only' kinds of explanations with which women have been policed for so long and which feminists have come to abhor. But acceptance of the fundamental realist ontological claim that there are intransitive realities does not commit one to a mechanical conception of cause any more than it commits one to a naive epistemology.

The theory of such a humble realist in sociology maps relationships, constructing concepts which constitute and specify patterns of articulation (many and diverse) and dis-connection between the relationships observed, identified and explored. The humble realist, while never forgetting the limits of her vision and her enterprise, is free to map the articulations between configurations of relationships of various scopes. She may relate observed teenage mating customs to any or all of domestic structures and ideologies, labour markets, religious beliefs, patriarchy or social class. She will do this without arguing that a segmented labour market causes young girls to flirt and mature women to cook. The concept of underlying mechanism does not give her enough precision to deal with her deviant cases or enough space for cross-cultural manoeuvre. She will need a subtler and gentler concept than either mechanism or constant conjunction, with much more room for fall out (Marsh, 1982).

Because she has not yet thought of a concept of cause that will do this work she will be content, for now, to constitute and record the signs, the characteristics of the connections, until in tranquility she finds a philosophic name for what she has been almost doing all the while. The new concept will not be one like cause, in which one relationship is deemed to dominate another. Whatever the name for the explanatory device, there will be more room for interchange and resistance within it.

These are explorations in reconstruction: for a theory of openings rather than closure. And in the meantime they raise questions of the observer's transitive understandings and of the relationships between these and the transitive understandings – the world views if you will – of those observed.

Standpoints, theories, fractured identities and difference

There can be no getting away from the fact (*sic*) that we all think (speak, write, create and distribute knowledge) from somewhere in our society, from some site or other. Putting it another way, we all have relationships.

The particular intersection of these relationships in us is the site from which we produce knowledge and in that sense each site is unique, historical and changing. Some of these relationships form part of our identity, others are part of the way we think about the world but are not conscious of at all. I was not really aware of my ethnic identity until I lived in a country where virtually everyone else was African or Indian (Afro- or Indo-Caribbean). Before then being white was like being male (I assume). I knew that I was white but I regarded that as the normal thing to be. It was always other people who had something non-normal called ethnicity.

But as a realist I have to accept that I am certainly also involved in relationships of which I have no knowledge at all and which no one else knows anything about either (yet or maybe ever). Harding (1983a) has argued that the sex–gender structure used to be like that, but now it usually causes a laugh when men talk about themselves as if they were everybody. That laughter (which succeeds rage) means that one is in the presence of both politics and theory. Both are essential to the generation of standpoint-specific knowledges, as standpoint specific knowledges are reciprocally necessary for both theory and successful politics.

A standpoint, then, is a site which its creator and occupier has agreed to occupy in order to produce a special kind of knowledge and practice and of which he or she is aware in a special, theoretical way. If knowledge is site specific then changing what it is possible to know involves changing your site. This is why agreement, the decision to change or not, is fundamental to the concept of standpoint. Changing one site for another involves changing relationships. If you want to know *for* women, say, you must connect yourself 'organically' (Gramsci, 1972) *with* women, move to an appropriate site from which to generate this knowledge. Both men and women can and have to do this. Goodwill is not enough. Being a woman does not mean that one can automatically speak for women from a feminist standpoint. This is because 'being' a woman means, precisely, being caught up in 'womanish' relationships, in multiple ways. We are not talking about biological givens. So too women have to agree or choose to speak as feminists and this agreement often means that they have to make an effortful choice to align themselves with other women or change their relationships.

The implication of this is that the production of subversive knowledge is an activity *constitutive* of a feminist standpoint. It is in this sense that standpoint-specific knowledges are integrally knowledges for women. But this sense of the pronoun *for* also makes it clear that we are not speaking of knowledge which is guaranteed to be right or, sadly, even successful. The successor science remains a science of uncertainties.

This brings me to the last point of the definition, the question of awareness. In presenting our field work we have to be *personally reflexive*, that is, present a description of our changing relationship with the researched population based on feminist common (or co woman) sense. But in order to decide which site to speak from or to understand a pre-given site we have to engage in *theoretical reflexivity*, based on the new kind of theories we are constructing. Theoretical reflexivity is a key concept and a key practice in the identification of standpoints and in the production of knowledge from a feminist standpoint. Theoretical reflexivity means thinking about oneself in terms of a theory and undertanding theoretically the site one finds oneself in. For us this means understanding theoretically how being a professional criminologist articulates both with personal and particular relationships, as well as with relationships of more general scope such as class, race, age and gender.

Such theoretical knowledge about oneself is what makes it possible to say that if I want to work from a feminist standpoint I must make connections with feminist struggle – join a women's group or get involved in feminist teaching, lobbying, advocacy, cooperative marketing or child minding. Theoretical reflexivity makes it possible to continue working on one's standpoint in order to improve the fit between its constitutive relationships and one's ideological claim to speak *for*. Theoretical reflexivity tells you whether anything in your personal site must be changed in order for a standpoint claim to be made for it. It is simultaneously structural and personal, more than a site and more than an opinion. (See Val Kerruish (forthcoming) for an elaboration of the distinction between standpoint and opinion.) People who share standpoints have differing views. The standpoint does not cause one to have a thought but it does both discursively and structurally shape the thoughts, whether creative or established, that one is likely to have.

In defence of standpoints

To what extent does this realist elaboration of the concept of standpoint make it possible to defend it against the new feminist critics? It is necessary to deal with this defensive question, to make sure that we can now hold our ground, before moving on to examine the considerable advantage for social science generally and for criminology in particular which is represented by realist epistemology, including the concept of standpoint.

The main criticisms can be reduced to three: standpoint epistemologies are essentialist; standpoints cannot be identified because of differences between women and across cultures; and finally there are problems of linking knowledges to presently existing theoretical sites.

Both in this paper and previously (1986a) I have argued that standpoint is a relational concept which, so far from being essentialist, uniquely explains how a man can work from a feminist standpoint. A standpoint is constituted by politics, theory, theoretical reflexivity and choice (of site), not biology.

This elaborated concept of standpoint also addresses directly the second criticism. First it must be reiterated that occupancy of a standpoint does not foreclose debate. Standpoints do not 'cause' knowledge so much as reshape possibilities for the imagination. Opinions between those generating/occupying a standpoint can, do and should differ. Secondly, what about fractured identities? Is a woman's class, femaleness or colour to shape her vision? Black women in Africa see differently from black women in the USA, the West Indies and Australia, as well as from white Americans, white Europeans, Polynesians and Asiatic women. Where on earth can a standpoint be found in all of this? If one thinks about it, however, it is this criticism which is essentialist not the concept of standpoint. The presumption is that identities are fixed and that sites may not be chosen or changed. This criticism also denies the role of theory in 'recognizing' fractured identities and in identifying unities of which occupants of sites may be unaware. Theory, or theoretical work by us, is an essential ingredient of the identification of standpoints. It enables us to abstract from the myriad differences between us without denying them, and to reunite around important samenesses. In that complex process our theory changes, we refine it and it gets better. It is only when we try to think more theoretically that we can work out where the fractures that matter are and why and when they matter. It is hard work. But the alternative is to base our alliances on essentialist (common-sense, ideological) identifications of sameness and difference or on a political whimsy.

There is also a positive aspect to diversity. Rather than succumbing to impossibilism we should, perhaps, begin to see our divisions as evidence of the potential richness of women's contributions to knowing and to welcome the challenges, both intellectual and political, posed by our wondrous variety. I am left with the criticism that standpoint-specific knowledges are linked to presently existing historical sites. What seems important here is that standpoints are not just given sites in an intersection of relationships: they are agreed to or chosen and that choice involves a politics, a theory and theoretical self-reflection, all of which are brought to bear on an only partially transitive site. The people constituting standpoints may, therefore, be aware of their own historicity, not trapped by it, and of the historicity and temporality of the knowledge they generate.

Why bother with standpoint epistemologies?

We can now address some of the things the standpoint epistemologist can do. She can evade dominant knowledges. She can share the knowledges she produces with others in the standpoint and also with others who share the site (recruitment) or who are sympathetic (alliance). She can generate new knowledge from repressed common senses. She can make shareable decisions about how to treat those she investigates. (This is discussed more fully by Loraine Gelsthorpe and Liz Kelly in this volume and in Cain, 1986a). She can change things. She is strong. But there are three particular things that I wish to dwell on, from among all that the standpoint epistemologist can do: she can make alliances; she can be accountable; and she can be scholarly in a way denied to all other theorists so far. There are particular advantages for the criminologist in all of this.

Standpoint epistemologies and alliances

In an earlier paper (1986a) I argued that it is not possible to work from two standpoints at once. I received several letters from people saying they agreed with all the rest of the argument but not that. Now I am not sure about the answer in logic: it is a bit like asking whether three or only two angels can dance upon the point of a needle. If a person fully occupies two standpoints then it must be that she will be aware of the contradictions between them and try to theorize and make sense of these in order to achieve an improvement in the position of both groups, say women as a whole and black people or the working class or children too. For my part, I can usually only direct my energies, whether intellectual or political, to one thing at a time. And I, therefore, prefer the concept of an alliance to describe my relations with the full range of groups whose causes I may from time to time espouse. I do not think my problem is unique. Black women in the West Indies are more aware of four centuries of denigration and oppression of blackness than they are of the problems of white women in Europe. What is important is to reflect upon a uniquely fractured site, reclaim it as a standpoint for knowledge production and political work and use this theoretical reflection to understand the relationships with others sites and standpoints.

What is also important is to allow this continuing process of theoretical reflection to determine not only who shares the standpoint and who does not, but also to shape the decision about which groups we should be *in alliance* with at any point in time and the nature of that alliance. We have not got an adequate understanding of the fractures and contradictions yet. But I suggest that feminist standpoint epistemologists, in the wake of those who are already engaged with the issue at a practical level, are in a strong position to produce one. Moreover, because standpoints are relational as well as theoretically reflective, we can understand that the sites and standpoints of both individuals and groups change as people go their own ways or work together.

This way of thinking resolves some dilemmas for feminist criminologists who, for example, may find that their work with incarcerated girls leads to alliances with decarceration movements generally or with children's rights movements or with black or radical social workers. They will have to decide with whom they share a standpoint in order to devise an appropriate research strategy. But they must be prepared – theoretically and politically – to decide which alliances will be fruitful, which carry dangers of co-option and how to deal with these risks, and which alliances could be diverting or damaging for those whose standpoints they share. This brings me to the issue of accountability.

Standpoint epistemologies and accountability

Once we have admitted the historical specificity of knowledges we cannot rely on truth or discovery procedures and their professional guardian to deal with the problems of accountability for us (Feyerabend, 1978). For the person working from a standpoint the objective is to produce knowledge from a site that one has identified theoretically and agreed or chosen to occupy *for* those people whose standpoint one shares. Standpoint epistemologists take that inevitability one stage further arguing that it can be made positive use of if brought to a theoretical consciousness which enables the criminologist to understand and control or choose the site from which she produces knowledge. This means that she can theoretically determine, and choose, for whom the knowledge she produces will be most useful. As I have argued, it is in this sense that all knowledge is produced for those whose standpoint (or site) you share.

That preamble leads me to a rather simple point about accountability. Accountability is to those whose standpoint you share, based on a full understanding of the configuration of relationships which constitutes the standpoint. The knowledge is for them. And because they make use of this knowledge, it is to them that the feminist criminologist, say, is answerable for the quality of the knowledge she produces. This is why polemic, cooking the books or inadequate or insufficiently public evidence cannot be accepted. Those whose standpoint you share will be more likely to make mistakes if the knowledge they have to work with is not of a high quality. They are the ones who stand to lose, so it is to them that the feminist criminologist is accountable (see also Cain and Finch, 1981). Just think of the suffering that has been caused to women by mistheorizations of their atypical behaviours, by the rending of families by practices of 'care' (Carrington, 1989) and you will know to whom you are accountable for the quality of the knowledge you produce.

For good quality knowledge: feminist criminology as a successor science

Those who argue that all knowledge is historical and site specific have two big problems about science and scholarship. They have the problem as to whether or not their knowledge is determined by the site. (Did being a middle-class white female sociologist in the West Indies with a particular career and personal biography 'make' me write this paper the way I have?) They also have the problem as to whether any criteria for assessing knowledge exist at all, other than temporary conventional agreements within various scientific and other communities which have achieved enough power to establish the conventions. In one sense or another, and coming from totally opposed directions, both these arguments boil down to the view that knowledge is *only* politics. I profoundly disagree.

The first argument has, I think, already been dispensed with adequately. A realist ontology which views the social world as configurations of *relationships*, some intransitive, others transitive, creates a space in which human agency can change the sites people speak from. It can then be argued that people can have some degree of choice about the sites they occupy. One aspect of a standpoint theory of knowledge stems from this. Add this to the non-causal theory of explanation which I have argued for in these pages and the first problem is simultaneously acknowledged and dispensed with by realist historicism.

The second problem is the one that has more recently been vexing feminist philosophers and social scientists, because the relativism which had seemed the only alternative to essentialism and empiricism left no possibility of guidance for those setting out to do research. The concluding sections of this essay address this issue.

Guidelines for the conduct of social research

In 1987 I presented a long account of the guidelines for social research which might be developed from an elaboration of realist ontology and epistemology (Cain, 1987). I present them here in an abbreviated form.

Guidelines derived from realist ontology

1 Intransitive relationships require: (a) open techniques (to allow for the hitherto unthought about to impinge or impact upon knowledge production) and technical inventions (the most recent example is probably the videoed group interview (Lees, 1986)); (b) theory (the practice which enables the constitution and reconstitution of new experiences and relationships); (c) open-mindedness about thought processes leading to theory building (see Keat and Urry, 1975); and (d) technical outreach (if the multidimensional mapping which constitutes explanation is to conclude only when the multiple and contradictory connections with configurations of relationships of the most general scope have been discerned, then *empirical* routes out from the

unit of observation must be identified. This is why technical outreach is required rather than mental abstraction.)

2 Transitive relationships require: hermeneutic techniques, so that the discursive worlds of those investigated can be included in the investigation.

Guidelines derived from realist epistemology

1 *Constant change in the relationships observed requires*: building duration into the investigation. This could take the form of a historical analysis of an institution studied, follow up studies, biographical data on those investigated, or just staying in the field a long time.

2 *The site specificity of knowledges produced requires*: theoretical reflexivity, choice of site, a politics (each working from a standpoint) and acknowledgements of accountability to those whose standpoint you work for, your scholarship and your ethics.

If all this begins to sound even more stringent than positivism, well, it is. Oppositional knowledges will always be under attack and it would be stupid to leave ourselves vulnerable to criticisms on avoidable technical grounds. But realism is nothing if not realistic. This realist methodology is able to allow for, say, access problems or dispersed populations which rule out observations or budgets which rule out follow up studies or relationships which are only investigable by survey techniques. These real-life occurrences are dealt with by means of a final guideline: *theoretical pragmatism*. This means quite simply that with an elaborated and emerging theory of method, and elaborated and emerging theory of what you are investigating, you are in a position to assess the loss resulting from non-adherence to the guidelines and to take account of this assessment in your analysis.

What is good quality knowledge?

The argument has reached its denouement. For a successor science to achieve credibility it (we) must be able to distinguish between good and poor quality knowledge. Just as the guidelines are not rules, because they can be broken without total loss, so the distinction between good and poor quality knowledges is not an absolute one. We are not so much interested in damning knowledges as in finding out how much is in them for us. To do this we do need criteria which we can justify and which are not simply *ad hoc*. The theory of knowledge outlined here offers the following criteria:

1 Good quality knowledge is knowledge produced according to the guidelines just discussed.

2 Good quality knowledge is integrally political. This is the way in which

we reclaim the inevitably value-full (site-specific) character of all knowledge. We embrace the fact that we are creating knowledge for a collectivity, from their standpoint. If this is so then the knowledge can be evaluated in terms of how well it works for those from whose standpoint it was produced. To 'work' is to explain relationships in a way that enables the occupants of the standpoint to assess their situation and to act upon those assessments in ways they find useful. This second criterion, then, is a *retrospective heuristic*, an academic way of saying that only time will tell.

3 If knowledge is to be useful then it must be capable of being very thoroughly assessed by those for whose use it was intended. This third criterion, therefore, is *publicity* (see also Cain and Finch, 1981). Publicity has three elements: (a) The knowledge must be *theoretical*, in the sense that the relationships between concepts and terms deployed must be clear. In other words, the knowledge itself must be public or 'objective' in its form. (b) The mode of production of the knowledge must be public. This is where *personal reflexivity* is relevant. We need to know the researcher's standpoint (that is taken care of by adherence to the guidelines) but we also need to know the particular circumstances of the knowledge's making. (c) The mode of production of the knowledge is made public by *displaying techniques*. It is here that incidence statements and quantification of observation categories can be helpful. Within criminology, Mary Eaton's work (1986) on the deployment of familial discourse in magistrates' courts is exemplary here.

4 Lastly, the theory we produce should account for our own knowledge as well as for that of those we investigate. I call this *theoretical inclusion*, deliberately choosing a term which does not imply a smooth or continuous theoretical totalization but which allows for contradictions and discontinuities. As in the case of the subject–object relation (Cain, 1986a), if we accept that our input to the knowledge we make is inevitably considerable, then we need one theory to explain both ourselves and those whom we investigate. Otherwise we have two discrete theories purporting to explain the same result: one of us and one of them. Instead we should ensure that we push our knowledge outward until we identify a configuration of relationships of sufficient scope to include both us and them. If we can do this to identify our standpoint relations then we can do it, too, in order to explain our knowledge. The process also encourages a healthy scepticism about our own expertise.

If these four criteria of conformity with the guidelines are met then we have knowledge of a very high quality indeed. And they are not impossible criteria. They are relatively often met by feminist scholars.

Feminist criminology?

This has been a long theoretical journey. As each word has been developed into a concept, page by page I have had the reader, the feminist criminological reader, very much in mind. For it is feminism that has insisted that we get away from silly dichotomies like science/unscience and silly exam questions like 'is history, sociology, criminology a science or not?' It depends how good the history, sociology, criminology is, if we want to keep the term science at all. The questions we should be asking now, using the new criteria, are does this particular work meet the realist standard for good quality knowledge? And how can we evaluate theoretically the extent of any fall from perfection?

It is criminology, uniquely within sociology, which has insisted that there are at least two sides to every knowledge: that of the authorities and that of the defendant, that of the victim, that of the police(man) and that of the culprit, that of the non-conforming girl and that of her tormentors. So this is a theory for feminists and criminologists which accepts those glorious uncertainties and opens a way to live with and create uncertainties while still retaining a great pride in our craft as knowledge makers. This essay, like all knowledges, now has to wait a retrospective heuristic.

Note

1 I am indebted to Sandra Harding (1986) for this term as, indeed, for much else.

PART 3

Feminism, politics and action

'You're women. You're going to be engineers. You're all a bunch of feminists. I hate feminists.'

(Attributed to Marc Lépine who shot fourteen female students in Montreal on 6 December 1989.)

We referred in the previous section to contrasts between conventional and feminist research methods and took as an example men's violence against their female partners. This contrast in perspectives can be broadened. Gender is of central and critical concern to feminists. It is not for conventional writers who refer to wife-battering in such neutral terms as 'domestic violence', 'family violence' and 'inter-spousal violence' (Ohlin and Tonry, 1989; Straus *et al.*, 1980; Gelles and Cornell, 1985). These give little clue as to who is beaten and who does the beating. Indeed, the implication is that spouses of both sexes act violently towards each other in even amounts. But this is not the case. Feminist research findings indicate that it is (primarily) men beating (primarily) women and that violence against women is not 'rare', 'unusual' or 'exceptional' (Hall, 1985; Borkowski *et al.*, 1983 and essays in this Part). Feminist researchers have both *illuminated* and *named* the violence – wife abuse.

This is not a simple definitional issue. Such distinctions have implications for the way in which these phenomena are explained. Conventional writers look, for example, to *family* dysfunctioning. Feminist writers seek to explain why *men* beat their *female* partners rather than, say, their bosses or their neighbours (Yllö and Bograd, 1988). Also, in both conventional and early feminist writings, particular forms of violence – rape, sexual harassment, pornography and child sexual abuse – were treated as discrete units of analysis. Now it is thought more appropriate to refer to a continuum of violence and to ask not 'why are men violent?' but rather 'why are men violent towards women?' (Hanmer and Maynard, 1987; Kelly, 1988).

Conventional theorists focus on the pathological and structural aspects of violent individuals in an attempt to explain their violence. The behaviour is seen as the product of mental illness, low self-esteem, psychological disturbance, alcoholism, poverty, stress, sexual frustration, strong sexual drives or whatever (Roy, 1982; Gayford, 1975; 1976; 1978). Conventional writers have also blamed women for violence against them: that is, they must have been provocative, frigid, aggressive or the like (Gayford, 1975; 1976; Pizzey and Shapiro, 1981; 1982). But there is no simple association between any of these factors and violence against women. Research which has described the characteristics of particular samples – for example, arrested or imprisoned men, men in treatment programmes, women in refuges, women who contact social services – and which purports to make such connections is not generally valid. The findings – if that is what they are – are peculiar to that particular sample, but we would argue that such 'findings' were 'produced' only by ignoring more significant dimensions. The men who abuse women and the women who are abused come from all age, cultural, ethnic, socio-economic and religious groups – in short, they come from all walks of life (Russell, 1982; Morash, 1986; Smith, 1989a). What conventional research ignores is the extent of violence againt women. Its sheer prevalence means that individual, social or personal factors alone cannot explain it (Borkowski *et al.*, 1983; Hall, 1985).

Feminists, rather than trying to explain why a particular man assaults a particular woman at a particular moment, attempt to explain why men *as a group* direct their violence at women (see generally Yllö and Bograd, 1988). The fact that not all men are violent towards women does not matter to this thesis. Some men choose not to abuse their power – or to abuse it in non-violent ways (for example, by restricting their partners' freedom of movement or their female co-workers' access to information and resources). The fact remains: men have the power to choose and to act abusively. Men's privilege is not restricted to the men who abuse; it is endemic in our culture. A feminist perspective makes it clear that if patriarchal structures did not give men the power to abuse women and, importantly, to get away with it in large measure, then they would not abuse them, regardless of the state of their finances, level of stress or whatever. Feminist writers have begun to explore the ways in which social institutions and traditional relationships between the sexes can interact to produce, condone and exacerbate violence against women. They stress that the supposedly 'private trouble' of violence against women must be transformed into public and political issues.

This takes us to the question 'what's to be done about violence against women?' Traditionally there has been a marked reluctance amongst criminal justice and other related professionals to get involved, except where the violence has been committed by a stranger or has occurred in a situation which conforms to the stereotype: in a public place, late at night and so on (Binney *et al.*, 1981; Smith, 1989b). Feminist responses are different and have been broadly of two types. First, they have addressed the needs of victims directly through the creation of refuges, shelters and rape crisis centres. Secondly, they have addressed victims' needs indirectly through pressure for law reform – for example, the introduction of restrictions on the admissibility in court of the prior sexual experiences of the victim of a sexual assault – and changes in police practices – for example, the 1983 Home Office circular to all Chief Officers of Police which advocated, among other suggestions, the need to deal sensitively with the victims of sexual assault and special training for officers dealing with such cases. In particular, some feminists have pressed for the criminalization of violence against women and, with respect to sexual violence, for longer prison sentences, mandatory prison sentences and the like (Crites, 1987; rhodes and McNeill, 1985). In the United States some feminists have also pointed to the Minneapolis experiment which seemed to indicate that arresting men who abused their partners was more effective in terms of subsequent violence than mediation and counselling or separation of the parties (Ferraro, 1989). This evidence that arrest – irrespective of subsequent prosecution or sentence – could act as a deterrent has led in many areas of the United States to either mandatory or presumptive arrest policies. Similar changes are occurring in England. In 1987, for example, the Metropolitan police issued new guidelines on how the police should respond to violence within the home.

Susan Edwards, in her chapter in this volume, discusses the tensions evident in feminists' attempts to change legal practice. She refers in brief to debates surrounding the legal regulation of pornography, prostitution and child sexual abuse and explores the issues raised there in more detail with respect to wife abuse. Problematic for feminists, however, is the possibility that law reform may be counterproductive: for example, it can lead to fewer rather than more convictions and to plea bargaining. Maria Los's chapter provides convincing although depressing evidence of this with respect to rape law reform in Canada. The law there was changed in response to and in accordance with some feminist demands. However, this apparent success masks a failure in real terms to make a fundamental impact on the legal structure.

Although Susan Edwards and Maria Los both accept that some law reform is better than none, they also accept that there are a number of problems with relying on law reform *per se* as a mechanism for change. First, the law tends to frame issues in terms of individual pathology and, consequently, to offer individual remedies. Law reform, therefore, leaves untouched the institutions and practices which are at the root of violence against women and, in particular, of women's subordination. Legislation in England in the 1970s with respect to violence against wives, for example, may, in theory, have improved the legal rights of women but, as Freeman (1980) and others have pointed out, actual improvements in women's position are less pronounced. Law reform must be accompanied by more fundamental changes – changes in women's social and economic position and in the power relations between men and women. Without this, deep-rooted attitudes and patriarchal values will remain.

Second, and this is in many ways linked to the first point, the law has traditionally encompassed *men's* accounts of events because it is men who both legislate and then interpret the law. With respect to rape, Catherine MacKinnon writes that 'rape, from a *woman's* point of view, is not prohibited, it is regulated. . . To them [some men], it is sex. Therefore, to the law it is sex' (1983: 651–3) (our emphasis). Thus feminists must endeavour to substitute *women's* accounts, *women's* experiences, *women's* demands. Betsy Stanko in her chapter attempts to do this creatively in terms of crime prevention advice. She rejects men's accounts of what women need and takes the first tentative steps towards creating a feminist crime prevention strategy.

11 Violence against women: feminism and the law

Susan Edwards

There never has been nor is there one feminist movement. Indeed, there are fundamental differences within feminism and nowhere is this more apparent than in discussions of violence against women. According to Segal: 'opposing attitudes to heterosexuality and to the significance of male violence blew apart the women's movement of the seventies' (1987: 67). Issues of race are also relevant to the tensions in these debates. In their criticism of early feminist writings, both Sa'adawi (1980) and Joseph (1981) showed that feminism was blind to the experiences of black and Third World women. Moreover, as Joseph wrote, 'Black women in American society have at least as much in common with Black men as white women' (1978: 95). Southall Black Sisters demonstrate the consequences of this in their discussion of black women's responses to wife abuse: 'We are forced to make demands of the police to protect our lives from the very same men along whose side we fight in anti-racist struggles' (1989: 40). Marcia Rice in her essay in this volume refers to these tensions.

Nor is there one feminist criminology or feminist approach to law. There exist different conceptualizations of the relationship of the law to the state, different views as to appropriate ways of dealing with the problem of crime generally and with crimes against women in particular and differences in preferred approaches towards offenders and victims. Some feminists' support for the victim is such as to totally exclude consideration of the offender. At a recent European Conference on Critical Legal Studies at which I presented a paper on rape, I made an *en passant* reference to the appalling conditions in British prisons for rapists and to their high rate of recidivism. This led to an outburst from one woman who declared that what happens to rapists should not properly be an issue for feminists. Similarly, calls for more humane and effective treatment of sex offenders by Box–Grainger (1986) and others is, to some feminists, a betrayal of the victim. Though I believe this to be a misguided criticism, such a separatist view characterizes one of the many faces of feminist criminology.

During the last decade especially, the difference in feminist positions both within and outside criminology has become increasingly apparent. Where matters of crimes against women are concerned, some feminists, instead of rejecting the law, have systematically pressed for more penal laws and especially for the stricter application of the law, for more inten- sive policing, for more prosecutions, for harsher sentencing and for more severe punishments for specific categories of offending by men against women and children (Edwards, 1989d). This chapter explores how this state of affairs can arise, how it can be explained and how it is that the same women who identify with the abolitionist perspective[1] for specific categories of offending are now calling for more control of men's power by increased state intervention, policing and punishment (Edwards, 1989d; Horley, 1988; Walker, 1989).

What I wish to argue is that feminists who argue for decriminalization of certain offences are not necessarily confused when they also call for increased legal intervention for certain crimes against women and chil- dren. This state of affairs is not a contradiction, since there is no consis- tent, fixed relationship between the state, its laws and social interests. As Taylor rightly points out:

> Nowhere is the contradictory character of law, as an oppressive in- strument of a particular social interest as well as an immediately important area of struggle, more apparent than in the relationship of law to women.
>
> (1981: 180)

Feminists and law

The paradox outlined above exists not only in feminist writings. Nelken, for example, recognizes that: 'critical writers, including those writing from a feminist perspective, now seem to be arguing for more rather than less use of the criminal law' (1987: 108). In their work feminists have drawn attention not only to the absence of substantive law relating to rape in marriage and violence against women but also to the lack of enforcement of existing laws and, in those instances where the law is applied, to the trivial sentences meted out by a largely ageing, male judiciary. Recent comments made by the judiciary in cases of rape and wife assault either exonerating rapists or trivializing male abusers have incensed many people, not just as feminists (Pattullo, 1983).

Men who rape women and sexually abuse children have been the subjects of feminist pressures for reform. Feminists have argued that for too long the interests of offenders have been given priority over and above the protection of victims who are at the same time the least powerful. The rapist, the wife abuser, the child sexual and physical abuser, the punter, the pimp, the distributor and seller of pornography have all been the foci of feminist concern.

But alongside these concerns there has also been considerable unease since it is well known that it is not axiomatic that more laws and more intensive policing can transform society or ensure justice, equality and empowerment for women. The words of Dorie Klein, quoted in Andriessen, reflect this dilemma:

> The women's movement, at least in this country, has, according to me, made the mistake to believe that the criminal justice system could be transformed into a vigorous feminist instrument.
>
> (1982: 138)

Smart, similarly, reminds us of 'the paucity of gains for women arising out of the pursuit of law reform' (1986: 109) and more recently warns feminism 'to avoid the siren call of law' (1989: 160). But there are other problems too.

Many writers have puzzled over an apparent alignment of feminists on the left and reformists on the right who both call for more law and order. But it is a fundamental mistake and fallacy to link left feminists with traditional conservatives. Those who have argued that left feminists are linking arms with right-wing reactionaries have misunderstood feminist politics and feminist demands with respect to violent crime against women and have also misunderstood the complex nature of law. This misunderstanding arises out of an assumption that there is an inexorable relationship between capitalism, repressive penal structures, patriarchy and the *laissez-faire* position adopted by the state regarding men's relationship to women and to the family.

The state has traditionally intervened, controlled and intruded in what it regards as 'proper' state matters – namely, security, public order and street crime. At the same time, the state has retreated and determinedly maintained this retreat from controlling or regulating behaviours between those in familial relationships. It is also a mistake to assume an unproblematic alignment between feminism and left politics. Eileen Fairweather, for example, argues that left politics fails to grasp the significance of the two countervailing modes of intervention and non-intervention mentioned above:

I am sick of those socialists and sociologists, mostly male or living in the safety of suburbia, who dismiss the 'law and order' debate as just another Tory vote catcher . . the far left continues to push its lunatic line: that all criminals no matter how vicious are in some way rebell-ing against capitalism.

(1982: 375)

Such a monist, determinist analysis of crime ignores the fact that some 'crimes' are committed by women in rebellion against patriarchy and that many male 'criminals' walk free because their behaviour towards women is socially sanctioned by patriarchy.

Moreover, the interests of those women who campaign for the legal regulation of men's sexual behaviour and men's violence and those who are caught up in the web of patriarchal dependence for their existence are not always the same. Radical feminists in North America and in the United Kingdom have organized demonstrations to 'reclaim the night'. They have endeavoured to highlight the symbolic curfew which controls women's lives. Yet there are tensions between radical feminists and the views and perspectives of women who work as prostitutes or in the sex industry. Nickie Roberts writes about how Women Against Violence Against Women picketed Peter Terson's play *Strippers* while she and others, together with the English Collective of Prostitutes (ECP), picketed the pickets (1986: 18).

What this section indicates is the complexity of feminist responses to justice and law. It is my view that the law has an important symbolic function to play and that a society which presses for changes without at the same time expressing and codifying these sentiments within its legis-lative framework cannot effect any real change. Indeed, the law is the most symbolically powerful tool we have at our disposal (O'Donovan, 1985: 20).

The non-regulation of familial relationships

The point which some critics fail to grasp is that laws do not control or oppress all people with the same tenacity, tyranny or consistency. Cous-ins, for example, argues that

Marxists frequently treat the law and the legal apparatuses as a homogeneous field, one that can be conceived as a general instance, operating in a unitary mode, singular in its source and punctual in its effects.

(1980: 110)

The law, however, is palpably neither homogeneous nor consistent. When black people are the subject, the law is extremely oppressive; and when it comes to the regulation of men's conduct towards family members this domain is called 'private' and is characterized by minimal regulation (Radford, 1987). As O'Donovan maintains, it is wrong to regard state intervention as unmitigatedly bad and 'to pretend that the private is free leads to a false analysis' (1985: 15). This privacy persists through the absence of laws, or through the unequal application of law in its various aspects, and is a fundamental and persistent component of judicial ideology and thought. Consider the following judicial statements. Thomas J., referring to the family, opined:

> There could hardly be anything more intimate or confidential than is involved in that relationship, or than in the mutual trust and confidences which are shared between husband and wife. The confidential nature of the relationship is of its very essence.
> (*Argyll* v. *Argyll* [1967] cited in O'Donovan 1985: 126)

And Lord Wilberforce (in *Hoskyn* v. *Commissioner of Police for the Metropolis* [1978] 2 All ER 138 – a case I will refer to again in due course) stated that to allow a wife to give evidence against a husband 'would give rise to discord and to perjury and would be, to ordinary people, repugnant'. Lord Salmon agreed that to compel a wife to give evidence against a husband would 'probably destroy the marriage' (*ibid.*, at 148).[2] This non-regulation meant that familial relationships were abandoned to the exploitation of power advantages by men under the guise of respect for privacy.

Feminist demands for more law and order

Feminist demands for more law and order function at a symbolic rather than at an instrumental level. Feminists argue that it is the absence of law, the lack of application of the law or the selective enforcement of law which has created a cultural climate in which particular behaviours, including violence against women, is condoned. The law then serves symbolically to support a climate of violence against women and sets the scene for that climate. Hall *et al.* (1978) argue that the law also orchestrates public opinion and Michael Freeman (1980) goes further: the symbolic function of the absence of penal law in this area means that *the law itself* constitutes the problem. Put simply, the argument is that the legal regulation of men's behaviour towards women and children and men's behaviour within the family has not been adequately addressed through legal regulation. Thus we cannot just dismiss the arguments of feminists who want more intensive policing, stricter laws, more control of men's power and the regulation of men's violence.

At the same time, within these demands for more law and order, there are different perspectives. Dworkin (1981), for example, bases her claims

for increased legal intervention in the realm of pornography on the premise that 'the reality is that men commit acts of forced sex against women
systematically' (quoted in Segal, 1987: 12). But many feminists, who are
also supportive of more law and order, find Dworkin's position excessive.
As Hanmer, Radford and Stanko point out:

> If reforms are geared only to curbing the more obvious excesses of
> men's violence and to protecting women the police define as deserv-
> ing of male protection, then women's demands will only shore up
> the existing relations between men and women rather than secure
> the feminist aim of autonomy for all women irrespective of class,
> race, and relationship to heterosexuality.
>
> (1989: 5)

I explore these tensions further by examining feminists' views on legal
regulation in three areas in brief – pornography, prostitution and child
sexual abuse – and more fully with respect to wife assault.

The legal regulation of pornography

Feminists are divided over the question of how far legal regulation
is appropriate here, since censorship would extend into other areas of
sexual and social relations. As Ecklersley (1987: 158) points out, anti-
pornography campaigns have attracted strong criticism from lesbian
groups and this has resulted in a number of fresh attempts to reformulate
feminists' objections to pornography. Indeed, censorship debates have
always posed grave problems for the left in its endeavour to preserve
democratic freedoms. Thus some feminists in favour of the censorship of
pornography are against censorship in other areas. Clare Short, for example, has consistently campaigned for the prohibiton of semi-nude
photographs in daily newspapers as representations which objectify
women in a way similar to though less obviously than pornography – but
she takes a rather different line on the Salman Rushdie *Satanic Verses*
issue.

> It is a fine book, it's been misrepresented. It's absolutely crucial that it
> should be published in hardback, paperback, and any other version.
> If we didn't publish all the books that offend Christians, agnostics,
> atheists, Buddhists, Muslims, Hindus, Sikhs, we wouldn't have any
> books in Britain.
>
> (Quoted in *The Independent* July 22 1989)

Dworkin (1981), Griffin (1981) and others have consistently argued for
stricter laws, more intensive policing and more severe punishments for
the creators, sellers and distributors of pornography. Dworkin, for example, in her evidence to the Meese Commission on Prostitution and

Pornogrpahy expounded the dangerousness of pornography and on the need for censorship:

> I am a citizen of the United States and in this country where I live, every year millions of pictures are being made of women with our legs spread. We are called beaver . . . our genitals are tied up . . . real rapes are on film and are being sold in the market place, women are penetrated by animals and objects for public entertainment . . . urinated on and defecated on, women are made to look like five year old children for anal penetration . . . there is amputee pornography . . . there is a trade in racism as a form of sexual pleasure . . . there is concentration camp pornography . . . and this material exists because it is fun, because it is entertainment, because it is a form of pleasure and there are those who say it is a form of freedom.
>
> (1988: 769–70).

The kind of pornography to which Dworkin alludes is of the extreme kind and it is easy to get support for the wholesale rejection of this. It is not so easy to take this line on representations of women which are less obviousy harmful but which many feminists feel create a culturally sanctioned mysogyny.

It is in response to these representations that many feminists like Brants and Kok remain sceptical about the role of the criminal law in curbing pornography and sexism. Instead, they argue that 'penal law must always be *ultimum remedium*: a last resort' (1986: 19). Experience has shown that law in itself cannot change attitudes overnight and that social changes develop in a context of education and formal rules (Soetenhorst, 1986: 7). However, other feminists on the left believe that all censorship is harmful and repressive and that censorship of pornography of necessity implies censorship of other matters essential to democracy and freedom of speech.

But perhaps the last word in this debate should be given to women working in the sex industry who feel that *all* sides of the debate have excluded them. Nickie Roberts, an ex-stripper, says:

> Feminist anti-porn campaigners or the Whitehouse brigade: it makes no difference to us. Both factions clamour for more repression and censorship at the hands of the state; both divert attention away from the real issue of women's poverty in this society; and both are responsible for the increased hounding and vilification of women who work in the sex industry.
>
> (1986: 16)

The legal regulation of prostitution

Feminists are similarly divided over the role the penal law should play with respect to prostitution. Several feminist organizations are in favour of the decriminalization of all laws relating to prostitution. Both the English Collective of Prostitutes (ECP) and Programme for the Reform of the Law on Street Offences (PROS), for example, were against the criminalization of the kerb crawler, a measure introduced in the Sexual Offences Act 1985, because they believed that 'any further criminalization of prostitution would only serve to penalise the prostitute further' (Edwards, 1989d: 16). Some women on the left, however, welcomed this Act.

Indeed, women on the left (and Conservative Party feminists such as Janet Fookes MP) were responsible for the introduction of the bill. They argued that, as women who were prostitutes were already penalized, measures to penalize the client introduced some measure of 'equality'. Besides, as many women recognized, women from all social classes were regularly being harassed, canvassed and intimidated by male kerb crawlers. Fairweather provides a sense of how women feel:

> Several women on Hillview were sexually attacked. Over the years you get used to being kerb crawled every night, every day asked if you do fellatio when you just pop out to the shops.
>
> (1982: 377)

Women, however, remain unprotected from such harassment.[3]

The legal regulation of child sexual abuse

It is well recognized that the legal process, the standards and requirements of evidence, the court process and the trial may be as damaging for the victim as the initial victimization (Weis and Borges, 1973). Thus, although there are deep divisions of opinion about legal intervention in cases of child sexual abuse, many feminists have campaigned for changes in the law which would simultaneously result in more prosecutions being brought against men and which would lessen the burden on victims of giving evidence (Woodcraft, 1988). Criticisms of the traditional view that children are liars and unreliable as witnesses, for example, have led to the development of methods to test the veracity of children (such as the use of anatomically correct dolls). However, the courts' view of the uncorroborated evidence of children still· presents a major obstruction to prosecution and conviction. This year the Court of Appeal ruled in two separate cases involving allegations by young girls of sexual abuse that they were too young to give uncorroborated evidence.[4] This has been followed in subsequent cases. The indication is that the protection of the child depends very much upon her age at the point of the allegation. This continues to leave very young children largely unprotected. As Campbell points out:

Usually there is little to withstand the suspect's denial; it is only the child's word against his. It has always been the case of men's word against children's: men have been believed and children have been silenced.

(1988: 71)

However, a question which is not yet resolved is whether or not the criminalization of child sexual abuse is the way forward. That is to say is the prosecution of the offender, and the requirement that the victim gives evidence in court in the event of a not guilty plea, the best way of dealing with these cases? While, as Woodcraft argues, condemnation and prosecution is undeniably important at the symbolic level, until there are changes in the treatment of the child witness/victim, the effects on children are often devastating (1988: 126). Adler has already argued for major reforms in the treatment of child victims in the criminal justice process. For example, she has called for new procedural and legislative reforms 'to mitigate the trauma induced by participation in the legal process' and 'to end the discrimination that is currently denying judges and juries the opportunity to hear and process children's evidence on a par with information received from adults' (1989: 146).

The Criminal Justice Act 1988 did introduce some major changes including the introduction of video links (s. 32 (1)) and the abolition of the corroboration requirement in the unsworn evidence of children (s. 34 (1)) but these still do not go far enough. The corroboration warning must still be given where the child is the complainant in a case involving a sex offence and although the use of video equipment in the courtroom may allow the witness to give evidence behind a screen it does nothing to change the adversarial contest. Victims are still cross-examined and suggestions are still put to the child witness that he or she is lying or has imagined the incident. The use of video links, therefore, does little to reduce the damage of the contest on the victim. Similarly, the Law Commission No. 177, Criminal Code Draft Bill 1989 contains nothing in it to ease the child's burden of giving evidence. On the other hand, the *Report of the Advisory Group on Video-Recorded Evidence*, published on 19 December 1989, states that no child witnesses in such cases should be required to appear in open court. It remains to be seen whether this and other proposals mooted in the report are adopted.

The symbolic function of law in wife abuse

Analysis of law at the level of statute, precedent, evidence and procedure provided the starting point for feminists' and legal scholars' critique of the lack of protection afforded victims of wife assault and homicide. In sum, their argument is that the law, through essentially non-regulation of this sphere, constitutes the problem and because of the absence of legal intervention, it reinforces the cultural climate of acceptance of wife abuse. There are three key points within the legal process itself which, independently and collectively, symbolically reinforce a cultural acceptance of violence against women.

First, there is the existence of dual jurisdictions. This substantive division of remedies into civil and criminal carries with it a clear symbolic function which goes beyond the actual process of law itself. This dichotomy is translated into juridical, policing and everyday common-sense perceptions which reinforce conventional opinion that violence against wives or female partners is in certain ways distinct from violence towards non-family members in the street.

Second, within the criminal jurisdiction, a clear distinction is made between behaviour on the streets (public disorder and street crime) and behaviour in the home; the latter is not the responsibility of the state but of individual family members. This conceptual distinction is formalized by the legal rules and procedures which govern police responses on the street and in the home and pertains to the gathering of evidence from strangers and spouses. Threatening or suspicious behaviour on the streets – public order – depends largely on police evidence; the police are the chief prosecution witnesses. Private order in the home is not similarly circumscribed and, while not arguing for the same extension of powers into the home, the difference is there and the fact remains that, notwithstanding considerable evidence of threats or violence, the police traditionally rarely intervened. Instead the *victim* had to make a complaint and press charges.

Third, there have been significant differences between the rules of evidence and procedures governing the assault of a wife, a female partner or cohabitee who had not entered into a marriage contract, and a female stranger. In violence by a stranger and violence between persons acquainted or well known to one another, the complainant/victim can be compelled to give evidence against the aggressor. On the other hand violence perpetrated within the family and against wives was not dealt with in this way. Wives were traditionally not compellable witnesses.[5] The law thus then served to symbolically reaffirm social mores and values regarding the family and the hegemony of men's power within it.

In the following sections I elaborate on each of these points.

Dual jurisdictions

The present system of justice in the civil and criminal courts in England and Wales, Europe, North America, Canada and Australia presents a major obstacle to the protection of women from men's violence in the home. Despite feminist support for the campaign to introduce civil legislation in

England and Wales with the aim of giving women greater protection, these provisions in fact reinforce the different symbolic significance attaching to these two jurisdictions. This distinction, rather than providing more options for women, perpetuates the public/private dichotomy which exists in the substantive law and categorizes violence against wives as private rather than public. From wife assault to marital rape, the criminal law has conventionally never been regarded as the best instrument for dealing with 'family matters' (Criminal Law Revision Committee, 1980; paras 33–6). Some go even further and argue that *Family* Court is the most appropriate domain for resolving violence and sexual assault between husband and wife. Yet Family Court symbolically serves to remind us that even where a crime has been committed the very nature of the forum reduces the seriousness of the offence in the eyes of the legal system and society.

The symbolic function of the civil law

Since 1976, in England and Wales, battered wives/cohabitees have been able to seek legal redress through the civil courts. The introduction of the Domestic Violence and Matrimonial Proceedings Act 1976 and the Domestic Proceedings and Magistrates' Courts Act 1978 provided women with some protection from the abuse of men through the granting of injunctions and ouster (exclusion) orders. Traditionally the police were reluctant to support or suggest a criminal prosecution as an appropriate mechanism and, in practice, they encouraged women to seek solutions in the civil courts to the violence perpetrated against them by their male partners. However, also in practice, the various civil orders are difficult to get and are largely ineffective without the attachment of a power of arrest. Moreover, the symbolic function of the civil law in these cases seems primarily to be to reaffirm the fact that society and the courts regard wife abuse as less serious than other forms of violence and to view attempts at resolution in the criminal court as inappropriate. The existence of civil law remedies thus has *obstructed* the recognition of violence in the home as a criminal offence.

The symbolic function of the criminal law

The criminal law regulating violence is derived from the Offences Against the Person Act 1861 and, in theory, the criminal law applies equally to all regardless of the relationship of the victim to the suspect. Previously, the legal criterion necessary for a prosecution was the presence of a prima-facie case. Since the introduction of the Prosecution of Offences Act 1985 the prima-facie case test has been reformulated and now 'sufficiency of evidence' and 'a reasonable prospect of conviction' are the predominant considerations. In practice, insofar as wife abuse is concerned, the criminal law is rarely invoked.

The criminal statistics, especially in this area, bear no relation to the extent of violence against wives; wife abuse and marital rape probably have 'dark figures' higher than most other crimes. Homicide statistics indicate that over one-fifth of all violence resulting in death involves wives as victims. Feminists internationally are pressing for more prosecutions of assault against wives (Stanko, 1985; Horley, 1988; Edwards, 1989d), supported by evidence that intervention and prosecution does have an impact on deterring subsequent violence (Sherman and Berk, 1984). Although impossible to measure, it must also be the case that prosecutions of violent men have a powerful effect on the social tolerance of violence and hence some impact on other men in their behaviour towards women.[6]

The symbolic function of evidence

In law, for many years, one spouse could not be compelled to give evidence against the other. In England and Wales, the infamous decision in *Hoskyn* v. *Commissioner of Police for the Metropolis* [1978] 2 ALL ER 138 reaffirmed this guiding principle, *inter alia*. In *Hoskyn*, the wounds inflicted on the wife were extremely grave: she was found to have sustained two stab wounds in the chest, a nine centimetre cut from the temple to the right ear, smaller cuts to her right lip and chin and a four and a half centimetre cut on the left forearm. Notwithstanding these appalling injuries, the doctrine of family privacy was given priority over and above the right of an individual wife to protection. This sentiment is reflected in many other jurisdictions (Hanmer *et al.*, 1989).

Reshaping the symbolic function of law in wife abuse

Attempts to change police policy and prosecution practice has characterized much of the feminist response to violence against women. There is no doubt that while attempts to change these policies have not met with complete success they do challenge the cultural climate created by non-regulation and reaffirm that violence against women will not be condoned. Moreover, it is not certain that the law is *incapable* of introducing some degree of reform in this area.

Police policy: the symbolic function

In 1987 the Metropolitan Police extended their working definition of violence to include threats and attempts:

> A domestic dispute is defined as any quarrel including violence between family or members of the same household. Domestic violence occurs when a person or persons causes, attempts to cause, or threatens to cause physical harm to another family or household member.
>
> (Metropolitan Police Press Notice 199/87)

New instructions were then issued to police officers in the form of a force order which states that 'an assault which occurs in the home is as much a criminal act as one which may occur in the street'. The order emphasized the need to improve training and procedures for wife abuse, to arrest abusive men and to support the victims. Since 24 June 1987, officers have been required to write up such incidents either in a crime report book or in an incident book. Officers are encouraged to use their powers of arrest in accordance with section 25(3)(e) of The Police and Criminal Evidence Act 1984 where 'the constable has reasonable grounds for believing that arrest is necessary to protect a child or other vulnerable person from the relevant person'. In considering the appropriate criminal charge, officers are encouraged to use section 47 of the Offences Against the Person Act 1861 and, where the victim is reluctant to substantiate the charge, the police are encouraged to prosecute in accordance with section 80 of the Police and Criminal Evidence Act 1984 which now makes the wife a compellable witness. The force order emphasized also the need for a multi-agency approach with local organizations such as Women's Aid and Victim Support. It further envisaged 'follow up' calls to the victim to ensure that she was well, to offer her advice or to warn her when the suspect was to be released from custody.

Edwards (1989a, 1989b, 1989c, 1989d) shows that the implementation of this policy has been variable depending on individual divisions' and stations' within divisions willingness to embrace the policy and translate it into practice, especially by front line officers. In a study conducted in 1984–5 and in a follow-up study in 1988, I examined police recording practices and police attitudes to policing 'domestic situations' in two Metropolitan Police divisions, Holloway and Hounslow. The earlier (1985) study revealed the extent of the traditional police view which regarded wife assault as a non-police matter: trivial and inconsequential. In 1985 approximately 54,000 calls were received in the Metropolitan Police district (with a population of 7.6 million); only 12 per cent of these calls were treated as crimes. Seventeen per cent of these resulted in an arrest and prosecution. On the whole, the earlier research showed that many cases involving physical assault were entered in an incident book instead of a crime record and that 83 per cent of the cases entered in a crime record (where there was evidence of assault or criminal damage) were later written off and disposed of as 'no crimes'.

The new police policy has had a significant impact on these matters. In 1988 95,500 calls were made to the police: 21 per cent of these resulted in a crime report being completed. In 26 per cent of the crimes recorded an arrest was made. There was a decline in the use of 'no crime' to dispose of cases and a decline in the use of the incident report book as an alternative but illegitimate means of recording cases involving physical assault. However, at the end of the day, a smaller proportion of cases was actually prosecuted: 16 per cent. This indicates that although police work on the ground is changing and that front line officers are arresting men more frequently it is difficult to pursue these cases through to prosecution. It is also important to mention that Holloway and Hounslow stations differed in respect of the proportion of arrests made, the proportion of cases crimed and the prosecution rates. This indicates the difficulty of translating policing policy in a uniform manner within one police force.

The symbolic function of legislative change

Feminists have also worked towards changing the rules of evidence which have traditionally resulted in the differential treatment of wives. The Police and Criminal Evidence Act 1984 (section 80 (8)) introduced a significant provision which, for the first time, made spouses legally compellable. This means that wives can be compelled to give evidence against physically abusive husbands. If realized this provision promises to revolutionize the success rate of the prosecution of physically abusive husbands and, in theory at least, has the potential to influence the police to report cases to the Crown Prosecution Service even when the witness is reluctant to give evidence. It also has the potential to influence the decisions of the Crown Prosecutor since, if the complainant is reluctant to testify, the prosecutor can compel her to do so. This legislation places a wife on exactly the same footing as any other witness with regard to giving evidence for the prosecution. The removal of this unique treatment of the wife in such cases is very important and serves to convey the message to police officers and others working within criminal justice that an assault committed against a wife is no different from other violent assaults.

Conclusion

The law alone is unable to provide the degree of change demanded by feminists. While it is important not to place too much faith in the ability of the law to reform patriarchal society, it is also the case that the law and its corollaries, that is the courts, the legal system, the police, the judiciary and the legal profession must not and cannot be ignored. Feminists must continue to press for legal change and to make efforts to infiltrate and inform the legal, criminological and policing debates about the extent and prevalence of crimes against women and about the experiences of women at the hands of men despite awareness that the law is intransigent and 'resistant to the challenge of feminist knowledge and critique' (Smart, 1989: 2). Feminists must also continue to challenge malestream academia. The male-dominated criminological enterprise – whether left realist, idealist or conventional – has paid little regard to gender dimensions in discussions of law and the state. For example, left criminology (both idealist and realist) focused its main attack on the state through exploring such issues as race and crime, urban problems and the inner city. Thornton (1989) refers to this tendency within academia to ignore women as 'hegemonic masculinity'. This has obstructed the analysis of violence against women as a problem in its own right and, on a more theoretical and conceptual level, prevented awareness of the role of patriarchy as an important dimension in the analysis.

Notes

1 This perspective is largely based on a class analysis of the definition of crime and the development of criminal sanctions. The fundamental guiding tenet is that laws are defined and maintained by the state in the interests of those who have power (Fine, 1984). It argues that the needs and interests of victims have been ignored and that it is necessary to retreat from the persistent use of penal sanctions in order to change or modify social behaviour (Van Swaaningen, 1989). This aspect has appealed to some feminist victimologists though the perspective generally, in its obsession with class as the appropriate dimension of analysis, is blind to the importance of patriarchy as an equally defining, constraining and repressive arm of the state apparatus. It performs its task in a similarly oppressive and suffocating manner.

2 The law relating to the status of evidence of spouses has now been changed in the Police and Criminal Evidence Act 1984. I refer to this later.

3 A clause in the Sexual Offences Bill 1985 which would have offered some protection was dropped.

4 There are two separate issues here: whether a child gives sworn or unsworn evidence and what the corroboration requirement is when children give evidence. (See the *Guardian* 8 June 1989.)

5 This rule, of course, applied equally to husbands but cases in which wives abuse husbands are rare and appear less frequently in the criminal courts.

6 Attempts to increase the effectiveness of both civil and criminal law depend on how these laws are implemented. While at present some police officers receive training regarding wife abuse, prosecutors are not obliged to undergo similar extensive training. This is also the case for magistrates and judges.

12 Feminism and rape law reform

Maria Los

While real enough for the women who experience or fear it, rape is a social construction. Being the ultimate expression of gender conflict, the act of rape is particularly susceptible to cultural–ideological interpretations instrumental to the interests of the gender groups involved. One of the most powerful tools of symbolically defining an act is its inclusion into the law. Given the fact that legal language, the legislature and the judiciary have traditionally been men's domain, it can be safely assumed that the process of the legal construction of rape has been shaped by ideological and cultural perceptions and assumptions that are shared by men rather than by both men and women. Moreover, it is the interests of men rather than women which are likely to be served by the resultant legal definitions. These interests can be conceptualized in terms of group-status maintenance strategies.

A group's status maintenance requires the utilization of cultural and political resources (including law) to project the legitimacy and natural permanency of the group's position within the existing power structure and the validity and benevolence of the power itself. The group's image which is consistent with its rank within the hierarchy must be symbolically affirmed, possibly through conveying an impression that the subordinate group – due to its specific deficiencies or dispositions – has justifiably been relegated to a lower status.

Historically, rape laws have been instrumental in ideologically reinforcing the relations of domination and subordination between genders. This assertion applies both to early formulations when rape was defined as a property crime whereby compensation was paid to the woman's rightful owner, be it her father or her husband, and to modern day rape laws and interpretations (see, for example, Schwendinger and Schwendinger, 1982; Clark and Lewis, 1977).

In this chapter,[1] I describe first the definition of rape and surrounding legal concepts contained in the Canadian Criminal Code's sections on rape prior to their reform in 1983 and assess in what explicit and implicit ways this law projected images and symbolic messages instrumental to male-status maintenance. In the second section I examine the new law on sexual assault introduced ostensibly to satisfy the demands of the feminist lobby. In the third section, I analyse women's groups' efforts to redefine rape on their own terms and try to assess the viability of utilizing the law on rape to project women's interests and to enhance their status. Finally, I point to several reasons why women's groups were not able to detach the issue of rape from the dominant male-gender ideology.

The Canadian rape law prior to the 1983 reform: its symbolic content

The normative messages projected by the law dealing with rape prior to 1983 (The Criminal Code of Canada, secs 143–5) point to sexual double standards and cultural perceptions of gender relations which were functional to male-status maintenance. The most important of these messages are listed below. They are only briefly discussed here because there already exists an abundance of publications on the sexist nature of Canadian rape laws and of similar legal enactments in other countries (for example, Borgida, 1981; Boyle, 1984; Brownmiller, 1975; Clark and Lewis, 1977; Goldsmith Kasinsky, 1978; LeGrand, 1973; Schwartz and Clear, 1980; Snider, 1985).

The patriarchal basis of marriage must be protected

This is reflected in three ways:

1 Husbands had unlimited access to their wives sexually.[2]
2 Rape required heterosexual penetration. The possibility that a woman might conceive a child outside marriage was viewed as more important than her own definition of sexual violence, which could include forced oral sexual acts, penetration with objects and so forth.
3 A man who seduced a young virgin under a false promise of marriage was guilty of an indictable offence. This implies that women are weaker and dependent partners in a relationship.

Women are morally underdeveloped

This is reflected in two ways:

1 Women's testimony under oath could not be trusted. Thus the judge

was obliged to inform the jury that it would not be safe to convict the defendant solely on the basis of the complainant's testimony: such warnings were required otherwise only in cases involving testimony by children.

2 Rape complaints which were not made immediately after the attack were invalidated since otherwise the woman would have had enough time to make up a story about the incident.

Women's credibility depends on her sexual reputation, while men's does not

Before 1983 nothing prevented the use of information about the complainant's sexual conduct and reputation in assessment of her credibility.[3] On the other hand, information about the accused's past convictions – including those for rape and other sexual offences – was inadmissible in evaluation of his testimony.

Some women do not deserve legal protection and men are entitled to take full advantage of it

Particularly prior the 1975–6 amendments,[4] women did not have the right to refuse sexual access to some men if they had granted it liberally to others. The complainant's sexual conduct with men other than the accused was considered crucial in establishing her consent. The underlying rationale appears to have been that men should be able to safely assume that some women are available to all of them without discrimination.

Women's sexuality is complementary to and defined by men's sexuality

This is reflected in two ways:

1 The requirement of penetration by the man's sexual organ defined it as the only instrument with which a woman's body could be sexually violated.

2 A unique usage of the legal concept of consent underlies the pre-1983 law's definition of intercourse as rape when the woman's consent was 'extorted by threats or fear of bodily harm' (s. 143). Insistence on using the notion of 'consent' in this context reflected well men's incredulity that a woman could be raped totally against her will: she must *somehow* have consented, even if out of fear. Implicitly, every rape victim is thus perceived as a *participant* in sexual intercourse rather than a victim of sexual violation.

These symbolic messages were further reinforced in the course of the interpretation and implementation of the law dealing with rape which resulted in the dismissal of a majority of complaints (Canadian Advisory

Council on the Status of Women (CACSW), 1982: 3; 28–35; Clark and Lewis, 1977; Minch and Linden, 1987; for non-Canadian sources, see Box, 1983: 120–64; Chappel, Geis and Geis, 1977; Hindelang and Davis, 1977; LaFree, 1989; Renner and Sahjpaul, 1986). In short, far from being effective in controlling sexual violence against women, the law reinforced the informal control of women and helped to perpetuate the ideological premises of the traditional gender order.

The Sexual Assault Law of 1983: its ultimate purpose

The current law, promulgated on 1 January 1983 was preceded by a prolonged campaign by feminist writers and women's organizations. Despite frequent official references to women's demands as one uniform entity, several women's groups put forward different proposals which varied in their degree of adherence to the internal conventions and principles of the extant legal system. Eventually, however, most groups accepted the proposal submitted to Parliament by the National Association of Women and the Law (NAWL) (Macdonald, 1982: 13–16). The Association supported in principle Bill C–53 introduced by the Minister of Justice in 1981 but strongly disagreed with several specific clauses both in the initial bill and in its final, amended version (Bill C–127) (see NAWL, 1979; 1981; 1982a; 1982b).

The sudden pressure from the Ministry of Justice to reform the law on rape after years of stalling can, however, be explained by factors other than a tardy but genuine recognition of the women's lobby. The enactment, in 1982, of the Canadian Charter of Rights and Freedoms (as part of the Constitution Act) was bound to lead to constitutional challenges to those parts of the law which were likely to fail the equal rights test. The sections on rape in the Criminal Code would have been an obvious target, with their clearly discriminatory vocabulary and unusual procedures. Furthermore, the existence of an organized women's movement made such challenges virtually inevitable. Consequently, the primary goal of the reform – explicitly stated by the Ministry of Justice – was to make these sections formally compatible with the rest of the criminal law (Senate of Canada, 25: 19, 1982).

The reforms were as follows. First of all, the offence was redefined in gender-neutral terms. Therefore, by including female offenders but, more importantly, male victims (homosexual assault), the definition of sexual violation had to be changed and could no longer be limited to the traditional understanding of sexual intercourse. Since a whole range of sexual activities had to be covered, the term 'rape' was no longer appropriate and 'sexual assault' – suggested by both women's groups and the Law Reform Commission – appeared to be a good substitute. The term 'sexual assault' allowed for a multi-tiered offence to account for different degrees of severity. Furthermore, under the Charter, it was clearly no longer feasible to discriminate against married women. The peculiar usage of the term 'consent' had also to be corrected simply because 'at common law you do not have consent if it is not predicated upon a voluntary act' (Senate of Canada, 25: 35, 1982). Similarly, rules of evidence had to be made consistent with those in comparable offences: the 'recent complaint' requirement and the special rules of corroboration could no longer be sustained. Finally, with rape classified as a type of assault, inquiries into the complainant's sexual conduct with people other than the accused became harder to justify and were, therefore, further restricted.[5]

Redefining rape: women's role

Many aspects of the new sexual assault legislation were prompted by or coincided with the demands of major women's groups, but the latter were often informed and motivated by considerations other than the internal consistency of the law, formal equality and gender neutrality. In their demands for rape law reform, women acted as an interest group determined to use the legal process to reconstruct the meaning of rape from the one which was shaped by men to one more reflective of women's interests and experience.

In the process they defined rape as a women's issue, an exclusive concern of women. No men were allowed in anti-rape marches or rape crisis organizations. Because of their cultural conditioning and the sexualization of violence, all men were believed to be potential rapists just as all women were believed to be potential victims. Regardless of the possible – but clearly problematic – long-term integrative impact of the anti-rape mobilization, the overriding aspiration of the movement's activists was to provide a voice to this victimized gender group and to empower it to make itself less vulnerable. To achieve this goal, women's groups undertook two major initiatives: the reform of patriarchal rape laws and the development of feminist services for rape victims. Within the latter sphere they did not have to compete with or conform to any established standards as such services were simply invented by the women involved. They did not have to accept any external, institutional frames of reference (for example, they did not have to advise the victims to report the attack to the police). They were, however, inevitably perpetuating the focus on women's ability to cope with their victimization, rather than on its roots and on ways of reducing, its prevalence. Their desire to be agents of change notwithstanding, these workers' social status was low as a result of belonging to a helping profession which had long been relegated to the zone of low-paid, low-visibility *women's* occupations. Moreover, their mission of helping sexually victimized women – the 'pariah' category among crime victims – lowered further their standing within the man-made status hierarchy.

The law reform campaign, on the other hand, forced women into direct competition with men but it also required their acceptance of established standards and frames of reference. While their identification with the victimized gave them a legitimate standing as a lobby with a clear constituency, it was unlikely to become a source of power. Just as rape symbolized unequal power relations between genders, the lobbying for law reform on behalf of rape victims put women automatically in a subordinate, easily trivialized position.

In their campaign for legal change women had no choice but to accept the legal system as given and try to adjust their objectives to its language and philosophy. Their ambition to redefine rape in a way true to the complex socio-political context of this crime was thus compromised and reduced to a set of formal demands congruent with the formidable legal machinery adjusted and perfected throughout modern history in the name of the protection of individual rights. Yet, the rights assigned to men and women – ostensibly equal and universal – have grown out of a reality of inequality justified by disparity in culturally exalted gender ideals. The obvious advantages of liberal philosophy thus disguise its dangerous potential for entrapping those who have been excluded from active participation in the law-making process.

The philosophical concept of social contract (or 'the original position' elaborated by John Rawls, 1972) is based on an assumption that rationally minded law-makers (or legal philosophers) are bound to produce fair rules as long as they know that they are not exempt from them, no matter what position in life they are destined to occupy eventually. But the real-life law-makers of the past not only knew that they were not going to end up being women; they were as a rule unable to appreciate what women's existence was like and what would matter to them if indeed they were women. Their neutrality and the vision of their 'original position' was, thus, by necessity crippled. Nevertheless the rules they passed were perceived as genuinely universal: see, for example, Dawson, 1987–88: 314. Women's efforts to reform the law may in turn be perceived as a test of whether these underlying, formal legal rules can be applied to remedy their well-entrenched but biased modes of application[6] or whether the rules themselves are inherently flawed.

With this question in mind, the main legal demands formulated by women's organizations engaged in lobbying for rape law reform are discussed below in the context of the broader interests of women, expressed in non-legal terms. What transpires from this analysis is the essential tension between legal and feminist discourses.

All women's groups agreed that in order to correct the inequities of the existing law, the double standard and the differential treatment inherent in the offence of rape had to be abolished. Within legal discourse, this could only be done in the name of gender-neutrality and legal consistency. Yet such an approach negates an argument which many women feel strongly about, namely that rape is a unique crime in that it involves predominantly the victimization of members of one gender group by members of the other.[7] The new offence of sexual assault does not stress the right to sexual autonomy in a manner which would have required men to alter, accordingly, their view of women's sexuality. The abolition of husbands' immunity from prosecution for rape has remedied the blatant discrimination against married women in this respect but the overall problem has not been addressed by the new law. The controversial issue of 'consent' (discussed below) and its implications for the accused's defence exemplify well the law-makers' reluctance to support unequivocally women's right to sexual autonomy.

Since conviction for most offences requires *mens rea*, an *intent* to commit sexual assault was demanded by women's groups (for example, NAWL, 1979: 2) and was explicitly included in the new legislation. An honest belief that the complainant consented to the conduct which is the subject matter of the charge constitutes a defence. While the presence of reasonable grounds for such a belief must be considered by the jury, it is *not a necessary condition* for a successful defence. In short, the honest belief in consent does not have to meet the test of the reasonable man, let alone the reasonable woman. What women's representatives demanded, even in their relatively early proposals was an *objective* test whereby mistake of fact as to consent would be accepted as a defence at a rape trial only if it were based on reasonable grounds.

Men and women's notions of consent are very different. To a man, a woman's resistance often presents a challenge, an invitation to 'rough sex', or a sign that she must yet be shown what she really wants. This is part of the prevailing mythology of sexual conquest. As the Action Committee's spokeswoman argued in vain before the almost all-male Senate Committee, 'they may have a belief that is indeed honest, but if prohibition of sexual assault is to have a meaning at all, this cannot be a valid defence' (Senate of Canada, 27: 10, 1982). In fact, 'many men believe a woman consents to sex when she accepts a ride from him, goes to his house or invites him to hers, accepts a drink or a dinner' (NAWL, 1981: 28). The legislators remained unmoved by these pleas, however. Consequently, the new law endorsed men's right to define women's sexuality.

Another contradiction which underlies women's lobbying for rape law reform is related to the highly publicized replacement of rape with a broader category of sexual assault. There were good legal and social reasons for women's groups to demand and support such a change. It promised to highlight the violent nature of the crime, to remove the condition of vaginal penetration, to alleviate the stigmatization of the victim and the humiliating nature of questioning in court and consequently to increase the rate of reporting and conviction.

The focus on the legal relabelling, however, creates a fiction that somehow the sexual degradation of women, integral to the traditional notion of rape, is, or is going to be, reduced (Cohen and Blackhouse, 1980). The shift in terminology offers some practical and legal advantages: it reflects the results of the research which show that rape tends to be motivated by the wish to dominate or punish rather than by sexual desire, and it more easily locates the offender within the broader culture which promotes or perpetuates men's domination over women and increasingly ties sex with violence. But the shift in terminology also gives exclusive attention to the perpetrator's motives, while deliberately underplaying the women's experience of rape as a *sexual* violation. Rape or sexual assault is not merely physically painful; it is repulsive, humiliating and degrading: the ultimate violation of women's privacy and sense of control over their bodies.

A major drawback in this stress on violence is that it may send a message both to the courts and to the public that only really brutal rapes are criminal and that sexual imposition itself is not of much consequence. Indeed, a survey of several hundred sexual assault sentencing reports, conducted in the late 1980s by the Metro Action Committee on Public Violence Against Women and Children, confirms this (Marshall, 1988). It found that judges repeatedly commented on the absence of injury or damage to the victim: 'no lasting and permanent damage to the complainant' was a comment made by the judge in a case where the victim was taken 'to a secluded area and raped. . . The complainant struggled a great deal but the accused overpowered her'; another victim according to the judge involved had 'no injury to her person or damage to her clothing'; and the stepdaughter and daughter of a man who raped them over an eight-year period were said to show 'no evidence of a lasting impact' (Marshall, 1988: 11–12).

Ironically, for feminists, the desexualization of rape has obscured the economic and cultural content of heterosexual relations and the related victimization of women. A unique aspect of the subordination of women – attacking their sexual identity as women – is blurred by the stress on the threat to their physical integrity as genderless legal persons.

In its rhetoric, the anti-rape women's lobby was trapped in the same myopic pespective which most victim's groups seem to adopt: the victimizers were perceived as an enemy to be crushed. Thus more diligent law enforcement and the wider application of punishment was a key objective for lobbyists. While some women's groups recommended moderation in penalties, they did it in the hope that this would increase juries' readiness to convict (NAWL, 1981: 13; 1982a: 2, 1982b: 6; Snider, 1985: 343).[8] Moreover, a number of feminists explicitly opposed any lowering of penalties, warning that it would symbolically downgrade the seriousness of the crime of sexual assault relative to other crimes (for example, CACSW, 1982: 9; Chase, 1983: 54; Cohen and Blackhouse, 1980: 102–3).

The desire to put rapists behind bars is more than understandable. It does not make it less myopic, however. The same research findings which moved women to press for a re-interpretation of rape suggest that prison can only aggravate the problem. By stripping convicted rapists of all power, prison is bound to make them even more power frustrated and angry and even less able to relate to women as equals. Yet, for women activists who sustained on a shoestring budget the network of vital support centres for rape victims, the idea of lobbying for massive funding for alternative programmes for sexual offenders was not one likely to even be considered. The thinking about crime and punishment that permeates dominant (man-made) images of justice was thus accepted by these women who were caught between the escalating fear of rape and the paucity of alternative, non-legal avenues for action.

In their legal proposals the unresolved dilemmas of the criminal justice system were glossed over and the well-documented class and race biases in the application of the penal law were overlooked due to exclusive concern with gender-based discrimination. The hope that toughening up the law on sexual assault and its increased enforcement would at least send an appropriate symbolic message to society is also questionable. This hope is either unrealistic or, more critically, misguided. Tamar Pitch has pointed to the dubious wisdom of 'the attribution to the penal system of the function of symbolic organiser of the hierarchy of general goods' (1985: 43). Commenting on Italian feminists' proposals for rape law reform, she wondered how – given the existing reality of conflict and inequality – penal law could be expected 'to perform the symbolic function of establishing and supporting universal values, to provide a focus for political and cultural consensus' (1985: 44). Yet various Canadian women's groups expected that a changed legal formula would facilitate and symbolize a fair consensus; see, for example, CACSW 1975: 1.

The question whether their legal proposals could have been better devised to serve women's interests and philosophy more accurately is a hypothetical one. The changes women's groups asked for were always developed and assessed with reference to existing practices and biases. They were not necessarily searching for the best legal solutions, but rather the legal formulae which would cause relatively less damage in the hands of sexist implementors. Yet, as Boyle seems to suggest, any legal solution may be easily distorted and adjusted to serve existing gender relations:

In essence both a gender neutrality and a recognition of difference approach can be used against women . . . Recognition of real differences may in fact invite the perpetuation of differences, e.g. may allow the continuing discrimination against women under the guise of 'protective' legislation and the perpetuation of stereotypes . . . Gender neutrality may be a vehicle to deny women's reality.

(1985: 17)

Women, rape laws and the mass media[9]

LeGrand in 1973 claimed that 'If [rape] laws were changed to relate more rationally to the reality of the crime and to the goal of sexual equality, attitudes about the crime might also change' (1973: 919). Now, however, when Canada and elsewhere have revised their laws, studies show that their impact is rather minimal (see, for example, Horney and Spohn, 1987; Loh, 1980; Polk, 1985; Renner and Sahjpaul, 1986; LaFree, 1989). Carringella-MacDonald (1985), for example, established, in her study in Michigan, that attrition and high acquittal rates persisted. There was, however, an increase in the number of cases resolved by plea-bargaining. This produced lower sentences but spared victims the ordeal of a court appearance. Overall, the new rules seem to continue to serve old stereotypes. Women's efforts to redefine rape have not been particularly advanced. One reason for this is that they had to face, and try to resolve, a number of contradictions stemming from the fact that they undertook the project of re-appropriating the definition and meaning of rape through the legal channels which are structured and dominated by the very group whose control over this issue they wanted to break. The following discussion attempts to address some of the reasons why these law reforms – based to a significant degree on feminist blueprints – *failed to redefine rape* on women's terms.

For women's organizations, rape became a suitable issue to organize around (Edwards, 1987). To make their mark as a political lobby they had to get involved in the official process of law reform rather than concentrating simply on the process of consciousness raising. To mobilize and demonstrate their power and their distinct interests as women, they excluded men – the very group whose consciousness needed to change. The mass media aggravated this symbolic gender separation by presenting rape completely out of its cultural and structural context and by depicting rape as an emotional issue for women but a legal quandary, and a trap, for men.

By participating in the law reform process, women created the impression of a shared definition of rape (sexual assault). Everyone appeared to agree that rape is a very serious, coercive, usually violent crime, that occurs mainly against women. However, they might all have had in mind quite different images. The prevailing ideology still assumes that a certain measure of domination and coercion is normal for men in sexual relations. This is not shared by an increasingly large number of women who want recognition of their right to sexual autonomy.

The multitiered offence of sexual assault acknowledges the existence of a continuum of sexual coercion. But it would be totally unrealistic to expect any significant changes in law enforcement with respect to sexual assault in dating and marital relationships. Indeed, the unrestricted right of the defence to introduce evidence concerning the victim's past sexual activities with the accused may actually serve as a 'natural' deterrent for women to report this type of sexual abuse. The amendments may, therefore, have the effect of encouraging the reporting and perhaps the prosecution of those rapes which have been traditionally perceived as 'real' rapes (i.e. those involving total strangers, public places and violence: LaFree, 1989; Sebba and Cahan, 1973), rather than those traditionally ignored or considered problematic. Indeed, it has been argued already that 'one of the problems in "proving" rape in a court is that forced or coerced sex are common experiences for women' (Kelly, 1987: 55). Lawmakers and law-enforcers are thus likely to 'endorse' the lines which demarcate uncommon forms of sexual coercion from those practised almost routinely in contemporary societies.

Feminist analysis has demonstrated quite convincingly that sexual violence and the fear of violence constitute an integral part of the social control of women (see, for example, Brownmiller, 1975; Smart and Smart, 1978; Edwards, 1987; Radford, 1987). It also shows that some types of violence have in practice been legitimated by the refusal of the criminal justice system to intervene or through its displacement of blame from the offender to the victim. Indeed, it has been suggested that as long as the state is guided by men's ideologies and interests, it will continue to define 'the limits of violence appropriate for the control of women' (Radford, 1987: 43).

What the women's lobby was allowed to do was to negotiate these limits, but not the principle itself. Indeed, in the aftermath of the law reform, the mass media – fed by the appropriate criminal justice agencies – reinforced the distinction between legitimate and criminal sexual coercion by highlighting cases disqualified by the courts due to the complainants' characteristics or the circumstances of the alleged assaults. They helped create the impression that while some liberties and forms of aggression in sexual relations are justified, or at least excusable, for men, the law reforms and the women's movement created a situation in which no man was safe from accusations by hysterical women. Feminist counter-arguments, while given a certain amount of attention, were unlikely to be as effective as these dramatic court and police stories or the interviews with representatives of the criminal justice system, who drew on their professional experience and exuded authority.

Various studies of convicted rapists and general populations have shown that rape cannot be explained apart from the dominant culture and structure with their well-defined gender roles and power lines. The focus of the women's groups on law reform and the accompanying publicity from the media blurred this connection and reinforced an individualized view of rape. While the feminist campaign gave sexual violence against women new visibility, its legal objectives might have distorted the message.

The fact that the reformed law included many of the suggestions of women's groups has contributed to the impression that gender inequality is a myth: when women care enough about an issue they can exercise considerable influence. Moreover, the legislation, widely depicted as a victory for the women's lobby, symbolically closed the issue and makes it difficult for women to campaign against the conditions which generate rape. The law has been improved and, logically, the task of eradicating sexual assault should now be left to the courts. Thus interest in the issue has dropped dramatically and the anti-rape movement has lost its momentum and focus.

In sum, the range of legal solutions which Canadian women's groups advocated was dictated both by the demands of legal discourse and their mistrust of the legal system. They were not fully effective in lobbying for rape law reform. Some of their postulates were ignored and the reform itself seems to have resulted from the introduction of the Charter of Rights and Freedoms rather than been brought about solely by women's pressures. Their actual impact notwithstanding, the frequent official references to the women's lobby, and the mass media presentation of the new law as a victory for the women's movement, put women on the political map more effectively than any other campaign. This, however, created a backlash, whereby defenders of the gender status quo mobilized their forces to trivialize and block women's attempts to reconstruct the notion of rape and unmask the role of sexualized violence in men's efforts to 'keep women in their place'.

Notes

1 This is an abbreviated version of a longer text. I would like to acknowledge the help of Colleen Gilbert whose research assistance was funded by a grant from the Solicitor General of Canada.
2 Section 143 explicitly states: 'A male person commits rape when he has sexual intercourse with a female person who is not his wife . . .'. In 1978, the Minister of Justice introduced – albeit unsuccessfully – a bill (C–52) that not only proposed to maintain the spousal exemption – with the exception of separated spouses living apart – but recommended its *extension* to all forms of indecent assault.
3 While amendments in 1975 appeared to limit the admissibility of such evidence, the 1980 ruling of the Supreme Court of Canada (*Forsythe* v. *The Queen*) interpreted these amendments as permitting evidence of the past sexual history of the complainant to be used to attack her credibility.

4 According to these amendments no questions could be asked about the sexual conduct of the complainant with a person other than the accused unless notice in writing had been given to the prosecutor and a hearing in camera concluded that the exclusion would prevent a just determination of an issue of fact, including the credibility of the complainant.

5 The new section (s. 246.6) which requires written notice and an in camera hearing permits the inclusion of evidence which rebuts evidence of the complainant's sexual activity (or its absence) adduced by the prosecution. It also permits evidence of sexual activity which took place on the same occasion as the activity named in the charge if it relates to the person who had the sexual contact described in the charge or relates to the issue of consent. The complainant is not a compellable witness at the in camera hearing.

6 For a well-documented pessimistic assessment of this option, see McCann, 1985.

7 For reviews of feminist writings on the issue of formal equality and gender neutrality, see Boyd and Sheehy, 1986; Boyle, 1985: 13–26; Sheehy, 1987.

8 It is difficult to agree with Snider (1985: 343) that 'the thrust . . . of the changes women's groups recommended . . . were liberalizing, a loosening of the net of social control.' While some of the groups did indeed ask for moderation in the upper limits of penalties for sexual assault (only to secure higher conviction rates), they also expressed dismay about the courts' leniency towards offenders and fought against provisions which made it possible (see, for example, Senate of Canada, 27: 17, 1982). Moreover, they reacted very negatively to a proposal to lower the maximum penalty for the offence of 'assault causing bodily harm' and insisted on raising penalties instead (CACSW, 1982: 9; NAWL, 1982b, 1981: 16).

9 In this section some of the results of my research on the reporting of rape and rape law reform by the Canadian press are mentioned, but due to limited space are not elaborated on.

13 When precaution is normal: a feminist critique of crime prevention

Elizabeth Stanko

You realize there's no safe place. I think people who can sort of say, 'well, you know, the deviants out there, you recognize them and they have squinty eyes or whatever and it's only .02 of the population who is degenerate. I think they can operate within a more sense of safety. But I think when you realize it's not those [men], those are only a very small percentage, you know, your brother, and the man at the corner, and your stepfather, all that. That really changes the perception that indeed you really can be safe. There's *degrees* of safety and circumstance, but. . .

(Linda, quoted in Stanko, 1990)

Women's safety in public places has increasingly become a focus for the tabloid press and women's magazines. Police, too, have published pamphlets advising women about routine practices of avoiding danger. *Practical Ways to Crack Crime*, the Home Office (1989) crime prevention booklet, is now in its third edition. Under the section entitled 'Your family' there are three pages devoted to specific strategies to aid women to reduce the risk of victimization. While there is the occasional mention of violent spouses, boyfriends or relatives, the advice from all of these sources emphasizes the potential danger of strangers. However, available evidence from the Home Office itself (for example, Smith 1989a and 1989b), from police statistics (for example, Dobash and Dobash, 1979), and from feminist research (for example, Stanko, 1985; Kelly, 1988) tells us that women should protect themselves from their friends, acquaintances, husbands, boyfriends, relatives and former intimates much more than from the anonymous man.

This chapter examines the conundrum of what is now commonly termed the 'fear of crime': on the one hand, women report levels of fear about personal safety at three times those of men, yet it is men who, as the British Crime Surveys tell us,[1] are the most likely targets of violence (Hough and Mayhew, 1983; Chambers and Tombs, 1984; Gottfredson, 1984; Maxfield, 1984; 1988).[2] On the other hand, the crime prevention literature produced by the police and the Home Office has responded to women's fear by issuing reassuring statements and designing advice documents. And yet, to date, they have not issued advice to young men whom they believe to be most likely to be victimized by violence. Using a radical feminist perspective, I also explore in this chapter the usefulness of crime prevention initiatives which attempt to reduce women's fear of crime and suggest how we might construct a feminist crime prevention strategy.

Women, fear and sexual danger

'Fear of crime' presents a political dilemma. Increasingly, the popular media call for 'safe' streets so that citizens can enjoy the full benefits of community life. Concern for personal safety, they assert, limits full participation in the wider sphere by restricting the use of public space and this affects women more than men. 'Fear of crime', largely a construct of opinion poll researchers and examined by criminologists through the use of large-scale surveys, is typically measured by asking women and men about their perception of safety on neighbourhood streets after dark. Generally, fear of crime is taken to represent individuals' diffuse sense of danger about being physically harmed by violence. It is associated with concern about being outside the home, probably in an urban area, alone and potentially vulnerable to violent crime.

Criminological surveys examine the extent of crime and individuals' concern or fear of it through the legal categories of what constitutes a serious threat to safety. Questions in the British Crime Survey (BCS), for example, asked respondents how worried they were about being burgled, 'mugged' or raped. The local surveys conducted in Merseyside (Kinsey, 1985) and Islington (Jones *et al.*, 1986) widened their inquiry to include street sexual harassment, incidents which are not easily classified as criminal incidents. While the local survey analyses clearly show women are subjected to sexual harassment and wife assault at levels much higher than the BCS found, the overall context of the inquiry focuses on women's experiences during a period of only one year. Women's fear of rape and experiences of sexual indignity are accumulated over a lifetime.

Moreover, what these researchers fail to realize is that women's fear of crime is in reality a fear of sexual danger – a fact well documented by feminist researchers (Gordon and Riger, 1988; Warr, 1984; 1985; Stanko, 1987; 1990). From childhood and throughout adulthood, women learn from both direct and indirect experience that they must protect themselves from various forms of sexual assault, threat and harassment. Kelly (1988) describes this as a continuum of sexual violence. Central to the understanding of this sexual intrusion is the concept of men's power over women's sexuality (MacKinnon, 1982; 1983). On an individual and institutional basis, men's dominance creates the context for sexual violence, maintains the legal and social structures of inquiry about the potential harm and consequences of such violence and forgives the so-called indiscretions of men by defining the majority of instances of men's violence as 'unintentional' (Stanko, 1985).

While initial concerns about sexual danger focused on the malevolence of faceless men, familiar and familial men in women's lives – intimates, acquaintances, authorities and service providers – pose the greatest threat to women's physical and sexual safety (Smith, 1989a). Women's lovers are more dangerous than the stranger on the street. And because many of women's social, educational and economic situations take place primarily within a framework of heterosexuality, they are at risk of violence merely because they are in some form of a relationship with a man. Characterized as the protectors of women from the violence of other men, husbands and boyfriends who are violent rarely meet the wrath of the criminal justice system for their assaultive behaviour.

Women's sexuality thus becomes the linchpin of subordination (MacKinnon, 1987). Feminist researchers have revealed that the more women articulate their experiences of heterosexuality, the more they disclose the common and widespread features of physical and sexual abuse, threats and harassment within their everyday lives (Radford, 1987; Hanmer and Saunders, 1984; McGibbon, Cooper and Kelly, 1989).

The first study of the prevalence of sexual abuse among the general population is now under way and the results of that work will reveal some baseline information about women's lives.[3] However, some information is currently available from other sources. *Elle*'s 1988 survey about personal safety found that, in the past 12 months, over 70 per cent of its respondents reported 'unwelcomed approaches'; almost half (49 per cent) had received obscene phone calls; 45 per cent reported 'threatening behaviour'; two in five (39 per cent) recalled being 'groped'; and one in ten had experienced a physical assault. While this survey is not representative of all women, it reveals the experiences of over 2,100 women. The September 1989 survey published in *Living* explored women's experiences of 'minor' sexual offences. Nearly half of the 1,000 women interviewed had experienced an obscene phone call, had been groped by a stranger or had been flashed at. The 60 in-depth interviews which Kelly (1988) conducted in the mid-1980s also showed the various forms of violence which women experience. Only four of these women did not name sexual harassment as a common experience.

The face of danger, however, remains 'officially' as the stranger because it is extremely difficult to include the fear of known men into criminological knowledge and the legal discourse of serious crime. Because women typically hide experiences of criminal violence from the police and survey researchers alike, much of the violence against women remains hidden from official bodies (Stanko, 1988a and 1988b). While police are publicly attempting to take on board the fact that women experience sexual and physical violence more often from known men, their approach to crime prevention remains firmly focused on increasing women's safety on the street and in the home through vigilance against strangers.

Keeping safe: women's own strategies for safety

As a consequence of their understanding of sexual danger, most women have developed an elaborate set of precautionary strategies which they use in every day life (Gordon and Riger, 1988; Stanko, 1990). How and where they walk, shop, live, and spend leisure time is fused with individual rules for safekeeping. Most women don't simply walk down the street at night – the walk involves being aware of who is on the street, where others are and what their sex is; they assess alternative routes, carry grasped keys and act assertively. Some women sacrifice financial flexibility in order to afford a car so that they do not have to use public transport at night. Women who do not own cars may decide to use taxis after certain times in the evening. Whatever the circumstances, most women negotiate and manage situations to avoid those which they feel are potentially dangerous.

Women also use rules for safety with intimates, friends and co-workers. Women beaten by boyfriends or husbands describe how they 'know' when a beating is imminent and use avoidance tactics to delay the beating as long as possible. Women may cook a particular meal, wear a particular dress or keep the children out of sight to keep the 'peace'. Women sexually harassed at the office devise strategies to minimize the harassment. They may change the way they dress, decline to have lunch with colleagues or request transfers because of the harassment.

Women's strategies for personal safety are continuously adjusted throughout adult life. Direct and indirect experience of violence and danger, together with gathering tips from other women on how they cope with safety and danger and the accumulated advice about safety gleaned from the media, friends, relatives and others merge to inform 'rules of caution'. Women learn to exercise 'common sense' and to take responsibility for their personal safety. They learn, too, that there are sanctions for not being sensible, particularly if they are harmed (Stanko, 1985). They may be blamed for not adequately protecting their safety, particularly their sexual safety.

Although it is impossible to guarantee safety, the manoeuvres which women use in negotiating danger give them a feeling that they can in some ways control the possibility of violence. Bart and O'Brien's (1986) study of rape avoidance, for example, shows that women who managed to avoid rape used two or more tactics of confronting men. They screamed, fought, ran or actively negotiated safety with their attackers. The authors suggest that women should not 'act like ladies' when confronted by intimidating men. What women learn is to try to avoid men's sexual and physical violence through an active, alert demeanour and this posture is used with the men women know as well as with strangers. Indeed, women can already be described as experts in surviving danger (Kelly, 1988). But survival is not without costs: women pay the emotional cost of feeling anger, anxiety and resentment in their relationships with others or in their own assessments of self-worth and personal esteem; incur financial loss through shouldering the expense of transport, locks and bolts, and 'safer' housing; and suffer social isolation because of concern about the dangers of the unknown.

The crime prevention literature assumes that women do not ordinarily take precautions in their daily lives and do not already have elaborate strategies devised to minimize their experiences of men's violence. This is not so and thus we need to ask how useful crime prevention advice is to women and whether it acknowledges women's own knowledge about the sexual dangers in their everyday lives.

Stranger danger: official crime prevention advice

The proliferation of advice literature in the past two years in Britain (and elsewhere) illustrates that the police, local authorities and the Home Office have all read the message of women's fear of crime. The multi-million pound effort by the Crime Prevention Unit, *Practical Ways to Crack Crime* (1989), acknowledges women's high levels of concern about their personal safety. This booklet, and others published by local police forces, aims to reassure women that crimes against them are rare (an assumption that can only be made, as I have made clear, by ignoring violence by known others) and that the proposed precautions *can* (emphasis in the text) reduce the risk of victimization.

Practical Ways to Crack Crime suggests the following precautions. Behaviour at home should include checking the security of one's home; keeping curtains drawn at night; using only initials on the flat or telephone directory to avoid being identified as a woman; calling the police from a neighbour's house if signs of entry are observed; installing a telephone extension in the bedroom; changing the locks when moving into a new dwelling and using them; showing prospective house buyers around with another person present; never giving one's phone number when answering and never saying one is alone in the house; and hanging up on obscene phone callers. While the booklet correctly points out that in most situations of rape the attacker is known to the woman, there is no advice about how to avoid men's violence in the home, especially from husbands, boyfriends or ex-lovers. The pamphlet also assumes that all women have telephones and that all they need is another extension. Many single mothers on a limited income have difficulty purchasing weekly provisions, let alone having the resources for a telephone or an extension.

The pamphlet goes on to suggest ways to ensure safety on the street when on foot. Women are advised to avoid short cuts through 'dimly lit alleys' or waste grounds; to face traffic when walking down the street and to walk on the road side of the pavement 'so that an attacker lurking in an alley has further to come to reach you'; to scream if approached by a car (it is important to note that the advice avoids making it explicit that the danger lies with *the man* in the car) and to run away (noting the registration number and a description of the car at the same time); to refuse rides from strangers and to avoid picking up hitch-hikers; to hide 'expensive looking' jewellery; to take a lift home when out late; to consider carrying a screech alarm ('their piercing noise can frighten off an attacker'); to keep your handbag close to your body; to cross over if you feel you are being followed and, if you are suspicious, to go to a place and call the police (but avoid using a callbox as 'the attacker could trap you inside'); to vary your route when exercising and stick to well-lit roads with pavements (presumably this means jogging on the road side); and to think about taking self-defence courses.

There are additional tips for taking public transport and when driving alone. Women are advised to avoid 'dimly lit bus stops', and to sit near the driver or guard on the train (difficult, indeed, if there are no guards); and to sit near the exit when on a train and in a compartment where there are other 'people' (again, note the avoidance of the mention of *men* as presenting the danger). If driving (and one must assume that they mean when driving alone), the pamphlet suggests that your vehicle should be in good working condition. On your journey you should use 'main roads' and you should have enough petrol and money in case you get lost. You should also have a phone card or spare change available in case you need it (but you should not use a call box because your attacker could trap you). If you do use the phone while on the hard shoulder, keep 'a sharp look out'. Keep your purse and valuables away from windows and lock the doors. Always park in a well-lit, 'preferably' trafficked area, and 'take a moment or two' to look about you before leaving your car. Have the key ready when approaching your car and check to see that there is no one lurking in the car waiting for you. Most, though not all, women I have interviewed already use these strategies as second nature. They do not need to be told.

The third edition of *Practical Ways to Crack Crime* does include a new section which provides advice to men on how to take 'care not to frighten women' so men can help women 'feel safer' in public. Men are reminded that a woman might feel threatened by what they think are 'admiring looks' and are asked to keep their distance from women on their own, especially after dark. The emphasis, therefore, continues to be on men's behaviour in public places rather than in the home.

The *Personal Security Handbook* (Drake, 1987) also devotes space to women's safety. It does point out that over half of all crimes of violence are committed by men known to women, but nevertheless concentrates on giving guidance to protect against the danger presented by strangers. In the special section for women living alone it suggests that women hang up men's clothing when drying their own clothes, presumably to indicate to these 'strange' men lurking behind the clothes line that these women are in the protection of a man who can fend off the stranger. This handbook is even more explicit than the Home Office booklet. It states categorically: 'The primary responsibility for preventing opportunistic crime rests *with you*, and *The Personal Safety Handbook* shows you how you can do it' (1987: 143, my emphasis).

Feeling safer: crime prevention and women's knowledge

These approaches to crime prevention may raise women's fears rather than lessen them, do not take into account women's own knowledge and precautionary strategies, normalize women's concern for personal safety and keep the burden of safety firmly upon individual women's shoulders – formulating a new version of blaming women for their victimization. It is important to ask whether or not it is possible to align crime prevention advice with women's experiences of danger from supposedly 'safe' men and to alert girls and women to the potential danger which they might meet from trusted men.

The stony silence in the crime prevention literature and in the popular press about violence from known men leads to countless dilemmas about how to advise women about safety within the context of women's relationships and interactions with men who are assumed to be safe and, even more ironically, are assumed to be the protectors of women. Advising women about safety is currently necessarily flawed because we have no idea of the extent to which knowledge about the danger posed by familial and familiar men is fear producing.

Are we doing women a service by omitting this thorny contradiction of the danger of known men in the advice literature? I think not. Eileen, a 22-year-old London accountant, was devastated by her rape, and stated:

> I took all the general precautions, like not opening the door, always knowing who was on the other side of the door before opening it, especially at night when there's no people around. All these precautions I took. I didn't expect that somebody I had met two or three times would . . , who had been in my home, who had been invited into my home would do this [rape] to me, after having known him.
>
> (quoted in Stanko, 1990)

To provide women with advice about how to sort out the 'safe' from the 'unsafe' men is an extremely difficult task. Crime prevention advice spotlights the dangers of the outside because it can focus on specific situations where danger could arise and where it might be possible to negotiate a bit more safety. What becomes dangerous is darkness, or a bus stop, or an alley, or a phone box – a place where dangerous men might lurk. There is, of course, a degree of myopia in this. The onus of responsibility for safety, according to traditional advice, is *women's*.

What would happen if the responsibility for the safety of women were to be thrown back to *men* to sort out. Characterizing the problem of women's safety as men's, not women's, responsibility changes the nature of the debate. I use the word 'safety' here and not protection intentionally. Safety implies a level of managing danger from a position of equality. Safety is a positive action. It demands that the seeker of safety is an autonomous individual capable of making positive choices, not having to choose among unpalatable options.

It also means that women do not have to be 'men' to be safer nor do they have to display their 'man' as their protector. 'Protection' demands that women are subordinate to the protector. Protection, after all, can be withdrawn at any time if the target of the protection does not comply with the rules for proper behaviour. Women already know that if they breach notions of respectability (as defined from men's point of view) they will not – and probably should not expect to – receive the benevolent protection of a man, the police, the criminal justice system and so forth. The fact that so many women feel unsafe, change their everyday behaviour because of it or assume that reasonable precautions are the best policy ('better safe than sorry') is a reflection of men's violence, not women's hysteria. And women's feelings of unsafety are not caused by a small band of men hell bent on making all women's lives uncomfortable and, indeed, for far too many, frightening. Typically, women's danger arises within their friendship and kinship relationships with men. While the most recent edition of *Practical Ways to Crack Crime* (1989) acknowledges the need for men to participate in promoting women's safety, it falls short of addressing men's behaviour behind closed doors, the behaviour that is most likely to threaten women's physical and sexual integrity. To promote women's safety, men need to take responsibility for their own and their 'brothers'' behaviour in both private and public spheres.

Official crime prevention cannot and, most likely under the present government, will not confront the power of men in the family. The present stance, reflected in the growing police attention to personal safety and in the crime prevention literature, is one of paternalistic concern, fostering an orientation of protectionism rather than autonomous safety for women. Women are advised to hide the fact that they are women alone, on the street or at home or to adopt a 'siege' mentality when they are in public. While many women already adopt such a stance, taking this further is not a solution to increasing women's safety or to reducing women's fear.

To address the issue of men's violence head on, the issue of men's treatment of wives, lovers, children, co-workers must be at the top of the agenda. Such an approach will set the stage for a collision with ideologies that emphasize the sanctity of the family, men's roles as protectors and, ultimately, the benefits which men receive directly and indirectly through a society founded on women's sexual, economic, political and social subordination; a system which could be termed 'heteropatriarchal'.[4]

Crime prevention from a feminist perspective necessarily includes a direct challenge to men's dominance in all spheres of everyday life. Preventing the victimization of children and women, therefore, entails crime prevention strategies aimed at boys and men. In part, this means challenging traditional notions of masculinity which are so interwoven with women's experiences of threat and victimization. Looking ahead, good crime prevention would demand that all aspects of community life, especially the institutions which might assist women to escape and complain about the violence of men, promote women's economic, sexual and political independence.

We must, if women are ever to feel less threatened, keep our sights on the eventual goal of women's equality. Challenging the institutional and individual foundations of men's power goes hand in hand with creating a climate where safety for women is a possibility. When women are not socially and economically dependent upon men we may find that women are able to leave violent relationships without the devastating social and economic consequences that result when women, primarily responsible for their children, take on the financial burden of caretaking when their options for well-paid waged labour are limited.

What does this mean in the short term? Obviously, we cannot afford to sit back and wait for women to inch their way towards equality. Short-term goals must embrace the support systems for women which confront violence at the hands of familial and familiar men. Thus a feminist crime prevention strategy would include:

1 A policy statement on the right of all citizens to sexual and physical integrity (perhaps in a bill of rights) with powers to sanction violations apart from (or in addition to) criminal sanctions.

2 School curricula which address safety not only as a problem of strangers, but provide children and adolescents with personal strengths and strategies to avoid the dangers of the uncle, the father or the teacher. The national curriculum could include a section on violence modelled after the New Zealand programme *Standing Strong*, which teaches adolescents about wife abuse and sexual integrity. This programme teaches girls about their right to challenge authority in the interests of safety. It also opens up discussions with boys about masculinity, aggression and violence. Such a programme combines both strengthening young women's self-awareness and esteem and confronting the cultural permission granted to young men to dominate women.

3 The full funding of refuges, safe networks, crisis lines, women's centres, advice centres and support systems which provide options for women and children to escape violence.[5] These women's networks should be considered crime prevention networks and given top priority for funding, even if it means diverting funds from other crime prevention efforts.

4 Advertising campaigns which address the commonness of sexual and physical assault among known others and which reach out to provide information about the above support networks. These campaigns should acknowledge women's experiences of violence and validate their present worry about sexual violation without at the same time frightening women. Women are already afraid and do not need fear-producing advertising to convince them to take precautions. Moreover, the campaigns could include components addressed directly at men, modelled along the lines of the drink–driving campaigns, stating that men's behaviour such as unwelcome sexualized comments does frighten and intimidate women and is socially irresponsible within a community concerned with the well-being of all its members. While not all men will immediately alter their behaviour, some men will and others may take a more active role in intervening when men behave inappropriately.

No doubt the claims of women's 'unsafety' have been heard in many different sectors. There are no simple solutions, only solutions which open up the possibility of fundamental changes in women's and men's relationships. It is now crucial that the wider issues of women's experiences of men's violence be taken on board by crime prevention from a feminist perspective. Difficult, yes, but it is not impossible.

Notes

1 The crime surveys carried out in Britain in recent years have their roots in the US President's Commission on Law Enforcement and Administration of Justice which funded a survey of victimization to provide information on the extent of unreported crime and on the risks of crime. This work led to the setting up of the National Crime Survey (NCS) programme which started in 1972 and which continues to the present day. Undoubtedly, it was the NCS which provided the impetus for similar surveys in many other countries, including Britain. There were British surveys on crime funded by Office of Population Censuses and Surveys (OPCS) before the NCS but the more clearly defined focus on victimization did not emerge until the 1970s (see, for example, Bottoms *et al.*, 1987 and Tuck and Southgate, 1981). Indeed, the Home Office took a lead in funding and directing studies in this area. The British Crime Survey is a national survey designed to elicit information on unreported and unrecorded crime. Police statistics of recorded crime are adequate as an indication of police workload, but deficient as an index of crime and as a measure of the fear of crime. At the time of writing, the BCS has carried out three studies, in 1982, 1984 and 1988.

2 Findings from the first sweep of the Survey suggest that the odds of being a victim of violence are much higher for those who are male, under 30-years old, single, widowed or divorced, spend several evenings a week out, drink heavily and assault others (Hough and Mayhew, 1983: 21). On the other hand, Hough and Mayhew (1983) found that a third of the women in their sample, but very few men, said they they sometimes avoided going out after dark. The proportion was even higher for young, middle-aged and old women in inner cities.

3 The research is being conducted under the direction of Dr Liz Kelly, Child Sexual Abuse Studies Unit, Polytechnic of North London.

4 Heteropatriarchy is a term used to signify a system of social relations based on men's dominance in social, political, sexual, and economic systems. The term describes a social context wherein women's sexual relationships with men create and maintain a structure of subordination.

5 As it now stands, many of these centres and refuges are facing closure due to lack of funding and changes in the benefits system by the Department of Social Security.

References

Abercrombie, N., Warde, A., Urry, J., Walby, S. and Soothill, K. (1988). *Contemporary British Society*. Cambridge: Polity.

Acker, S., Barry, K. and Esseveld, J. (1983). 'Objectivity and truth: problems in doing feminist research', *Women's Studies International Forum*, **6**, 4, 423–35.

Adams, D. (1988). 'Treatment models of men who batter: a pro-feminist analysis', in K. Yllö and M. Bograd (eds), *Feminist Perspectives on Wife Abuse*. Beverly Hills, CA: Sage.

Adler, F. (1975). *Sisters in Crime*. New York: McGraw-Hill.

Adler, F. and Simon, R. (eds) (1979). *The Criminology of Deviant Women*. Boston: Houghton Mifflin.

Adler, Z. (1989). 'Prosecuting child sexual abuse: a challenge to the status quo', in M. Maguire and J. Pointing (eds), *Victims of Crime: A New Deal?*. Milton Keynes: Open University Press.

Ahmed, S. (1986). 'Cultural racism with Asian women and girls', in S. Ahmed, J. Cheetham and J. Small (eds), *Social Work with Black Children and their Families*. London: Batsford.

Allen, H. (1987). *Justice Unbalanced: Gender, Psychiatry and Judicial Decisions*. Milton Keynes: Open University Press.

Amos, V. and Parmar, P. (1984). 'Challenging imperial feminism'. *Feminist Review*, 17, 3–19.

Andriesson, M. (1982). 'We moeten de realiteit van vrouwenlevens leren begrijpen: interview met Doris Klein (We must learn to understand the reality of women's lives). *Tijdschrift voor Criminologie*, **24**, 131–44.

Anthias, F. and Davis-Yuval, Y. (1983). 'Contextualising feminism – gender, ethnic and class divisions', *Feminist Review*. 15, 62–77.

Balkan, S., Berger, R. and Schmidt, J. (1982). *Crime and Deviance in America*. Belmont: Wadsworth.

Bankowski, Z., Mungham, G. and Young, P. (1977). 'Radical criminology or radical criminologist?' *Contemporary Crises*, **1**, 1, 37–52.

Barker, H. (1986). 'Recapturing sisterhood: a critical look at "process" in feminist organising and community work', *Critical Social Policy*, 16, 80–90.

Barrett, M. (1980). *Women's Oppression Today*. London: Verso.

Barrett, M. and McIntosh, M. (1982). *The Anti-Social Family*. London: Verso.

Barrett, M. and McIntosh, M. (1985). 'Ethnocentrism and socialist feminist theory', *Feminist Review*, 20, 23–47.

Bart, P. and O'Brien, P. (1986). *Stopping Rape: Successful Survival Strategies*. Oxford: Pergamon.

Bartky, S. (1988). 'Foucault, femininity, and the modernization of patriarchal power', in I.D. Diamond and L.Q. Quinby (eds), *Feminism and Foucault*. Boston: Northeastern University Press.

Bauman, Z. (1988).'Is there a postmodern sociology?', *Theory, Culture and Society*, **5**, 2/3, 217–38.

Becker, H. (1967). 'Whose side are we on?' in H. Becker (ed.), *Sociological Work*. London: Allen Lane.

Becker, H. and Horowitz, I. (1972). 'Radical politics and sociological research', *American Journal of Sociology*, **78**, 1, 48–67.

Beechey, V. and Whitelegg, E. (eds) (1986). *Women in Britain Today*. Milton Keynes: Open University Press.

Bernstein, B. (1977). *Class, Codes and Control*, Vol. 3 *Towards a theory of educational transmissions*. London: Routledge and Kegan Paul.

Bhaskar, R. (1971/1989). *The Possibility of Naturalism*. Brighton: Harvester.

Bhavani, K. and Coulson, M. (1986). 'Transforming socialist feminism: the challenge of racism', *Feminist Review*, 23, 81–91.

Binney, V., Harknell, G. and Nixon, J. (1981). *Leaving Violent Men: A Study of Refuges and Housing for Battered Women*. Leeds: Women's Aid Federation.

Blackburn, R. (1969). 'A brief guide to bourgeois ideology', in A. Cockburn and R. Blackburn (eds), *Student Power: Problems, Diagnosis, Action*. Harmondsworth: Penguin.

Blair, I. (1985). *Investigating Rape: A New Approach for the Police*. London: Croom Helm.

Bleier, R. (ed.) (1988). *Feminist Approaches to Science*. New York: Pergamon.

Borgida, E. (1981). 'Legal reforms and rape laws', in L. Bickman (ed.) *Applied Social Psychology Annual*, Vol. 2. Beverly Hills, CA: Sage.

Borkowski, M., Murch, M. and Walker, V. (1983). *Marital Violence: the Community Response*. London: Tavistock Publications.

Bottomley, K. and Pease, K. (1986). *Crime and Punishment: Interpreting the Data*, Milton Keynes: Open University Press.

Bottoms, A., Mawby, R. and Walker, M. (1987). 'A localised crime survey in contrasting areas of a city', *British Journal of Criminology*, **27**, 125–54.

Bourne, J. (1984). *Towards an Anti-Racist Feminism*. London: Institute of Race Relations.

Bowles, G. and Klein, R. Duelli (eds) (1983). *Theories of Women's Studies*. London: Routledge and Kegan Paul.

Bowker, L. (ed.) (1978). *Women, Crime and the Criminal Justice System*. Lexington: D.C. Heath and Co.

Box, S. (1981). *Deviance, Reality and Society* (second edition). London: Holt, Rinehart and Winston.

Box, S. (1983). *Crime, Power and Mystification*. London: Tavistock.

Box-Grainger, J. (1986). 'Sentencing rapists', in R. Matthews and J. Young (eds), *Confronting Crime*. London: Sage.

Boyd, S. and Sheehy, E. (1986). 'Feminist perspectives on law: Canadian theory and practice', *Canadian Journal of Women and the Law*, **2**, 1, 1–52.

Boyle, C. (1984). *Sexual Assault*. Toronto: The Carswell Co.

Boyle, C. (1985). 'Constitutional implications of reform', in C. Boyle *et al.* (eds), *A Feminist Review of Criminal Law*. Ottawa: Status of Women Canada and Ministry of Supply and Services.

Brants, C. and Kok, E. (1986). 'Penal sanctions as a feminist strategy: a contradiction in terms? Pornography and criminal law in the Netherlands', *International Journal of the Sociology of Law*, **14**, 3/4, 269–86.

Braverman, H. (1974). *Labour and Monopoly Capital*. New York: Monthly Review Press.

Bridges, L. (1983). 'The British Left and law and order', *Sage Race Relations Abstracts*, 8. 1.

Brittan, A. (1989). *Masculinity and Power*. Oxford: Basil Blackwell.

Brittan, A. and Maynard, M. (1984). *Sexism, Racism and Oppression*. Oxford: Basil Blackwell.

Brown, B. (1986). 'Women and crime: the dark figures of criminology', *Economy and Society*, **15**, 3, 355–402.

Brownmiller, S. (1975). *Against Our Will: Men, Women and Rape*. London: Secker and Warburg.

Bryan, B., Dadzie, S. and Scafe, S. (1985). *The Heart of the Race*. London: Virago.

Burstyn, V. and Smith, D. (1985). *Women, Class, Family and State*. Toronto: Garamond.

Cain, M. (1986a). 'Realism, feminism, methodology and law', *International Journal of the Sociology of Law*, **14**, 3/4, 255–67.

Cain, M. (1986b). ' Socio-legal studies and social justice for women', *Australian Law and Sociology Association Conference*. Brisbane: 1986 mimeo.

Cain, M. (1987). 'Realist philosophy, social policy and feminism: on the reclamation of value full knowledge'. Paper presented to the British Sociological Association Annual Conference, Leeds: 1988 mimeo.

Cain, M. (1989). 'Introduction: feminists transgress criminology', in M. Cain (ed.), *Growing Up Good. Policing the Behaviour of Girls in Europe*. London: Sage.

Cain, M. (1990). 'Towards transgression: new directions in feminist criminology', *International Journal of the Sociology of Law*, **18**, 1, 1–18.

Cain, M. and Finch, J. (1981). 'Towards a rehabilitation of data', in P. Abrams (ed.), *Practice and Progress: British Sociology 1950–1980*. London: Allen and Unwin.

Campbell, A. (1981). *Delinquent Girls*. Oxford: Basil Blackwell.

Campbell, B. (1988). *Unofficial Secrets: Child Sexual Abuse – The Cleveland Case*. London: Virago.

Canadian Advisory Council on the Status of Women (CACSW) (1975). *The Web of the Law: A Study of Sexual Offences in the Canadian Criminal Code*. Ottawa: CACSW.

Canadian Advisory Council on the Status of Women (CACSW) (1982). *A New Justice for Women*. Ottawa: CACSW.

Carby, H. (1982). 'White women listen! Black feminism and the boundaries of sisterhood', in *The Empire Strikes Back*. Birmingham Centre for Contemporary Cultural Studies: Hutchinson.

Carlen, P. (1983). *Women's Imprisonment: A Study in Social Control*. London: Routledge.

Carlen, P. (1985). *Criminal Women: Autobiographical Accounts*. Cambridge: Polity.

Carlen, P. (1988). *Women, Crime and Poverty*. Milton Keynes: Open University Press.

Carlen, P. and Worrall, A. (eds) (1987). *Gender, Crime and Justice*. Milton Keynes: Open University Press.

Carr, E.H. (1961). *What Is History?*. Harmondsworth: Penguin.

Carringella–MacDonald, S. (1985). 'Sexual assault prosecution: an examination of model rape legislation in Michigan', in C. Schweber and C. Feinman (eds), *Criminal Justice Politics and Women: The Aftermath of Legally Mandated Change*. New York: The Haworth Press.

Carrington, M. (1989). *Manufacturing Female Delinquency: A Study of Juvenile Justice*. PhD thesis, School of Behavioural Sciences, Macquarie University, Australia.

Carroll, L. (1947/1871). *Through the Looking-Glass*. London: Pan.

Casburn, M. (1979). *Girls will be Girls: Sexism and Juvenile Justice in a London Borough*. London: Women's Research and Resources Centre.

Central Statistical Office (CSO) (1988). *Social Trends*, **18**, London: HMSO.

Chambers, G. and Millar, A. (1983). *Investigating Sexual Assault*. Edinburgh: HMSO, Scottish Office Social Research Study.

Chambers, G. and Tombs, J. (1984). *The British Crime Survey: Scotland*. Edinburgh: HMSO, Scottish Office Social Research Study.

Chappel, D., Geis, R. and Geis, G. (eds) (1977). *Forcible Rape: The Crime, the Victim and the Offender*. New York: Columbia University Press.

Chase, G. (1983). 'An analysis of the new sexual assault laws', *Canadian Women's Studies*, **4**, 4, 53–4.

Chesney-Lind, M. (1973). 'The judicial enforcement of the female sex role: the family court and the delinquent', *Issues in Criminology*, 8, 51–69.

Chesney-Lind, M. (1977). 'The judicial paternalism and the female status offender: training women to know their place', *Crime and Delinquency*, 23, 121–30.

Chesney-Lind, M. (1988). 'Girls and status offenses: is juvenile justice still sexist?', *Criminal Justice Abstracts*, 20, 1, 144–65.

Clark, A. (1982). *The Working Life of Women in the Seventeenth Century*. London: Routledge and Kegan Paul.

Clark, L. and Lewis, D. (1977). *Rape: The Price of Coercive Sexuality*. Toronto: The Women's Press.

Clegg, S. (1975). 'Feminist methodology – fact or fiction', *Quality and Quantity*, **19**, 83–97.

Cloward, R. and Ohlin, L. (1961). *Delinquency and Opportunity: A Theory of Delinquent Gangs*. London: Routledge and Kegan Paul.

Cockburn, C. (1986). *Machineries of Dominance*. London: Pluto.

Cohen, A. K. (1955). *Delinquent Boys: The Culture of the Gang*. New York: Free Press.

Cohen, L. and Blackhouse, C. (1980). 'Desexualizing rape: dissenting view on the proposed rape amendments', *Canadian Women Studies*, **2**, 4, 99–103.

188   References

Cohen, P. (1972). 'Subcultural conflict and working class community', University of Birmingham, Centre for Contemporary Cultural Studies, *Working Papers in Cultural Studies*, 2.

Cohen, S. (1972). *Folk Devils and Moral Panics*. London: Paladin.

Cohen, S. (1981). 'Footprints in the sand: a further report on criminology and the sociology of deviance in Britain', in M. Fitzgerald *et al.* (eds), *Crime and Society: Readings in History and Sociology*. London: Routledge and Kegan Paul.

Cohen, S. (1985). *Visions of Social Control*. Cambridge: Polity.

Comte, A. (1853). *The Positive Philosophy of Auguste Comte*, translated by Harriet Martineau. London: Chapman.

Connell, R. (1985). 'Theorising gender', *Sociology*, **19**, 5, 260–72.

Connell, R. (1987). *Gender and Power*. Cambridge: Polity.

Cook, J. and Fonow, M. (1986). 'Knowledge and women's interests: issues of epistemology and methodology in feminist sociological research', *Sociological Inquiry*, **56**, 1, 2–29.

Coole, D. (1988). *Women in Political Theory: From Ancient Mysogyny to Contemporary Feminism*. Brighton: Wheatsheaf.

Corrigan, P. (1979). *Schooling The Smash Street Kids*. London: Macmillan.

Cousins, M. (1980). ' "Men's rea": a note on sexual differences, criminology and the law', in P. Carlen and M. Collinson (eds), *Radical Issues in Criminology*. Oxford: Martin Robertson.

Criminal Law Revision Committee (1980). *Working Paper on Sexual Offences*. London: HMSO.

Crites, L. (1987). 'Wife abuse: the judicial record', in L. Crites and W. Hepperle (eds), *Women, The Courts, and Equality*. Vol. 11, Women's Policy Studies, London: Sage.

Crow, I. (1987). 'Black people and criminal justice in the UK', *The Howard Journal of Criminal Justice*, **26**, 4, 303–14.

Curtis, L. (1984). *Nothing but the Same Old Story: The Roots of Anti-Irish Racism*. London: Information on Ireland.

Daly, K. (1989). 'Neither conflict nor labeling nor paternalism will suffice: intersections of race, ethnicity and family in criminal court decisions', *Crime and Delinquency*, 35, 136–68.

Daly, K. and Chesney-Lind, M. (1988). 'Feminism and criminology', *Justice Quarterly*, 5, 4, 497–538.

Davis, A. (1981). *Women, Race and Class*. London: Women's Press.

Dawson, T. (1987–88). 'Sexual assault law and past sexual conduct of the primary witness: the construction of relevance', *Canadian Journal of Women and the Law*, 2, 2, 310–44.

De Beauvoir, S. (1972/1949). *The Second Sex*. Harmondsworth: Penguin.

Deleuze, G. (1986). *Foucault*. Minneapolis: Minnesota University Press.

Delphy, C. (1984). *Close To Home*. London: Hutchinson.

Diamond, I. and Quinby, L. (eds) (1988). *Feminism and Foucault*. Boston: Northeastern University Press.

Dixon, V. (1976). 'World views and research methodology', in L. King, V. Dixon and W. Nobles (eds), *African Philosophy: Assumptions and Paradigms for Research on Black Persons*. Los Angeles: Fanon Centre.

Dobash, R. and Dobash, R. (1979). *Violence Against Wives: A Case Against Patriarchy*. New York: Free Press.

Downes, D. (1966). *The Delinquent Solution*. London: Routledge and Kegan Paul.

Downes, D. and Rock, R. (1982). *Understanding Deviance*. Oxford: Oxford University Press.

Downes, D. and Rock, P. (1988). *Understanding Deviance*. Oxford: Clarendon Press.

Drake, A. (1987). *The Personal Security Handbook*. London: Sphere.

Du Bois, B. (1983). 'Passionate scholarship: notes on values, knowing and method in feminist social science', in G. Bowles and R. Duelli Klein (eds), *Theories of Women's Studies*. London: Routledge and Kegan Paul.

Duchen, C. (1986). *Feminism in France*. London: Routledge and Kegan Paul.

Dunning, E., Murphy, P. and Williams, J. (1988). *The Roots of Football Hooliganism*. London: Routledge and Kegan Paul.

Dworkin, A. (1980). 'Pornography and grief', in L. Lederer, *Take Back the Night: Women on Pornography*. Toronto: Bantam.

Dworkin, A. (1981). *Men Possessing Women*. London: Women's Press.

Eagleton, M. (ed.) (1986). *Feminist Literary Theory: A Reader*. Oxford: Basil Blackwell.

Eaton, M. (1986). *Justice for Women? Family, Court and Social Control*. Milton Keynes: Open University Press.

Eckersley, R. (1987). 'Whither the feminist campaign?: an evaluation of feminist critiques of pornography', *International Journal of the Sociology of Law*, **15**, 2, 149–78.

Edwards, A. (1987). 'Male violence in feminist theory: an analysis of the changing conceptions of sex/gender violence and male dominance', in J. Hanmer and M. Maynard (eds), *Women, Violence and Social Control*. London: Macmillan.

Edwards. A. (1989). 'Sex/gender, sexism and criminal justices, some theoretical considerations', *International Journal of the Sociology of Law*, **17**, 2, 165–84.

Edwards, S. (1981). *Female Sexuality and the Law: a Study of Constructs of Female Sexuality as they Inform Statute and Legal Procedure*. London: Sage.

Edwards, S. (1984). *Women on Trial*. Manchester: Manchester University Press.

Edwards, S. (1985). 'A socio-legal evaluation of gender ideologies in domestic violence', *Victimology*, **10**, 186–205.

Edwards, S. (1989a). *An Evaluation of the Metroplitan Police Force Order on Domestic Violence: Report*. London: Police Foundation.

Edwards, S. (1989b). 'Stand by your man', *Police Review*, 19 May, 1016–17.

Edwards, S. (1989c). 'Compelling a reluctant spouse', *New Law Journal*, 19 May, 691–3.

Edwards, S. (1989d). *Policing 'Domestic' Violence: Women, the Law and the State*. London: Sage.

Eichler, M. (1980). *The Double Standard: A Feminist Critique of Feminist Social Science*. London: Croom Helm.

Eichler, M. (1988). *Nonsexist Research Methods: A Practical Guide*. Boston: Allen and Unwin.

Eisenstein, H. (1985). *Contemporary Feminist Thought*. London: Unwin Counterpoint.

Elias, N. (1978). *The History of Manners*. New York: Pantheon.

Elias, N. (1982). *State Formation and Civilization*. Oxford: Basil Blackwell.

Fairweather, E. (1982). 'The law of the jungle in King's Cross', *New Society*, 2 December, 375–7.

Farrington, D. and Morris, A. (1983). 'Sex, sentencing and reconviction', *British Journal of Criminology*, **23**, 3, 229–48.

Fekete, J. (1988). *Life after Postmodernism: Essays on Value and Culture*. London: Macmillan.

Ferguson, A. (1989). *Blood at the Root: Motherhood, Sexuality and Male Dominance*. London: Pandora.

Ferraro, K. (1989). 'The legal response to woman battering in the United States', in J. Hanmer, J. Radford and E. Stanko (eds), *Women, Policing and Male Violence*. London: Routledge.

Feyerabend, P. (1975). *Against Method*. London: New Left Books.

Feyerabend, P. (1978). *Science in a Free Society*. London: New Left Books.

Fine, B. (1984). *Democracy and the Rule of Law*. London: Pluto Press.

Finkelhor, D. (1986). *Child Sexual Abuse: New Theory and Research*. New York: Free Press.

Finkelhor, D., Gelles, R., Hotaling, G. and Straus, M. (eds) (1983). *The Dark Side of Families: Current Family Violence Research*. Beverly Hills, CA: Sage.

Firestone, S. (1981). *The Dialectic of Sex*. London: Jonathan Cape.

Fitzgerald, M. *et al.* (eds) (1981). *Crime and Society: Readings in History and Sociology*. London: Routledge and Kegan Paul.

Foucault, M. (1971). *Madness and Civilization: a History of Insanity in the Age of Reason*. London: Tavistock.

Foucault, M. (1973). *The Order of Things*. New York: Vintage Books.

Foucault, M. (1977). *Discipline and Punish: the Birth of the Prison*. London: Allen Lane.

Foucault, M. (1978). *The History of Sexuality*, vol. 1. New York: Vintage.

Foucault, M. (1980). *Power/Knowledge*, C. Gordon (ed.). New York: Pantheon.

Foucault, M. (1985). *The Use of Pleasure*. New York: Pantheon.

Foucault, M. (1988a). 'The ethic of care for the self as a practice of freedom', in J. Bernauer and D. Rasmussen (eds), *The Final Foucault*. Cambridge, MA: MIT Press.

Foucault, M. (1988b). *Politics, Philosophy, Culture*, L. Kritzman (ed.). London: Routledge.

Fraser, N. and Nicholson, L. (1988). 'Social criticism without philosophy: an encounter between feminism and postmodernism'. *Theory, Culture and Society*, **5**, 2/3, 373–94.

Freeman, M. (1980). 'Violence against women: does the legal system provide solutions or itself constitute the problem?', *British Journal of Law and Society*, **7**, 215–41.

Fudge, J. (1989). 'The effect of entrenching a Bill of Rights upon political discourse: feminist demands and sexual violence in Canada', *International Journal of the Sociology of Law*, **17**, 4, 445–463.

Gayford, J. (1975). 'Wife battering: a preliminary survey of 100 cases', *British Medical Journal*, January, 194–7.

Gayford, J. (1976). 'Ten types of battered wives', *Welfare Officer*, **25**, 1, 5–9.

Gayford, J. (1978) 'Battered wives', in J. Martin (ed.), *Violence in the Family*. Chichester: John Wiley.

Gelles, R. (1983). 'An exchange/social control theory', in D. Finkelhor *et al.* (eds), *The Dark Side of Families: Current Family Violence Research*. Beverly Hills, CA: Sage.

Gelles, R. and Cornell, C. (1985). *Intimate Violence in Families*. Beverly Hills, CA: Sage.

Gelsthorpe, L. (1985a). *Gender Issues in Juvenile Justice*. An Annotated Bibliography. Lancaster: Lancaster Information Systems.

Gelsthorpe, L. (1985b). *Girls, Crime and Justice*. Lancaster: Lancaster Information Systems (Audiocassette).

Gelsthorpe, L. (1986). 'Towards a sceptical look at sexism', *International Journal of the Sociology of Law*, **14**, 2, 125–52.

Gelsthorpe, L. (1989). *Sexism and the Female Offender*. Aldershot: Gower.

Gelsthorpe, L., Giller, H. and Tutt, N. (1989). *The Impact of the Crown Prosecution Service: Report*. Lancaster: University of Lancaster.

Gelsthorpe, L. and Giller, H. (1990). 'More justice for juveniles: does more mean better?', *Criminal Law Review*, March, 153–64.

Gelsthorpe, L. and Morris, A. (1988). 'Feminism and criminology in Britain', in P. Rock (ed.), *A History of British Criminology*. Oxford: Clarendon Press.

Giddens, A. (ed.) (1974). *Positivism and Sociology*. London: Heinemann.

Giddens, A. (1979). *Central Problems in Social Theory*. London: Macmillan.

Giddens, A. (1984). *The Constitution of Society*. Cambridge: Polity.

Gill, O. (1977). *Luke Street*. London: Macmillan.

Giller, H. and Morris, A. (1981). *Care and Discretion*. London: Burnett.

Giller, H. and Tutt, N. (1987). 'Police cautioning of juveniles: the continuing practice of diversity', *Criminal Law Review*, June, 367–74.

Gilligan, C. (1982). *In a Different Voice*. London: Harvard University Press.

Gilroy, P. (1982). 'The myth of black criminality', in M. Eve and D. Musson (eds), *The Socialist Register*. London: Merlin Press.

Gilroy, P. (1987). *There Ain't No Black in the Union Jack: The Cultural Politics of Race and Nation*. London: Hutchinson.

Glaser, B. and Strauss, A. (1967). *The Discovery of Grounded Theory: Strategies for Quantitative Research*. Chicago: Aldine.

Goldsmith Kasinsky, R. (1978). 'Rape: the social control of women', in W. Greenaway and S. Brinckley (eds), *Law and Social Control in Canada*. Scarborough: Prentice Hall.

Gordon, M. and Riger, S. (1988). *The Female Fear*. London: Macmillan.

Gottfredson, M. (1984). *Victims of Crime: Dimensions Of Risk*. London: HMSO, Home Office Research Study No. 81.

Gouldner, A. (1970). *The Coming Crisis of Western Sociology*. London: Heinemann.

Gramsci, A. (1972). *Selections from the Prison Notebooks*. London: Lawrence and Wishart.

Greater London Council (GLC) (1985). *Women's Imprisonment: Breaking the Silence*. London: Women's Equality Unit and Strategic Policy Unit.

Greenberg, D. (1988). *The Construction of Homosexuality*. Chicago: Chicago University Press.

Greenwood, V. (1981). 'The myth of female crime' in A. Morris and L. Gelsthorpe (eds), *Women and Crime*. Cambridge: Institute of Criminology.

Gregory, J. (1986). 'Sex, class and crime: towards a non-sexist criminology', in R. Matthews and J. Young (eds), *Confronting Crime*. London: Sage.

Griffin, C. (1985). *Typical Girls*. London: Routledge and Kegan Paul.

Griffin, S. (1981). *Pornography and Silence*. London: The Women's Press.

Gross, M. and Averill, M. (1983). 'Evolution and patriarchal myths of scarcity and competition', in S. Harding and M. Hintikka (eds), *Discovering Reality*. Dordrecht: D. Reidel.

Hall, R. (1985). *Ask Any Woman: A London Enquiry into Rape and Sexual Assault: Report of the Woman's Safety Survey Conducted by Women Against Rape*. Bristol: Falling Wall Press.

Hall, S., Critcher, C., Jefferson, T., Clarke, J. and Roberts, B. (1978). *Policing the Crisis: Mugging, the State and Law and Order*. London: Macmillan.

Hall, S. and Jefferson, T. (eds) (1976). *Resistance Through Rituals*. London: Hutchinson.

Hanmer, J. and Maynard, M. (1987). *Women, Violence and Social Control*, London: Macmillan.

Hanmer, J., Radford, J. and Stanko, E. (1989). *Women, Policing and Male Violence: International Perspectives*. London: Routledge.

Hanmer, J. and Saunders, S. (1984). *Well Founded Fear: A Community Study of Violence to Women*. London: Hutchinson in association with the Explorations in Feminism Collective.

Harding, S. (1983a). 'Why has the sex–gender structure become visible only now?', in S. Harding and M. Hintikka (eds), *Discovering Reality*. Dordrecht: D. Reidel.

Harding, S. (1983b). 'Common causes: toward a reflexive feminist theory'. *Women and Politics*, 3, 4, pp. 27–42.

Harding, S. (ed.) (1986). *The Science Question In Feminism*. Milton Keynes: Open University Press.

Harding, S. (ed.) (1987). *Feminism and Methodology*. Milton Keynes: Open University Press.

Harding, S. and Hintikka, M. (eds) (1983). *Discovering Reality*. Dordrecht: D. Reidel.

Hartmann, H. (1979). 'The unhappy marriage of Marxism and feminism: towards a more progressive union', *Capital and Class*, 8, 1–33.

Hartsock, N. (1983). 'The feminist standpoint: developing the ground for a specifically feminist historical materialism', in S. Harding and M. Hintikka (eds), *Discovering Reality*. Boston: D. Reidel.

Hearn, J. (1987). *The Gender of Oppression: Men, Masculinity and the Critique of Marxism*. Brighton: Wheatsheaf.

Hebdige, D. (1979). *Subculture: The Meaning of Style*. London: Methuen.

Heidensohn, F. (1968). 'The deviance of women: a critique and an enquiry', *British Journal of Sociology*, 19, 160–75.

Heidensohn, F. (1985). *Women and Crime*. Basingstoke: Macmillan.

Heidensohn, F. (1987). 'Women and crime: questions for criminology', in P. Carlen and A. Worrall (eds), *Gender, Crime and Justice*. Milton Keynes: Open University Press.

Hillyard, P. (1987). 'The normalisation of special powers: from Northern Ireland to Britain', in P. Scraton (ed.), *Law, Order and the Authoritarian State: Readings in Critical Criminology*. Milton Keynes: Open University Press.

Hindelang, M. and Davis, B. (1977). 'Forcible rape in the United States: a statistical profile', in D. Chappell, R. Geis and G. Geis (eds), *Forcible Rape: The Crime, the Victim and the Offender*. New York: Columbia University.

Hirst, P. (1975). 'Marx and Engels on law, crime and morality', in I. Taylor *et al.* (eds), *Critical Criminology*. London: Routledge and Kegan Paul.

Hirst, P. (1976). *Social Evolution and Sociological Categories*. London: Allen and Unwin.

Home Office (1989). *Practical Ways To Crack Crime*. London: HMSO.

hooks, b. (1982). *Ain't I A Woman: Black Women and Feminism*. London: The Women's Press.

hooks, b. (1984). *Feminist Theory: From Margin to Centre*. Boston: South End Press.

hooks, b. (1989). *Talking Black: Thinking Feminist, Thinking Black*. London: Sheba Feminist Publications.

Horley, S. (1988). *Love and Pain*. London: Bedford Square Press.

Horney, J. and Spohn, C. (1987). 'The impact of rape reform legislation', paper presented at the Annual Meeting of the American Society of Criminology: Montreal.

Hough, M. and Mayhew, P. (1983). *The British Crime Survey: First Report*. London: HMSO, Home Office Research Study No. 76.

Hough, M. and Mayhew, P. (1985). *Taking Account of Crime: Key Findings from the 1984 British Crime Survey*. London: HMSO, Home Office Research Study No. 85.

Hudson, A. (1985). 'Feminism and social work: resistance or dialogue?', *British Journal of Social Work*, **15**, 635–55.

Hudson, A. (1989). ' "Troublesome girls": towards alternative strategies and policies', in M. Cain (ed.), *Growing Up Good: The Policing of Girls in Europe*. London: Sage.

Hudson, A. (forthcoming). *'Troublesome Girls': Adolescence, Femininity and the State*. Basingstoke: Macmillan.

Hudson, B. (1985). 'Sugar and spice and all things nice', *Community Care*, 4 April, 14–17.

Hull, G., Scott, P. and Smith, B. (1982). *All the Women are White, All the Blacks are Men: But Some of Us Are Brave*. New York: The Feminist Press.

Hunt, A. (1986). 'Use of quantitative methods in researching issues which affect women', *Methodological Issues in Gender Research*, 10, 12–19.

Hutter, B. and Williams, G. (eds) (1981). *Controlling Women: The Normal and the Deviant*. London: Croom Helm in association with Oxford University Women's Studies Committee.

Inglis, A. (1975). *The White Woman's Protection Ordinance Act: Sexual Anxiety and Politics in Papua*. Brighton: University of Sussex Press.

Itzin, C. (1984). 'You can't do it like that: the conflict between feminist methodology and academic criteria for research on women and ageing', in O. Butler (ed.), *Feminist Experience in Feminist Research*. Manchester: Manchester University, Department of Sociology, Studies in Sexual Politics No. 2.

Jaggar, A. (1983a). 'Feminist politics and epistemology: justifying feminist theory', in A. Jaggar (ed.), *Feminist Politics and Human Nature*. Brighton: Harvester.

Jaggar, A. (ed.) (1983b). *Feminist Politics and Human Nature*. Brighton: Harvester.

Jardine, A. (1985). *Gynesis*. London: Cornell University Press.

Jayaratne, T. Epstein (1983). 'The value of quantitative methodology for feminist research', in G. Bowles and R. Duelli Klein (eds), *Theories of Women's Studies*. London: Routledge and Kegan Paul.

Jessop, B. (1982). *The Capitalist State*. Oxford: Martin Robertson.

Jones, T., MacLean, B. and Young, J. (1986). *The Islington Crime Survey*. Aldershot: Gower.

Joseph, G. (1981). 'The incompatible menage à trois: Marxism, feminism and racism', in L. Sargent (ed.), *Women and Revolution*. Boston: South End Press.

Kay, C. (1985). *At the palace: work, ethnicity and gender in a Chinese restaurant*. Manchester: Manchester University Press, Department of Sociology, Studies in Sexual Politics No. 3.

Keat, R. and Urry, J. (1975). *Social Theory as Science*. London: Routledge and Kegan Paul.

Keller, E. Fox (1980) 'Feminist critique of science: a forward or backward move?' *Fundamenta Scientiae*, **1**, 341–9.

Kellner, D. (1988). 'Postmodernism as social theory: some challenges and problems', *Theory, Culture and Society*, **5**, 2/3, 239–70.

Kelly, A. (1978). 'Feminism and research', *Women's Studies International Quarterly*, **1**, 225–32.

Kelly, L. (1987). 'The continuum of sexual violence', in J. Hanmer and M. Maynard (eds), *Women, Violence and Social Control*. London: Macmillan.

Kelly, L. (1988). *Surviving Sexual Violence*. Cambridge: Polity.

Kelly, L. and Radford, J. (1987). 'The problem of men: feminist perspectives on sexual violence', in P. Scraton (ed.), *Law, Order and the Authoritarian State: Readings in Critical Criminology*. Milton Keynes: Open University Press.

Kenney, S.J. (1986). 'Reproductive hazards in the workplace: the law and sexual difference', *International Journal of the Sociology of Law*, **14**, 3/4, 393–44.

Keohane, N., Rosaldo, M. and Gelpi, B. (eds) (1982). *Feminist Theory: A Critique of Ideology*. Brighton: Harvester Press.

Kerfoot, M. (1988). 'Deliberate self-poisoning in childhood and early adolescence', *Journal of Child Psychology and Psychiatry*, **219**, 3, 335–43.

Kerruish, V. (forthcoming). *Jurisprudence as Ideology*. London: Routledge.

Kersten, J. (1989). 'The institutional control of girls and boys: toward a gender specific approach', in M. Cain (ed.), *Growing Up Good*. London: Sage.

King, R. and McDermott, K. (1989). 'British prisons, 1970–1987: the ever-deepening crisis', *British Journal of Criminology*, **29**, 2, 107–28.

Kingdom, E. (1981). 'Sexist bias and law', in *Politics and Power*, 3. Edited Collection. London: Routledge and Kegan Paul.

Kinsey, R. (1985). *The Merseyside Crime and Police Survey*. Liverpool: Merseyside Metropolitan Council.

Kinsey, R. and Young, J. (1982). 'Police autonomy and the politics of discretion', in D. Cowell *et al.* (eds), *Policing the Riots*. London: Junction.

Kinsey, R. *et al.* (1986). *Losing the Fight Against Crime*. Oxford: Basil Blackwell.

Kleiber, N. and Light, L. (1978). *Caring for Ourselves*. Vancouver: University of British Columbia.

Klein, D. and Kress, J. (1976). 'Any woman's blues: a critical overview of women, crime and the criminal justice system', *Crime and Social Justice*, 5, 34–49.

Klein, R. Duelli (1983). 'How to do what we want to do: thoughts about feminist methodology', in G. Bowles and R. Duelli Klein (eds), *Theories of Women's Studies*. London: Routledge and Kegan Paul.

LaFree, G. (1989). *Rape and Criminal Justice: The Social Construction of Sexual Assault*. Belmont, CA: Wadsworth.

Lahey, K. (1985). '. . . until women themselves have told all that they have to tell. . .' *Osgoode Hall Law Journal*, **23**, 3, 519–41.

Law Commission (1989). *Criminal Law. A Criminal Code for England and Wales. Vol. 1: Report and Draft Criminal Code Bill*. London: HMSO, Law Commission No. 177.

Lea, J. and Young, J. (1982). 'The riots in Britain 1981: urban violence and political marginalisation', in D. Cowell *et al*. (eds), *Policing the Riots*. London: Junction.

Lea, J. and Young, J. (1984). *What is to be Done About Law and Order*. Harmondsworth: Penguin.

Lees, S. (1986) *Losing Out: Sexuality and Adolescent Girls*. London: Hutchinson.

Legal Aid Committee (1985). *Essays on Law and Society*. Kampala: Sapoba Bookshop Press.

LeGrand, C. (1973). 'Rape and rape laws: sexism in society and law', *California Law Review*, **61**, 919–41.

Leonard, E. (1982). *Women, Crime and Society: A Critique of Criminology Theory*. New York: Longman.

Lerner, G. (1986). *The Creation of Patriarchy*. New York: Oxford University Press.

Lewis, D. (1977). 'Black women offenders and criminal justice: some theoretical considerations', in M. Warren (ed.), *Comparing Male and Female Offenders*. Beverly Hills, CA: Sage.

Loh, W. (1980). 'The impact of common law and rape reform statutes on prosecution: an empirical study', *Washington Law Review*, **55**, 506–43.

Lombroso, C. and Ferrero, W. (1980/1895). *The Female Offender*. New York: Fisher Unwin.

Lombroso, C. (1911). *Crime: Its Causes and Remedies*. Boston: Little Brown.

London Rape Crisis Centre (1984). *Sexual Violence: The Reality For Women*. London: The Women's Press.

Lyotard, J. (1986). *The Postmodern Condition*. Manchester: Manchester University Press.

Macdonald, D. (1982). *The Evolution of Bill C-127*. Prepared for the Standing Committee on Legal and Constitutional Affairs, Ottawa, Library of Parliament.

MacKinnon, C. (1982). 'Feminism, Marxism, method and the state: an agenda for theory', *Signs*, **7**, 3, 515–44.

MacKinnon, C. (1983). 'Feminism, Marxism, method and the state: toward feminist jurisprudence', *Signs*, **8**, 4, 635–58.

MacKinnon, C. (1987). *Feminism Unmodified: Discourses on Life and Law*. Cambridge, MA: Harvard University Press.

Maguire, P. (1987). *Doing Participatory Research: A Feminist Approach*. Centre for International Education, Amherst.

Mair, G. (1986). 'Ethnic minorities, probation and the Magistrates' Courts', *British Journal of Criminology*, **26**, 2, 147–55.

Malson, M. (1983). 'Black women's sex roles: the social context for a new ideology', *Journal of Social Issues*, **39**, 3, 101–13.

Mama, A. (1984). 'Black women, the economic crisis and the British State', *Feminist Review*, 17, 20–35.

Manchershaw, A. (1988). *A Study of Sexual Abuse in Women Attending a General Practice: Prevalance, Disclosure and Psychological Adjustment*, unpublished research dissertation.

Mandaraka-Sheppard, A. (1986). *The Dynamics of Aggression in Women's Prisons in England*. Aldershot: Gower.

Marsh, C. (1982). *The Survey Method*. London: Allen and Unwin.

Marshall, P. (1988). 'Sexual assault, the Charter and sentencing reform'. Toronto, Metro Action Committee on Public Violence Against Women and Children, a paper presented to a conference of the Society for the Reform of the Criminal Law in Common-Law Jurisdictions, Ottawa, August 1988.

Matthews, R. and Young, J. (eds) (1986). *Confronting Crime*. London: Sage.

Matza, D. (1964). *Delinquency and Drift*. New York: John Wiley.

Matza, D. (1969). *Becoming Deviant*. Englewood Cliffs, NJ: Prentice Hall.

Maxfield, M. (1984). *Fear of Crime in England and Wales*. London: HMSO, Home Office Research Study No. 78.

Maxfield, M. (1988). *Explaining Fear of Crime: Evidence from the 1984 British Crime Survey*. London: HMSO, Home Office Research and Planning Unit Paper No. 43.

Mayhew, P., Elliott, D. and Dowds, L. (1989). *The 1988 British Crime Survey*. London: HMSO, Home Office Research Study No. 111.

Mays, J. (1954). *Growing Up in the City*. Liverpool: Liverpool University Press.

Mays, J. (1967). *Crime and the Social Structure*. London: Faber and Faber.

McCann, K. (1985). 'Battered women and the law: the limits of the legislation', in J. Brophy and C. Smart (eds), *Women-In-Law: Explorations in Law, Family and Sexuality*. London: Routledge and Kegan Paul.

McConville, M. and Baldwin, J. (1982). 'The influence of race on sentencing in England', *Criminal Law Review*, October, 652–8.

McGibbon, A., Cooper, L. and Kelly, L. (1989). *'What Support': Hammersmith and Fulham Community Police Committee Domestic Violence Project*. London: Hammersmith and Fulham Community Police Committee.

McRobbie, A. (1982). 'The politics of feminist research: between the talk, text and action', *Feminist Review*, 12, 46–57.

Meese Report, United States, Department of Justice (1988). *Attorney General's Commission On Pornography Final Report*, 2 vols. Washington DC: US Government Printing Office.

Messerschmidt, J. (1987). *Capitalism, Patriarchy and Crime*. Totowa: Rowan and Littlefield.

Midgley, M. (1988). 'On not being afraid of natural sex differences', in M. Griffiths and M. Whitford (eds), *Feminist Perspectives in Philosophy*. London: Macmillan.

Mies, M. (1983). 'Towards a methodology for feminist research', in G. Bowles and R. Duelli Klein (eds), *Theories of Women's Studies*. London: Routledge and Kegan Paul.

Mies, M. (1986). *Patriarchy and Accumulation on a World Scale*. London: Zed.

Millett, K. (1970). *Sexual Politics*. London: Jonathan Cape.

Minch, C. and Linden, R. (1987). 'Attrition in the processing of rape cases', *Canadian Journal of Criminology*, 29, 389–419.

Mitchell, J. and Oakley, A. (eds) (1986). *What is feminism?*. Oxford: Basil Blackwell.

Moi, T. (1985). *Sexual/Textual Politics*. London: Routledge.

Morash, M. (1986). 'Wife battering', *Criminal Justice Abstracts*, June, 252–71.

Morgan, D. (1981). 'Men, masculinity and the process of sociological enquiry', in H. Roberts (ed.), *Doing Feminist Research*. London: Routledge and Kegan Paul.

Morgan, R. (ed.) (1986). *Sisterhood is Global*. Harmondsworth: Penguin.

Morris, A. (1987). *Women, Crime and Criminal Justice*. Oxford: Basil Blackwell.

Morris, A. and Giller, H. (1987). *Understanding Juvenile Justice*. London: Croom Helm.

Morris, M. (1988). 'The pirate's fiancees: feminists and philosophers or maybe tonight it'll happen', in I. Diamond and L. Quinby (eds), *Feminism and Foucault*. Boston: Northeastern University Press.

Mort, F. (1987). *Dangerous Sexualities: Medico-Moral Politics in England Since 1830*. London: Routledge and Kegan Paul.

Mountain, A. (1988). *Womanpower*. Leicester: National Youth Bureau.

NACRO (1989). *Some Facts and Figures about Black People in the Criminal Justice System*. London: National Association for the Care and Resettlement of Offenders, Briefing Paper.

Naffine, A. (1985). 'The masculinity–femininity hypothesis', *British Journal of Sociology*, **25**, 4, 365–81.

Naffine, A. (1987). *Female Crime: The Construction of Women in Criminology*. London: Allen and Unwin.

National Association of Women and the Law (NAWL) (1979). *Recommendations on Sexual Assault Offences*. Ottawa: NAWL.

NAWL (1981). *A New Image for Sexual Offences in the Criminal Code. A Brief Response to Bill C-53*. Ottawa: NAWL.

NAWL (1982a). *Comments to Bill C-53*. Ottawa: NAWL.

NAWL (1982b). *Statement by the NAWL to the House of Commons Standing Committee on Justice and Legal Affairs re Bill C-53*. Ottawa: NAWL.

Nelken, D. (1987). 'Critical criminal law', *Journal of Law and Society*, **14**, 1, 105–17.

Nye, R. (1976). 'Heredity or milieu: the foundations of modern European criminological theory', *Isis*, **67**, 335–55.

Oakley, A. (1981). 'Interviewing women: a contradiction in terms', in H. Roberts (ed.), *Doing Feminist Research*. London: Routledge and Kegan Paul.

O'Brien, M. (1981). *The Politics of Reproduction*. London: Routledge and Kegan Paul.

O'Donovan, K. (1985). *Sexual Divisions in Law*. London: Weidenfeld and Nicolson.

O'Dwyer, J. and Carlen, P. (1985). 'Surviving Holloway and other women's prisons', in Carlen, P. (ed.), *Criminal Women*. Cambridge: Polity.

O'Dwyer, J., Wilson, J. and Carlen, P. (1987). 'Women's imprisonment in England, Wales and Scotland: recurring issues', in P. Carlen and A. Worrall (eds), *Gender, Crime And Justice*. Milton Keynes: Open University Press.

Ohlin, L. and Tonry, M. (eds) (1989). *Family Violence: Crime and Justice, A Review of Research*, Vol 11. Chicago: University of Chicago Press.

Parker, H. (1974). *View from the Boys*. Newton Abbot: David & Charles.

Pateman, C. (1988). *The Sexual Contract*. Stanford, CA: Stanford University Press.

Patrick, J. (1973). *A Glasgow Gang Observed*. London: Methuen.

Pattullo, P. (1983). *Judging Women*. London: National Council for Civil Liberties, Rights for Women Unit.

Pearson, G. (1975). *The Deviant Imagination*. London: Macmillan.

Pinchbeck, I. (1981). *Women Workers and the Industrial Revolution*. London: Virago.

Pitch, T. (1985). 'Critical criminology: the construction of social problems and the question of rape', *International Journal of the Sociology of Law*, **13**, 1, 35–46.

Pizzey, E. (1974). *Scream Quietly or the Neighbours Will Hear*. Harmondsworth: Penguin.

Pizzey, E. and Shapiro, J. (1981). 'Choosing a violent relationship', *New Society*, 23 April, 133.

Pizzey, E. and Shapiro, J. (1982). *Prone to Violence*. London: Hamlyn.

Poland, F. (1985). *Breaking the Rules*. Manchester: University of Manchester, Department of Sociology, Studies in Sexual Politics No. 4.

Polk, K. (1985). 'Rape reform and criminal justice processing', *Crime and Delinquency*, **31**, 2, 191–205.

Pollak, O. (1961). *The Criminality of Women*. New York: A.S. Barnes.

Popper, K. (1963). *Conjectures and Refutations: Growth of Scientific Knowledge*. London: Routledge and Kegan Paul.

Pym, L. and Lines, P. (1987). *Report on the Birmingham Court Social Inquiry Report Monitoring Exercise*. Birmingham: West Midlands Probation Service.

Radford, J. (1987). 'Policing male violence, policing women', in J. Hanmer and M. Maynard (eds), *Women, Violence and Social Control*. London: Macmillan.

Ramazanoglu, C. (1986). 'Ethnocentrism and socialist feminist theory: a response to Barrett and McIntosh', *Feminist Review*, 22, 83–91.

Rapoport, R. and Rapoport, R. (1976). *Dual Career Families Re-examined*. London: Martin Robertson.

Rawls, J. (1972). *A Theory of Justice*. Cambridge: Belknap Press.

Reich, W. (1975). *The Mass Psychology of Fascism*. Harmondsworth: Penguin.

Reinharz, S. (1979). *On Becoming a Social Scientist: From Survey Research and Participant Observation to Experiential Analysis*. San Francisco: Jossey-Bass.

Renner, K. and Sahjpaul, S. (1986). 'The new sexual assault law: what has been its effect?', *Canadian Journal of Criminology*, **28**, 4, 407–13.

rhodes, d. and McNeill, S. (eds) (1985). *Women Against Violence Against Women*. London: Onlywomen Press.

Rich, A. (1977). *Of Women Born*. London: Virago.

Riley, K. (1981). 'Black girls speak for themselves', *Multi-racial Education*, **10**, 3, 3–12.

Roberts, H. (ed.) (1981). *Doing Feminist Research*. London: Routledge and Kegan Paul.

Roberts, N. (1986). *The Front Line*. London: Grafton.

Robins, D. and Cohen, P. (1979). *Knuckle Sandwich: Growing Up in a Working Class City*. Harmondsworth: Penguin.

Rock, P. (ed.) (1988). *A History of British Criminology*. Oxford: Clarendon Press.

Rorty, B. (1985). 'Habermas and Lyotard on postmodernity', in R. Bernstein (ed.), *Habermas and Modernity*. Cambridge: Polity Press.

Rose, G. (1988). 'Architecture to philosophy – the postmodern complicity', *Theory, Culture and Society*, **5**, 2/3, 357–72.

Rosewater, L. (1988). 'Battered or schizophrenic? Psychological tests can't tell', in K. Ylló and M. Bograd (eds), *Feminist Perspectives on Wife Abuse*. Beverly Hills, CA: Sage.

Rousseau, J.-J. (1979/1762). *Emile or On Education*. New York: Basic.

Rowbotham, S., Segal, L. and Wainwright, H. (1979). *Beyond the Fragments: Feminism and the Making of Socialism*. London: Merlin Press.

Roy, M. (1977). *Battered Women*, New York: Van Nostrand Reinhold.

Roy, M. (1982). 'Four thousand partners in violence: a trend analysis', in M. Roy (ed.), *The Abusive Partner*. New York: Van Nostrand Reinhold.

Russell, D. (1982). *Rape in Marriage*. New York: Collier Macmillan.

Russell, W. (1988). *Shirley Valentine*. London: Methuen.

Rutherford, J. (1988). 'Who's that man', in R. Chapman and J. Rutherford (eds), *Male Order*. London: Lawrence and Wishart.

Sa'adawi, N. (1980). *The Hidden Face of Eve: Women in the Arab World*. London: Zed Press.

Sachs, A. and Wilson, J. (1978). *Sexism and the Law: A Study of Male Beliefs and Social Bias*. Oxford: Martin Robertson.

Schwartz, M. and Clear, T. (1980). 'Toward a new law on rape', *Crime and Delinquency*, **26**, 2, 129–51.

Schwendinger, J. and Schwendinger, H. (1982).'Rape, the law and private property', *Crime and Delinquency*, **28**, 2, 171–91.

Scraton, S. (1987a). 'Ideologies of the physical and the politics of sexuality', in S. Walker and L. Barton (eds), *Changing Policies, Changing Teachers*. Milton Keynes: Open University Press.

Scraton, S. (1987b).'Boys muscle in where angels fear to tread', in J. Horne *et al.* (eds), *Sport, Leisure and Social Relations*, London: Routledge and Kegan Paul.

Sebba, L. and Cahan, S. (1973). 'Sex offences: the genuine and the doubted victim', in I. Drapkin and E. Viano (eds), *Victimology: A New Focus*, Vol. 5. Lexington: D.C. Heath.

Segal, L. (1987). *Is the Future Female? Troubled Thoughts on Contemporary Feminism*. London: Virago.

Senate of Canada (1982). Legal and Constitutional Affairs Standing Committee. Minutes of Proceedings, Queen's Printer for Canada.

Shaw, M. (1972). 'The coming crisis of radical sociology', in R. Blackburn (ed.), *Ideology in Social Science: Readings in Critical Social Theory*. London: Fontana.

Sheehy, E. (1987). *Personal Autonomy and the Criminal Law: Emerging Issues for Women*. Ottawa: Canadian Advisory Council on the Status of Women.

Sherman, L. and Berk, R. (1984). The Minneapolis Domestic Violence Experiment, Police Foundation *Reports* 1. Washington D.C.

Shivji, I. (ed.) (1985). *The State and the Working People in Tanzania*. Dakar: Codesria.

Showalter, E. (1987). *The Female Malady: Women, Madness and English Culture, 1830–1980*. London: Virago.

Sim, J., Scraton, P. and Gordon, P. (1987). 'Introduction: crime, the state, and critical analysis', in P. Scraton (ed.), *Law, Order and the Authoritarian State: Readings in Critical Criminology*. Milton Keynes: Open University Press.

Simons, M. (1979). 'Racism and feminism: a schism in the sisterhood', *Feminist Studies*, **5**, 2, 384–401.

Simpson, S. (1989). 'Feminist theory, crime and justice', *Criminology*, 27, 4, 605–31.

Sivanandan, A. (1982). *A Different Hunger*. London: Pluto.

Smart, B. (1988). 'Modernism, postmodernism and the present', unpublished paper: University of Auckland.

Smart, C. (1976). *Women, Crime and Criminology: A Feminist Critique*. London: Routledge and Kegan Paul.

Smart, C. (1984). *The Ties That Bind: Law, Marriage and the Reproduction of Patriarchal Relations*. London: Routledge and Kegan Paul.

Smart, C. (1986). 'Feminism and law: some problems of analysis and strategy', *International Journal of the Sociology of Law*, **14**, 1, 109–23.

Smart, C. (1989). *Feminism and the Power of Law*. London: Routledge.

Smart, C. and Smart, B. (1978). 'Accounting for rape: reality and myth in press reporting', in C. Smart and B. Smart (eds), *Sexuality and Social Control*. London: Routledge and Kegan Paul.

Smart, C. and Smart, B. (eds) (1978). *Women, Sexuality and Social Control*. London: Routledge and Kegan Paul.

Smith, A. and Stewart, A. (1983). 'Approaches to studying racism and sexism in Black women's lives', *Journal of Social Issues*, **39**, 3, 1–15.

Smith, B. (1982). 'Racism and women's studies', in G. Hull, P. Scott and B. Smith (eds), *All the Women are White. All the Blacks are Men: But Some of Us Are Brave*. New York: The Feminist Press.

Smith, D. (1973). 'Women's perspective as a radical critique of sociology', *Sociological Inquiry*, **44**, 1, 7–13.

Smith, D. (1975). 'An analysis of ideological structures and how women are excluded: considerations for academic women', *Canadian Review of Sociology and Anthropology*, **12**, 4, 353–69.

Smith, D. (1980).'A sociology for women', in J. Sherman and E. Beck (eds), *The Prism of Sex*. Madison, Wisconsin: University of Wisconsin Press.

Smith, D. (1988). *The Everyday World as Problematic: A Feminist Sociology*. Milton Keynes: Open University Press.

Smith, D.J. and Gray, J. (1983). 'The police in action', in *Police and People in London*, Vol 4. London: Policy Studies Institute.

Smith, L. (1988). 'Images of women – decision-making in courts', in A. Morris and C. Wilkinson (eds), *Women and the Penal System*, Cambridge: Institute of Criminology.

Smith, L. (1989a). *Concerns About Rape*. London: HMSO, Home Office Research Study No. 106.

Smith, L. (1989b). *Domestic Violence: An Overview of the Literature*. London: HMSO, Home Office Research Study No. 107.

Snider, L. (1985).'Legal reform and social control: the dangers of abolishing rape', *International Journal of the Sociology of Law*, **13**, 4, 337–56.

Soetenhorst, de Savornin Lohman, J. (1986). 'Meer dan een belangenstrijd; zeden enstraffen ter discussie (More than a struggle for interests, morals and penalties in question)', *Nemesis*, **1**, 357–63.

Southall Black Sisters (1989). 'Two struggles: challenging male violence and the police', in C. Dunhill (ed.), *The Boys in Blue: Women's Challenge To The Police*. London: Virago.

Spender, D. (ed.) (1981). *Men's Studies Modified: The Impact of Feminism on the Academic Disciplines*. Oxford: Pergamon.

Stanko, E. (1985). *Intimate Intrusions: Women's Experience of Male Violence*. London: Virago.

Stanko, E. (1987). 'Typical violence, normal precaution: men, women and interpersonal violence in England, Wales, Scotland and the USA', in J. Hanmer and M. Maynard (eds), *Women, Violence and Social Control*. Basingstoke: Macmillan.

Stanko, E. (1988a). 'Fear of crime and the myth of the safe home' in K. Yllö and M. Bograd (eds), *Feminist Perspectives on Wife Abuse*. London: Sage.

Stanko, E. (1988b). 'Hidden violence against women', in M. Maguire and J. Pointing (eds), *Victims of Crime: A New Deal?* Milton Keynes: Open University Press.

Stanko, E. (1990). *Danger Signals*. London: Pandora.

Stanley, L. and Wise, S. (1979). 'Feminist research, feminist consciousness and experiences of sexism', *Women's Studies International Quarterly*, **2**, 259–379.

Stanley, L. and Wise, S. (1983). *Breaking Out: Feminist Consciousness and Feminist Research*. London: Routledge and Kegan Paul.

Straus, M., Gelles, R. and Steinmetz, S. (1980). *Behind Closed Doors*. New York: Anchor.

Sumner, C. (1976). 'Marxism and deviancy theory', in P. Wiles (ed.), *Sociology of Crime and Delinquency in Britain*, vol 2, *The New Criminologies*. London: Martin Robertson.

Sumner, C. (1979). *Reading Ideologies: An Investigation into the Marxist Theory of Ideology and Law*. London: Academic Press.

Sumner, C. (1981). 'The rule of law and civil rights in contemporary Marxist theory', *Kapitalistate*, **9**, 63–91.

Sumner, C. (1983). 'Rethinking deviance', in S. Spitzer (ed.), *Research in Law, Deviance and Social Control*, Vol 5. Greenwich: JAI Press.

Sumner, C. (1990). 'Rethinking deviance: towards a sociology of censure', in C.S. Sumner (ed.), *Censure, Politics and Criminal Justice*. Milton Keynes: Open University Press.

Sumner, W. (1906). *Folkways*. Boston: Ginn.

Sydie, R. (1987). *Natural Women, Cultured Men: A Feminist Perspective in Sociological Theory*. Milton Keynes: Open University Press.

Taylor, I. (1981). *Law and Order: Arguments for Socialism*. London: Macmillan.

Taylor, I., Walton, P. and Young, J. (1973). *The New Criminology*. London: Routledge and Kegan Paul.

Taylor, I., Walton, P. and Young, J. (eds) (1975). *Critical Criminology*. London: Routledge and Kegan Paul.

Thomas, W. and Znaniecki, F. (1974/1919). *The Polish Peasant in Europe and America*. New York: Octagon Books.

Thornton, M. (1989). 'Hegemonic masculinity and the academy', *International Journal of the Sociology of Law*, **17**, 2, 115–30.

Theory, Culture and Society (1987). **4**, 2/3, Special issue on Norbert Elias and Figurational Sociology.

Troyna, B. and Cashmore, E. (eds) (1982). *Black Youth in Crisis*. London: Allen and Unwin.

Tuck, M. and Southgate, P. (1981). *Ethnic Minorities, Crime and Policing*. London: HMSO, Home Office Research Study No. 70.

Van Swaaningen, R. (1989). 'Feminism and abolitionism as critiques of criminology', paper presented at a symposium of the European group For The Study of Deviance And Social Control, Bremen, West Germany, 27 January 1989.

Vedder, C. and Somerville, D. (1970). *The Delinquent Girl*. Springfield, IL: Charles C. Thomas.

Voakes, R. and Fowler, Q. (1989). *Sentencing, Race and Social Inquiry Reports*. Bradford: West Yorkshire Probation Service, Bradford Division.

Walker, B. (1981). 'Psychology and feminism – if you can't beat them, join them', in D. Spender (ed.), *Men's Studies Modified*. Oxford: Pergamon.

Walker, L. (1979). *The Battered Woman*. New York: Harper Colophon Books.

Walker, L. (1989). *Terrifying Love*. London: Harper & Row.

Walker, N. (1987). *Crime and Criminology. A Critical Introduction*. Oxford: Oxford University Press.

Walkowitz, J. (1980). *Prostitution and Victorian Society: Women, Class and the State*. Cambridge: Cambridge University Press.

Wardell, L., Gillespie, D., and Leffler, A. (1983). 'Violence against wives', in D. Finkelhor *et al.*, *The Dark Side Of Families: Current Family Violence Research*. Newbury Park, CA: Sage.

Warr, M. (1984). 'Fear of victimization: why are women and the elderly more afraid?', *Social Science Quarterly*, **65**, 3, 681–702.

Warr, M. (1985). 'Fear of rape among urban women', *Social problems*, **32**, 3, 328–50.

Weedon, C. (1987). *Feminist Practice and Poststructuralist Theory*. Oxford: Basil Blackwell.

Weis, K. and Borges, S. (1973). 'Victimology and rape: the case of the legitimate victim', *Issues in Criminology*, **8**, 71–115.

West, D. (1969). *Present Conduct and Future Delinquency*. London: Heinemann.

Whitehouse, P. (1983). 'Race, bias and social enquiry reports', *Probation Journal*, June, 43–9.

Wilkinson, C. (1988).'The post-release experience of female prisoners', in A. Morris and C. Wilkinson (eds), *Women and the Penal System*. Cambridge: Institute of Criminology, Cropwood Series No. 19.

Williams, J. and Dunning, E. (1984). *Hooligans Abroad*. London: Routledge and Kegan Paul.

Willis, P. (1977). *Learning to Labour*. London: Saxon House.

Woodcraft, E. (1988). 'Child sexual abuse and the law', *Feminist Review*, 28, Spring, 122–30.

Woodhull, W. (1988). 'Sexuality, power and the question of rape, in I. Diamond and L. Quinby (eds), *Feminism and Foucault*. Boston: Northeastern University Press.

Worrall, A. (1989).'Working with female offenders: beyond alternatives to custody', *British Journal of Social Work*, **19**, 1, 77–93.

Worrall, A. and Pease, K. (1986). 'Personal crime against women: evidence from the 1982 British Crime Survey', *The Howard Journal of Criminal Justice*, **25**, 2, 118–24.

Wright, E.O. (1978). *Class, Crisis and the State*, London: New Left Books.

Yllö, K. (1988). 'Political and methodological debates in wife abuse research', in K. Yllö and M. Bograd (eds), *Feminist Perspectives On Wife Abuse*. Beverly Hills, CA: Sage

Yllö, K. and Bograd, M. (eds) (1988). *Feminist Perspectives on Wife Abuse*. Beverly Hills, CA: Sage.

Young, J. (1979). 'Left idealism, reformism and beyond: from new criminology to Marxism', in National Deviancy Conference and Conference of Socialist Economists. *Capitalism and the Rule of Law*. London: Hutchinson.

Young, J. (1981). 'Thinking seriously about crime: some models of criminology', in M. Fitzgerald *et al.* (eds), *Crime and Society: Readings in History and Sociology*. London: Routledge and Kegan Paul.

Young, J. (1986). 'The failure of criminology: the need for a radical realism', in R. Matthews and J. Young (eds), *Confronting Crime*. London: Sage.

Zhana, (1989) (ed.) *Sojourn*. London: Methuen.

Index